LANDS TRIBUNAL CASES

VOL. 3

Edited by

FRANK OTHICK, M.B.E., F.R.I.C.S., F.R.V.A.

Published by

BARRY ROSE PUBLISHERS

CHICHESTER

SBN 85992 086 O

Printed by Lindsay & Co. Ltd., Edinburgh

INTRODUCTION

This, the third, edition of *Lands Tribunal Cases* brings the reported cases up to December 31, 1975. In this edition there are 230 items, covering the Tribunal's decisions on Capital Gains Tax, Compensation, Law of Property, Leasehold Reform and Rating. The edited reports are the work of Mr. Frank Othick, chartered surveyor and rating valuer, whose administrative and professional interests have, since the creation of the Lands Tribunal, been particularly identified with that important body.

Each decision is reported in a condensed form, but the essential points are included, together with dates, general location of the property, composition of tribunals, costs and headings indicating the subject of each appeal or reference. There is a separate index for each of the five sections and both the appeal (or reference) title and the subject matter are separately indexed. The object of these reports is to assist all property practitioners by bringing together in one volume each year's decisions in various professional fields. Over the years this speedy source of reference will be increasingly useful.

The jurisdiction of the Lands Tribunal is likely to grow as legislation extends the volume and complexity of land transaction problems and it now seems likely that the rating system will continue to exist in view of the terms in which it is discussed in the Layfield Report.*

It is intended that future editions will be published much earlier. As soon as the last December decisions of the Tribunal are available an effort will be made to publish within a few weeks.

* Local Government Finance—Report of the Committee of Enquiry (*Cmnd 6453 May 1976*).

CONTENTS

The reports are set out in chronological order for each of the five groups listed below. For each of those groups there is a list of cases reported and an index of the subject matter of each case. The order of presentation is shown below.

CAPITAL GAINS TAX

CAPITAL GAINS TAX. TAXPAYER'S BELIEF THAT NO CAPITAL GAIN OCCURRED IN VIEW OF VALUATION EVIDENCE NOT SHARED. DISTRICT VALUER'S EVIDENCE PREFERRED.

The reference *Marson* (*Inspector of Taxes*) v. *Hasler* was the first to the tribunal arising out of the capital gains tax provisions of the Finance Act 1965. Under s. 19(1) tax became payable on capital gains on the disposal of assets, s. 22(1) provides that all forms of property should be assets, sch. 6 (para. 25) permits a person to elect to have been owner on April 6, 1965, that the assets were sold, and immediately re-acquired by him at market value on that date, s. 44(1) provides that market value is to be related to a sale in the open market and s. 44(6) provides for disputes to be determined on a reference to the Lands Tribunal. In the present reference the interest to be valued was the fee simple subject to a lease for 21 years from March 25, 1951, at a rent of £150 exclusive for the first seven years, £160 for the next seven years and £180 for the last seven years, the lessee being responsible for all repairs and insurance of the property. In July 1965 there were discussions between the lessor and lessee about a possible purchase by the latter, and a firm of surveyors reckoned the current market value then was £10,000. In 1967 the lessee increased the offer to £9,000 (having offered £6,000 in 1965). On receipt of this offer the lessor again consulted the firm of surveyors who said that if the lessee was prepared to make an offer of £10,000 they would still advise their client, the lessor, to accept that figure. In due course a sale took place at that sum. The taxpayer (the lessor) therefore contended that as the property was worth the same at both dates there was no liability for capital gains tax. However, the Inland Revenue contended that the value in April 1965 was no more than £8,000. Expert evidence before the tribunal (Mr. R. C. Walmsley) disclosed differences of opinion. Although agreed on the value of the unexpired lease term, the lessor's valuer based the value of the reversion on a rent after the lease expired of a somewhat higher figure than did the valuer for the Inland Revenue. In addition the percentage for years' purchase was lower in the opinion of the taxpayer's valuer. The tribunal was more impressed by this valuer's evidence, based on actual transactions of comparables and agreed that the proper rate of return was certainly at least that applied by him, *i.e.* 9 *per cent*. It was not prepared to accept the 8 *per cent* table adopted by the taxpayer's valuer for capitalising the rental value, but then deferring that on the 7 *per cent* table. Had he analysed his comparables, devaluing them on the same basis, the multipliers used in his valuation for the reference property might have proved helpful. Supported valuations were to be preferred to those wholly unsupported. The tribunal contrasted the "analytical school" of valuers with the "forty years man and boy" school to the disadvantage of the latter, pointing out that the tribunal reached its conclusion on evidence. Market value fixed at £8,000. The tribunal went on to comment on related matters. It was, stated the tribunal, a characteristic of a freehold reversion that, all factors remaining equal, its value might be expected progressively to increase by the mere effluxion of time. Capital gains tax agreements on liability could only be regarded as secondary evidence. The third matter related to the history of the present proceedings and the tribunal, after examining that history, thought that the circumstances demonstrated that the taxpayer's criticisms of the Inland Revenue were wholly groundless; the Inland Revenue had no alternative but to refer the matter to the tribunal for determination. Taxpayer to pay the applicant's costs on County Court scale 4 if not agreed, with a certificate for increased fees to expert witness.

(*Decision March 4, 1975*)

COMPENSATION

LIST OF CASES REPORTED

SUBJECT MATTER OF CASES

1

INTER-RELATED COMPANIES. ONE RECOGNISED AS HAVING THE LEGAL OWNERSHIP OF THE FREEHOLD. COMPENSATION FOR DISTURBANCE TO THE OTHERS LIMITED IN POINT OF TIME AND ONLY AS ALLOWED UNDER S. 20 COMPULSORY PURCHASE ACT 1965.

The reference *Bronze Investments Ltd.* v. *London Borough of Tower Hamlets* involved the determination of preliminary points of law as to whether two other claimant companies associated with the above claimant company were entitled to compensation for disturbance (amounting to the extinguishment of their businesses) following compulsory acquisition of the premises in which the businesses were carried on. The other two companies were D. H. N. Food Distributors Ltd. and D. H. N. Food Transport Ltd. All three were in the process of voluntary liquidation. The two additional claimant companies were said by the acquiring authority not to have any interest in the land acquired entitling them to compensation for disturbance. The freehold interest in the land was transferred to Bronze in January 1964. Shares in Bronze were acquired by D. H. N. Food Distributors. The directors of the two companies were at all times the same. Bronze had no employees and no bank account. It did not trade. Its only asset was its legal ownership of the freehold. The whole of the issued capital of the transport company was owned by D. H. N. Food Distributors and the directors of the companies were the same. The transport company had no bank account but it owned vehicles used exclusively for D. H. N. Food and carried on no other business.

The preliminary legal issues were whether the two associated companies were confined to such compensation for disturbance as could be allowed under s. 20 of the Compulsory Purchase Act 1965, and, if so, whether such compensation had to be assessed on the basis that they could expect to remain in occupation of the subject land for only such period as would extend from March 17, 1971 (the date of possession by the acquiring authority) to the earliest date on which their tenancy could have been determined by a notice to quit served on that date. The acquiring authority did not concede entitlement even under s. 20.

Counsel for the two companies submitted the case for compensation under three heads—agency, trusteeship and subsisting contract. So far as agency was concerned Bronze was claimed to be no more than the agent or tool of D. H. N. Food but the tribunal (Mr. Douglas Frank, President) had no doubt that Bronze was carried on, and intentionally so, as a separate company, with all the advantages of a separate company. On trusteeship it was submitted that where a conveyance was made to one person but the purchase money was provided by another, there was a resulting trust in favour of the person providing the purchase money and that presumption could only be rebutted by evidence that the purchaser was intended to benefit. The tribunal found it impossible to conclude from the facts that there was any intention that when D. H. N. Food acquired the shares in Bronze from the bank it was intended that thereafter Bronze should hold the legal interest in the properties as trustees for D. H. N. Food. The facts pointed the other way. So far as the arguments on subsisting contract were concerned the tribunal stated that all the facts led to the conclusion that the parties impliedly rescinded the contract when the sale of the Bronze shares took place and that thereafter the contract no longer subsisted. The tribunal was unable to accept the companies' arguments on the second question involving the length of tenancy. Both questions were, therefore, answered in the affirmative, so that the two companies were confined to such compensation as could be allowed under s. 20 and it had to be assessed on the basis of the strictly limited period ended by notice to quit after the date of possession by the acquiring authority. Claimants to pay the acquiring authority's costs on the High Court scale if not agreed.

(*Decision January 30, 1975*)

2

FIRST CLAIM BEFORE TRIBUNAL UNDER PART I OF THE LAND COMPENSATION ACT 1973. NO COMPENSATION IN RESPECT OF ROAD IMPROVEMENT WORKS.

The reference *Hickmott* v. *Dorset County Council* was the first to come before the Lands Tribunal under part 1 of the Land Compensation Act 1973. This provides for compensation for depreciation caused by the *use* of public works. Road improvement works prompted the claimant to seek £8,000 in respect of a house near Beaminster, Dorset. The county council contended that there was no depreciation. The works entailed increasing the carriageway width from 15 ft. to 22 ft. The basis of the claim was noise and vibration. The tribunal (Mr. J. D. Russell Davis) explained that compensation had to be assessed by reference to prices current on the first day of the claim period, which was 12 months from the date on which the highway was first used after completion of the improvements. In this instance the date was August 1972. The claimant's valuer estimated the value of the house at £22,000 before the works and £14,000 afterwards. This estimate was not supported by any comparable transactions. The compensating authority's valuer thought the effect of the widening was to take traffic away from the claimant's house. Noise tests had been made and reference was made to the results. This witness thought the before and after value of the claimant's house was £18,000. The tribunal made appropriate visits and concluded that the traffic was light. It had not been proved to the tribunal's satisfaction that plaster cracks was not due to other factors than traffic vibration. The test was depreciation in market value and it did not think that a prospective purchaser in mid-1972 would have reduced his offer made before the improvements, and it could be argued that the greater road safety at the site in question would have enhanced the value. Claim dismissed. Claimant to make a contribution of £20 to the compensating authority's costs.

(*Decision February 6, 1975*)

3

COMPENSATION FOR LAND ACQUIRED FOR CONSTRUCTION OF RESERVOIR, AND FOR THE LOSS OF FISHING RIGHTS AND INJURIOUS AFFECTION.

The reference *Davies* v. *The Welsh National Water Development Authority* concerned the compensation following the compulsory acquisition of about 102 acres of land in the county of Powys for the construction of a reservoir. Before the construction of the reservoir the whole district was very remote and access was by a poor unclassified county road, mainly unfenced. Since construction the area had become attractive to visitors and tourists and a new road had been built on part of the land acquired. The tribunal (Mr. J. H. Emlyn Jones) thought there had been some misunderstanding about pursuing a claim for equivalent reinstatement and gave it as its opinion that the case was a clear one for compensation on open market value. The claimants sought £10,810. The acquiring authority contended for £6,032. The tribunal thought the acquiring authority's figures inadequately reflected the value of valley land and in adjusting for that reason it also thought a somewhat higher figure for timbered land to be appropriate. The tribunal's figure for the loss of fishing was rather less than the claimant's, and the total compensation determined by the tribunal was £7,590, plus a surveyor's fee and any legal costs properly incurred from the date of notice to treat up to the date of the notice of reference. The acquiring authority to pay the claimant's costs on the High Court scale unless agreed.

(*Decision February 13, 1975*)

4

COMPENSATION FOLLOWING COMPULSORY ACQUISITION FOR HOUSING PURPOSES. TRIBUNAL REJECTS CLAIM THAT IT LACKED JURISDICTION IN VIEW OF EARLIER HAPPENINGS ALLEGED TO CONSTITUTE AN ENFORCEABLE CONTRACT.

The reference *Allnatt* v. *London Borough of Barnet* concerned compensation for the freehold interest of a house in Edgware compulsorily acquired for housing purposes. The claimant alleged that he had entered into a binding contract with the acquiring authority to sell the dwelling to the authority for £14,000 together with his legal and surveyor's costs on that acquisition and upon purchase by him of an alternative property. This contract, in the claimant's opinion, deprived the tribunal of jurisdiction except as regards supplementary heads of claim. He referred to £500 removal costs and a sum of £1,000 to compensate him for the fact that without the compulsory purchase order he could have reasonably expected planning consent to conversion of the dwelling to one bedroom flats. Additionally, he sought a further sum of £500 in respect of the value of ground rents on the flats after conversion. The acquiring authority denied the existence of a binding contract or that the house had any conversion potential. The maximum compensation was £13,500 plus the agreed £500 for removal and other accepted costs.

The tribunal (Mr. V. G. Wellings) carefully examined the matters relevant to the question of a binding contract and concluded that the indications were that the acquiring authority no doubt desired to bring matters to a conclusion before the parties left a court where an attempt had been made to quash the compulsory purchase order but found, as a fact, that the relevant offer was expressly stated to be open for that day only. The offer was never accepted unconditionally and in any case a letter from the claimant introduced two new factors beyond the previous arrangement. In the view of the tribunal there was no binding contract and its jurisdiction was in no way inhibited. After hearing evidence on planning prospects and on values, the tribunal awarded £13,500 plus the agreed sum of £500, together with surveyors' fees and the claimant's proper conveyancing costs. The acquiring authority's sealed offer was exactly equal to the tribunal's award so the claimant was ordered to pay the acquiring authority its costs of the reference on the High Court scale unless agreed.

(*Decision February 26, 1975*)

5

POINT OF LAW, RELATED TO RULE 5 OF THE LAND COMPENSATION ACT 1961. ENTITLEMENT ESTABLISHED IN PRINCIPLE AT INTERIM HEARING.

The question whether the claimants, or one of them, were entitled to compensation under Rule 5 of s. 5 of the Land Compensation Act 1961, a matter of law, was the issue in the interim decision in the reference *Harpurhey Conservative and Unionist Club and Harpurhey Constitutional Club Ltd* v. *Manchester City Council.* The premises acquired, a club, were purpose built in 1877 and were acquired by the second named claimants in 1922, a company established for that purpose among others. In December 1971, the time of the notice to treat, the ground floor was let, but in any case did not form part of the Rule 5 claim. The remainder was let to the Conservative Club on an annual tenancy by the company which had never had any business other than the letting of the premises. Informally, the acquiring authority had offered to allocate a suitable alternative site for the club and there was no question but that the two claimants genuinely intended reinstatement of the club in some place.

In opposing the claim under Rule 5 the acquiring authority argued that there was no precedent for an application of that rule for premises let on a tenancy from year to year where the tenant's occupation was devoted to a Rule 5 purpose. Two questions had to be asked. For what purpose were the premises devoted, and who was going to reinstate them for that purpose? As to the first it was contended that the purpose for which the premises were devoted by the company were those of a property company, the letting at a profit. As to the second question it was agreed that the intention to reinstate must be by the payee of the compensation, which in this case must be the second named claimants, but they could not have any such intention because they had no money, and because notwithstanding s. 47 of the Land Compensation Act 1973, by reason of s. 20 of the Compulsory Purchase Act 1965, Rule 5 did not apply to a tenant from year to year at all. For the claimants it was said that if the authority's argument was right, that the company had no power to lease the premises for a members' club, then notwithstanding the club's occupation for 50 years, in law there had been no lease or licence and therefore the club had acquired a possessory title. However, that construction of the memorandum of association was not accepted. The first object under the memorandum stated that the acquisition was with a view to adopt and carry into effect an agreement dated 28 July 1922, made between the vendors and a William Gilgryst. That agreement had not been found, but, said the claimants, in regard to the club's use for 50 years, and applying the maxim *omnis praesumuntur rite acta est* it must be presumed that the lease to the club and its use of the premises was in furtherance of that agreement. So far as Rule 5 was concerned the question was whether the land was devoted to a particular purpose and not whether any particular interest in the land was so devoted. The question as to who would reinstate was also irrelevant because Rule 5 was in the passive voice. The realities should be looked at. It was not surprising that there was no precedent for the application of Rule 5 in a case where the purpose was being carried on by a tenant from year to year, because s. 47 of the Land Compensation Act 1973 had only been in operation for about a year.

The tribunal (Mr. Douglas Frank, President) was satisfied that:

1. The relevant part of the premises had been occupied by the club for many years as tenant from year to year.
2. The grant of the tenancy and the use to which the premises were put by the club were *intra vires* the company.
3. The use to which the premises were put by the club was of such a nature that there was no general demand or market for it.
4. Both the company and the club *bona fide* intended to reinstate elsewhere.
5. The club and the company jointly and severally intended that upon reinstatement elsewhere the new premises would be devoted to the same purpose as the existing premises.

The claimants, or one of them, would be entitled to compensation under Rule 5. The tribunal had not been asked to specify which; that would be dealt with at the substantive hearing. Acquiring authority to pay the claimants' costs of the hearing on the High Court scale if not agreed.

(*Decision March 14, 1975*)

6

FINAL DECISION ON REMOVAL AND "CRAWLEY" COSTS. EVIDENCE OF, AND RECEIPTS FOR, PAYMENTS LACKING. DECISION LEFT TO TRIBUNAL.

The reference *Roberts* v. *Greater London Council* followed an interim decision on compensation following compulsory acquisition of a house in north London. The parties could not agree on certain costs, in respect of which the acquiring authority had asked for receipts or other evidence to support certain items of claim. The tribunal (Mr. J. Stuart Daniel) went systematically through the particulars of claim, noting and accepting items on which there was agreement between the parties, but many items were questioned and disallowed. Examples were insurance cover on a house still occupied, imprecise claim on loss of earnings (partly allowed), surveyor's fees not vouched for, an exorbitant claim for travelling expenses by claimant visiting his agents and solicitors, excessive claim for telephone calls, reconnecting gas points (no receipts), excessive claim for floor coverings, unsupported fee to accountant, and one or two similar items. What the tribunal allowed was appreciably less than the claim total. On costs, a sealed offer by the acquiring authority was only about £170 below the tribunal's award. There had been an opportunity to amend this but details by the claimant had been lacking so that such an amended offer was inhibited. In the circumstances there was no order as to costs.

(*Decision March 14, 1975*)

7

SUBSTANTIAL EVIDENCE OF TRANSACTIONS SATISFIES TRIBUNAL ON DISTRICT VALUER'S FIGURE OF COMPENSATION.

The reference *Fleetwood* v. *London Borough of Lambeth* concerned compensation for an unfit house within a clearance area. Compensation under s. 59(2) of the Housing Act 1957 was on the basis of the land as a cleared site available for development in accordance with the requirements of the building byelaws for the time being in force in the district. The district valuer supported a sum of £850, reliance being placed on a schedule of settlements which had been reached with the owners of 26 other properties within the area of the same compulsory purchase order representing agreements with professional advisers in each case, 12 different firms being involved. The claimant could not understand how it was that property for which he paid £850 in 1925 should only be worth an identical sum in compensation 50 years later. The tribunal (Mr. J. H. Emlyn Jones) explained the basis of compensation for the site only and on the assumption that the other houses in the area of the compulsory purchase order were still standing, a rare set of circumstances. The tribunal was impressed by the schedule of agreed figures, the claimant had called no professional evidence, he had previously employed a surveyor but was not prepared to accept his advice. Compensation determined at £850, to which was to be added a surveyor's fee and legal fees properly incurred from the date of the notice to treat up to the date of the notice of the reference. No order as to costs.

(*Decision March 17, 1975*)

8

COMPULSORY ACQUISITION OF LEASEHOLD INTEREST. PLANNING PERMISSION NOT EXERCISED, TOO SPECULATIVE TO HAVE A VALUE.

The reference *J. Davy Ltd.* v. *London Borough of Hammersmith* concerned the compensation, following compulsory acquisition for housing purposes, for the leasehold interest of premises in Fulham. Agreement had been reached between the parties on all questions except one. In 1960 the claimants obtained planning permission for the erection of a petrol filling station on part of the land covered by their lease, and although this permission was never exercised the claimants contended that a prospective purchaser of the residue of the lease would have given, at the date the acquiring authority took possession of the land, a sum of £25,550 on account of the permission. Agreement had been reached on the value of the lease without the planning permission. The acquiring authority said that the tribunal should award nothing, or some very much smaller sum, in respect of the value of the planning permission. The British Transport Commission leased the premises to a firm for a term of 21 years from June 1953 with restrictive covenants regarding use, including the prohibition of keeping any combustible or inflammable material on the premises. Later, the lease was informally transferred to the claimants and written consent was given to a change of use to garaging and repairing of motor vehicles and only that. In 1959 the Commission provisionally agreed to a surrender of the existing lease and the granting of a new lease, part of the agreement being that the claimants should apply for planning permission for use of part of the land as a petrol filling station. But in 1960 the Commission told the claimants that it was not their wish to enter into any further lease arrangements, at least for the present. A month or so later the planning permission was given subject to certain conditions to safeguard amenities and the free flow of traffic. All the same this development could not take place without a licence from the Commission. Such a licence was never requested and of course the planning permission had not been used. In April 1965 the G.L.C. warned the claimants against any major redevelopment of their premises in view of the possibility of the then current thinking about extensive use of surplus railway land for housing purposes. By March 1968 the acquiring authority had made a compulsory purchase order for the freehold interest. In due course it was clear that the planning permission would have expired before the reversion fell in so that the freeholders would get no value from the permission unless they made terms with the tenants. But, it was claimed, they would be under considerable pressure to do so. The acquiring authority argued that a purchaser would not have given anything for the permission because its value was too speculative, and a landlord would have been more interested in his own more valuable development.

Detailed valuations were considered but the tribunal (Mr. J. Stuart Daniel and Mr. J. R. Laird) noted that calculations depended on the acceptance in principle that the planning permission had a value. When the Commission decided not to grant a new lease all the parties, it seemed, treated the petrol filling station as pigeon holed with the new lease. The tribunal was not satisfied that a prospective purchaser of the tail-end of the lease would have paid anything in the summer of 1970 for the planning permission. It accepted the simple proposition that the value of the planning permission was too speculative in 1970 for a purchaser to attach any value to it. Claim for compensation in respect of that permission dismissed. Costs against the claimants on the High Court scale if not agreed.

(*Decision March 19, 1975*)

9

COMPANY FORMATION 13 MONTHS BEFORE COMPULSORY PURCHASE ORDER. OWNER OF FREEHOLD WHO FORMED COMPANY NOT ENTITLED TO BUSINESS SUPPLEMENT.

The reference *Marzell* v. *Greater London Council* concerned the question of entitlement to a supplementary payment to the owner of a shop and premises in Bethnal Green following compulsory purchase for housing purposes. It appeared that the question involved in the reference had not previously been tested before the Lands Tribunal. Possession of the property was taken by the acquiring authority in February 1973, the date for valuation purposes. After holding the premises as tenant the claimant purchased the freehold in 1948 and in October 1963 a company was formed to take over the business. The claimant retained the freehold interest. The company paid nothing for goodwill, it was not granted a lease or any form of tenancy and no rent was charged against profits.

Paragraph 6 of Part 2 of the second schedule of the Housing Act 1957 has the headnote "Business Premises" and makes provision for the payment of a business supplement. The question raised by the reference was whether a person entitled to the receipts of the business held an interest in the property at all times during the two years preceding the date of the making of the compulsory purchase order. If the claimant was not so entitled he would receive only the site value, it then being open to the company to establish a claim for compensation for disturbance. The claimant spoke of tax advantages and business status when explaining the reason for forming the company. On his behalf it was claimed that the whole of the circumstances made the company artificial, appropriate case law being called in aid. The acquiring authority contended that the claimant and the company were distinct entities. The compulsory purchase order was made in November 1964 and the claimant had been in business on his own account up to October 1963, the date of incorporation of the limited company. The claimant lacked 11 months of the two-year qualifying period. He was not "entitled to the receipts" and, with his wife, an equal shareholder in the company, he was entitled to profits in the form of dividends, if dividends had been declared, and they had not.

The tribunal (Mr. J. D. Russell Davis) said each case had to be distinguished on its own facts and the nub of this decision was the identity of the company. The claimant was the victim of hardship on account of an unfortunate decision to form his business as a company, the consequences of which could not have been appreciated at the time, which was 13 months before the compulsory purchase order was made. Reluctantly, the tribunal found against the claimant, that he was not entitled to claim the business supplement.

(*Decision March 19, 1975*)

10

CLAIMANT ABSENT AND NOT REPRESENTED. ACQUIRING AUTHORITY'S VALUATION OF COMPENSATION ACCEPTED.

The reference *Graham* v. *Melton Borough Council* concerned the compensation payable for a property in Melton Mowbray, following compulsory acquisition for housing purposes. The property had been left empty for about five years. The authority's valuer had seen the claimant on a number of occasions, the claimant had promised to instruct solicitors, he had been advised of the hearing but had not appeared and was not represented. The only evidence before the tribunal (Mr. Douglas Frank, President) indicated an open market value of £7,700 and that in addition there should be a disturbance payment of £50 to cover the cost of removing certain chattels left on the premises. Compensation was determined at £7,750. No order as to costs.

(*Decision March 20, 1975*)

11

PROBLEM OF TITLE TO FREEHOLD. NO APPEARANCE BY CLAIMANTS. ALTERNATIVE DETERMINATIONS OF COMPENSATION TO COVER EVENTUAL PROOF OF OWNERSHIP.

The reference *Askey and Others* v. *Blackburn Borough Council* concerned the compensation payable for the freehold interest of a small terrace cottage in Blackburn, following a compulsory purchase order under the Housing Act 1957, the property being one of numerous unfit dwellings. There was a difficulty about title. In 1961 the claimants Askey had agreed to buy the cottage from a James Ridley. The price had been agreed, an initial payment had been made and weekly payments had followed, but by the date of the notice to treat there still remained a small balance due under the agreement. Mr. Ridley had died without having appointed an executor. At the hearing there was no appearance by or for the owners of the freehold interest. The authority's valuer produced evidence of settlements on similar interests under the same compulsory purchase order and the tribunal (Mr. R. C. Walmsley) was satisfied that if the freehold interest belonged to the Askeys the compensation payable was £30. This was the minimum payment equal to the gross value for rating purposes. If the freehold was still held by the personal representatives of the deceased James Ridley the compensation payable was £23 (s. 10 Land Compensation Act 1961, not applicable). In the event of the Askeys not establishing title the tribunal assumed that the compensation would be paid into court. No order as to costs.

(*Decision March 25, 1975*)

12

INTERIM DECISION ON EFFECT OF DEVELOPMENT SCHEME ON VALUATION FOR COMPENSATION.

The references *Sprinz and Others* v. *Kingston-upon-Hull City Council* concerned the compensation payable under compulsory purchase of 560 acres of land, but the main question was whether there was one scheme of development covering both the subject land and other land and the extent to which the effect on values of the development of the other land fell to be disregarded. The assessment of compensation could not be made until a decision had been reached on this point. Was it necessary in law to leave out of account any increase or diminution in the value of the properties which was attributable to the carrying out, or the prospect of, some other development? And if so, what was the precise extent of such other actual or prospective development? The first question arose because the authority contended that at all material times it had but one scheme covering not only the subject properties but also other land and it was that scheme which underlay the acquisition. The tribunal (Mr. Douglas Frank, President, Mr. V. G. Wellings and Mr. E. C. Strathon) was of the opinion that as a matter of strict law both s. 6 of the Land Compensation Act 1961, and the *Pointe Gourde* principle had to be applied where, on the facts, they were capable of applying, the one independently of the other. Was the proposed development of the subject land part of a wider proposal which had developed, by the material date, sufficiently to be described as a scheme, the scheme underlying the acquisition? Whether there was one scheme or two was a question of fact. The tribunal thought it right to find out on what date there was a scheme and then to ascertain if it included the subject land. It concluded that by the time the Council applied for planning permission in 1960 it had decided on a defined project for a defined purpose with defined boundaries and that it was a scheme complete in itself. Then there was a gap of eight years before the Council submitted a planning application for the scheme covering the subject land. Therefore there were at least two separate schemes. It followed that as a matter of fact and law the tribunal determined that it was not necessary to leave out of account any increase or diminution in the value of the subject properties other than was expressly provided for in Part 1 of Schedule 1 to the 1961 Act. The acquiring authority was ordered to pay three quarters of the claimants' costs to date on the High Court scale if not agreed.

(*Decision March 26, 1975*)

13

NO CLAIM BY MORTGAGOR. FREEHOLD VALUE COMPENSATION TO MORTGAGEE.

The reference *Ovolo Properties Limited and O'Connell* v. *Wirral Borough Council* concerned compensation for the freehold interest of a dwelling in Birkenhead which was within a clearance area (part 3 Housing Act 1957). A compulsory purchase order had been confirmed and the acquiring authority had served notices to treat and of entry on the reputed owner-occupier and also on the mortgagees. In due course the dwelling was demolished and the then owner-occupier was re-housed but subsequently his whereabouts could not be traced.

In August 1972 Ovolo Properties Limited claimed a sum of £1,200 plus costs and fees and the tribunal (Mr. J. R. Laird) considered that this was a claim for the value of the freehold interest. No formal claim had ever been made by the previous owner-occupier. In March 1975 the district valuer wrote to Ovolo Properties Limited stating that the full compulsory purchase value was £1,250 and surveyors for the claimants agreed. The district valuer spoke to a valuation in that sum and that was the only evidence before the tribunal. The compensation for the freehold interest was fixed at that figure and a lump sum of £68 costs was awarded, this to include the hearing fee and to be paid by the claimant company to the acquiring authority.

(*Decision April 10, 1975*)

14

COMPENSATION FOR REVOCATION OF PLANNING PERMISSION AND DISCONTINUANCE ORDER ON LIMESTONE QUARRY. BASIS RELATED TO LOSS OF PROFITS. DEFERMENT FACTOR. NO INTEREST ON AWARD. DEDUCTION FOR TAX.

The reference *Hobbs (Quarries) Ltd.* v. *Somerset County Council* concerned the compensation payable following revocation of a planning permission and the making of a discontinuance order on a limestone quarry at Webbington, Somerset. The land concerned had an area of about 6 acres and planning permission for working and winning limestone had been granted in 1947 but between June 1959 and the end of 1965 the quarry had been occupied as a depot by the county council. In July 1965 the claimants purchased about 57 acres of land, including the 6 acres comprising the quarry, for £50,000 but they were unaware of the intended revocation and discontinuance orders. In November 1965 the county council revoked the planning permission and the following month made a discontinuance order under s. 18 of the Town and Country Planning Act 1962, so far as quarry use was concerned. After a public inquiry the orders were confirmed.

At the time of this confirmation of the orders the limestone reserves amounted to two million tons and the quarry was convenient for the construction of a section of the M5 motorway. It was almost certain that the claimants would have secured a sub-contract for the supply of rock-fill and base material and the probability of such a sub-contract was the claimants' main motive in purchasing the quarry. The claimants would have made a profit of £295,805 but if it was correct to assume that the valuation date for compensation purposes was July 1, 1967, the date the orders were confirmed, and that it was correct to allow for deferment over the period of the contract, that amount would be reduced to £250,100. If the claimants had failed to win the contract they would still have been able to sell the limestone to the successful sub-contractor at a profit of

£199,700 and if there had been no motorway and the claimants had merely bought the quarry and installed plant to supply the general market the quarry would have had a life of $11\frac{1}{2}$ years and the profit as at November 1969 would have been £107,650 but if that amount had to be discounted back to June 1, 1967, it would have declined to £84,000.

The main issue before the tribunal (Mr. Douglas Frank, President, and Mr. J. D. Russell-Davis) was whether the claimants were entitled to compensation on the basis of loss of anticipated profits or whether they were restricted to the depreciation in the value of their interest in the land.

For the claimants it was stated that it was commonplace for compensation for loss of profits to be awarded in compulsory purchases cases subject to exclusion on the grounds of remoteness. There was no logic in the county council's argument that compensation for loss of profits was applicable only where the business on the site was an existing one. In a revocation case the question was whether the loss or damage was directly attributable to the revocation and there were three relevant questions. Would the company have made profits from the quarry? If so, was the loss of profits directly attributable to the revocation? If so, what is the quantum?

For the Somerset County Council it was stressed that the potentiality for making profits was reflected in the open market value of the land and if the owner was not already carrying on a business on the land the value was normally the open market value. Only in a case where the claimant had a better chance than a purchaser of making profits was he entitled to a payment for disturbance representing the additional value of the land to him. If the claimants' business had been a going concern compensation would have been on the capitalised loss of profits for the loss of the motorway contract and so it would if the claimants, instead of buying a quarry, had bought the shares in a company already operating the quarry.

The tribunal found the case very difficult because it saw force in the argument that the loss to the claimants could not be more than the depreciation in the market value but that argument pre-supposes that there was another quarry available to be bought at market value which could serve the claimants' purposes and provide them with an equal profit. There was no evidence to that effect. The damage resulting from the loss of the motorway contract was not too remote and it was conceded on behalf of the County Council that the claimants had been in a strong position to win the contract.

As there was no claim for the value of the land the question of double compensation did not arise. The tribunal found that the proper basis for compensation was by reference to the loss of profits from the motorway contract. On the question of deferment, the tribunal had not heard much argument as to the appropriate date for valuation, presumably because there was no alternative to the date of confirmation of the revocation order. If, therefore, compensation had been paid immediately after that date on the basis of estimated loss of profits the claimants would have the benefit of the use of the whole of that money for two years when, but for the revocation they would not have been earning any profits, and then, for a further two years, to profits of which they would have only had part until the exploitation was completed. The County Council's argument was well founded so far as deferment was concerned and the principal sum should be £250,100.

On the question of interest on compensation from the date of revocation the County Council claimed that there was an established principle that until compensation was quantified no interest was payable and he cited appropriate case law. This view was confirmed by the tribunal.

On the question of deductions for tax, the parties had agreed jointly to instruct counsel to appear *amicus curiae* on the understanding that neither party would be bound by his submission. In the event, neither party disputed counsel's submission but it was necessary for the tribunal to record that they reserved their right to do so elsewhere. Counsel, regarding tax deductions, referred to several reported cases and submittd that where compensation was assessed by reference to loss of anticipated profits it must be reduced where tax would be paid on those profits in the hands of a recipient, the sum reduced being grossed up by the amount of the extra tax payable. The tribunal awarded a sum of £193,418, which reflected a deduction for corporation tax and with a sum added back reflecting capital gains tax on the net compensation after tax and after deducting the cost of acquisition of the quarry. The acquiring authority was ordered to pay the claimants a surveyor's fee and any legal costs from the dates of confirmation of the discontinuance order and the revocation order up to the date of the notices of reference. The County Council's sealed offer was less than the tribunal's award and the County Council was ordered to pay two-thirds of the costs of the references on the High Court scale if not agreed.

(*Decision April 23, 1975*)

15

APPROPRIATE DATE OF ASSESSMENT OF COMPENSATION. DATE OF HEARING AGREED BUT WITHOUT PREJUDICE TO THE DATE OF THE REFERENCE BEING PUT FORWARD AS THE APPROPRIATE DATE.

The reference *The Corporation of Hull Trinity House* v. *Humberside County Council* concerned the compensation payable following the deemed compulsory acquisition of the freehold interest in 1·6 acres of land at North Ferriby. The site was unused but it was common ground that if the land had not been required for highway purposes it was likely that planning permission would have been granted for 12 detached dwellings. The first issue between the parties was the question of the appropriate date at which compensation should be assessed, the claimants arguing for December 1973 when a price was agreed by the parties' respective valuers. The respondents claimed that it was the date of the tribunal's hearing or August 1969 when there was an abortive agreement. There were also other disputes on the amount of compensation.

Late in 1968 and early 1969 the claimants' surveyors and the county land agent had agreed a figure of £230,050 plus fees and costs and although an abstract of title had been delivered and conveyancing procedures put in hand a dispute had arisen on the area of land involved. The county land agent, in correspondence, had expressed the view that the acquiring authority would soon be in a position to pay interest on the amount of the agreed settlement but the council had not proceeded to implement the agreement. On the contrary, in May 1969 the clerk of the county council had indicated in a letter that he was now asking the Ministry of Transport to accept responsibilty under the purchase notice. Solicitors for the claimants had written back indicating surprise at this turn of events and suggested that completion of the agreement should take place immediately. In the summer of 1973 there was an oral agreement on an offer of £83,600 but once again the clerk of the county council indicated unwillingness to shoulder the financial burden involved and pointed out that the county council still needed assurance about reimbursement from the central Government. Counsel for the acquiring authority, the successor authority to the original local authority, did not seek to justify these actions.

In March 1974 the claimants applied for an appropriate alternative development certificate under s. 17 of the Land Compensation Act 1961, and in July that certificate was issued, indicating frontage residential development of not more than 12 houses. Counsel for the claimants agreed that no enforceable agreement had been concluded in 1973 but as that was the time when the parties agreed to assess compensation then it should be adopted but counsel for the acquiring authority argued that where entry had not taken place and there was no enforceable contract, compensation should be assessed at the date of the hearing.

The tribunal (Mr. Douglas Frank, President and Mr. E. C. Strathon) thought that where there was a reference to the Lands Tribunal three dates fell for consideration, i.e. the date of the reference, the date or dates of the hearing and the date of the decision. After considering the circumstances the tribunal thought that common sense and convenience pointed overwhelmingly to the date of the notice of reference. Nevertheless as the parties seemed to be agreed on the date of the hearing that date was adopted ex concessis. That date was agreed without prejudice to the possibility that in some later case the date of the notice of reference might be put forward as being the right date. The claimants' valuer contended for £83,600 and the valuer for the acquiring authority supported two valuations, one for £49,200 and the other for £49,700. After considering supporting arguments and rejecting evidence claimed to indicate falling values, the tribunal accepted the valuation of £83,600. However, there were some subsidiary matters, one concerned with paired accesses and drainage and the tribunal thought that a purchaser in the market would probably reduce his bid by a small sum to £80,000 and that figure of compensation was determined, together with surveyor's fee and legal costs from the date of the confirmation of the purchase notice up to the date of the notice of reference. The sealed offer by the acquiring authority was less than the amount of the award so the acquiring authority was ordered to pay the claimants' costs of the reference on the High Court scale if not agreed.

(*Decision April 23, 1975*)

16

ENHANCEMENT IN VALUE DUE TO MARRIAGE OF SITES. ARGUMENT FOR ELIMINATION OF SUCH VALUE REJECTED. EARLIER RULE 42 VALUATION USED AS EVIDENCE. ABSENCE OF CLAIMANTS. GREATER BURDEN OF SCRUTINY OF EVIDENCE ON TRIBUNAL.

In the reference *Executors of G. A. and M. Cossey* (*deceased*) v. *City of Bristol* land at Kingsdown, Bristol, was the subject of dispute. The subject site had been included in a conservation area in 1972 and prior to that there had been a confirmed clearance order in October 1965 in respect of the subject land and the adjacent site. A compulsory purchase order had been made in April 1971 and it had been made because the authority knew of no one entitled to convey the land on behalf of the claimants.

On the question of the relevant date, counsel for the acquiring authority submitted that the date of valuation should be the date of the hearing, i.e. March 26, 1975, and as possession had not yet been taken the tribunal (Mr. J. D. Russell-Davis) accepted that date. The valuer to the acquiring authority considered that the subject site was incapable of development in isolation and could only be considered when married to adjacent land. At the tribunal's request the area planning officer had been called to give evidence and he confirmed that in his opinion the subject land was incapable of redevelopment in isolation. It could only be dealt with comprehensively because being in a conservation area, that was the only form of appropriate development and in addition the site dimensions and contours did not allow isolated development. Finally the small frontage was insufficient to allow the necessary obligatory space between a building on the site and any building adjoining.

The acquiring authority's valuer had no evidence to offer of private sales of individual sites but he did submit details of purchases by the acquiring authority. For the acquiring authority it was contended, as a matter of law, that because the authority had already acquired the adjacent site to that of the subject site any enhancement in value due to site marriage had to be eliminated. Therefore, the subject land could be said to have no hope value for anything more than the eighth schedule rights.

As the claimants were not represented the tribunal pointed out that it had not had the advantage of hearing counter arguments and it was, therefore, incumbent upon it to scrutinise most carefully the arguments and evidence of the acquiring authority and to question witnesses in much the same way as would have occurred if the claimant had been represented. The tribunal rejected the legal argument and valuation supported by the acquiring authority. The acquiring authority had submitted in May 1974 a rule 42 valuation prepared by the same valuer which, by implication, he had withdrawn because it was now claimed it had been made on the wrong premise, the subsequent acquisition of the adjoining property having altered the situation. After examining this lodged valuation the tribunal decided to adopt the figure of value therein, a sum of £4,500. There was a rentcharge on which there was no evidence before the tribunal but using its own experience, this rentcharge was capitalised at a sum which left the net figure of compensation at £4,150. This was the sum the acquiring authority was ordered to pay, less any accrued interest on the land charge in respect of the acquisition of the subject property. The authority would pay legal costs, if any, from the date of the notice to treat up to the date of the reference but no order was made as to the costs of the reference itself.

(*Decision April 24, 1975*)

17

ACQUIRING AUTHORITY'S OBJECTION TO BLIGHT NOTICE UPHELD.

The reference *Phillips* v. *Avon County Council* concerned a Bristol property and arose out of a blight notice under s. 193(1) of the Town and Country Planning Act 1971, as amended by s. 78(1) of the Land Compensation Act 1973. Proposed improvements and alterations to a highway led to the authority being required to purchase the claimant's interest and it was claimed that the blighted land fell within s. 192(1)(*d*) of the 1971 Act as amended, the claimant being qualified within the meaning of s. 203(3) of the 1971 Act. In November 1974 the acquiring authority objected to the blight notice by counter notice on the grounds that no part of the hereditament was comprised in land in any of the specified descriptions in s. 192 and that the authority did not propose to acquire any part of the hereditament in exercise of any relevant powers s. 194 (2) (*b*). The authority did not claim at any time or dispute that the claimant had not made reasonable endeavours to sell the property.

The tribunal (Mr. J. D. Russell-Davis) considered the relevant sections of the 1971 and 1973 Acts and in its opinion said there was no doubt that the claimant's property had been blighted in the usually accepted sense of the word. Evidence about the effects of traffic vibration and traffic noise were not seriously challenged and there was no dispute about endeavours to sell the property. However, although the claimant may have been badly advised at the time he did accept terms for the sale of adjacent land in full and final settlement of all claims. An offer by the authority had not been withdrawn and the tribunal understood that it was still open to the claimant to negotiate purchase on fair terms. The tribunal had been impressed by evidence that an appropriate officer had advised the acquiring authority that in all the circumstances, including grounds of hardship, the authority should purchase the property but the authority committee within their powers had decided not to do so and it was hardly credible that they should not when receiving the blight notice have taken into account the exercise of their powers under s. 22 of the 1973 Act. The authority had proved that the blight notice could not fall within s. 192(1)(*d*) of the 1971 Act, since the road in question at that point was neither a trunk nor a special road. Additionally the blight notice failed under s. 74(2)(*a*) of the 1973 Act because the property was not shown on plans approved by the highway authority as land proposed to be acquired. The tribunal had no alternative but to uphold the objection by the county council to the blight notice on the grounds that no part of the property was comprised in any of the specified descriptions and that the contention that the authority did not propose acquisition in exercise of relevant powers was well founded. The authority reluctantly asked for costs and a lump sum of £75 was awarded against the claimant.

(*Decision April 24, 1975*)

18

ROAD WIDENING. A STRIP OF GARDEN INVOLVED. BLIGHT NOTICE CONFIRMED. DEEMED NOTICE TO TREAT FOR WHOLE OF PROPERTY.

The reference *Randell* v. *West Glamorgan County Council* concerned a house in three-quarters of an acre of land at Caswell, Swansea, where the owner had served a blight notice under s. 193(1) of the Town and Country Planning Act 1971, requiring the authority to purchase the freehold interest in the property. The authority had lodged a counter notice objecting to the blight notice. The authority intended to acquire a strip of the garden of the subject property for road widening purposes. Of the total site area of about 3,450 square yards rather less than one-tenth was required. Before the acquisition of the strip the house at its nearest point was some 54 ft. 3 ins. from the boundary and after the strip had been taken the distance would be 34 ft. 8 ins.

The claimant wished the authority to acquire the whole of the property and unless they were required so to do the authority proposed to acquire only the strip. Reference was made to s. 202(2) of the Town and Country Planning Act 1971, which concerned part acquisition and the possibility of material detriment to the main property and evidence was given on behalf of the claimant that prospective purchasers had lost interest in the property once they became aware of the road widening proposals and expert opinion was offered indicating that the destruction of a large part of the existing screen of trees and shrubs would entirely affect the character of the house and would largely destroy its amenities and seclusion. This was disputed by the acquiring authority and on their behalf it was suggested that purchasers might be discouraged more by the separate sale of two parcels of the original plot, on one of which a bungalow had been erected.

In the view of the tribunal (Mr. J. H. Emlyn Jones) the strip of land in the present case could not be taken without material detriment to the house, nor could it be taken without seriously affecting the amenity of the house. The blight notice provisions of the 1971 Act provided a remedy whereby the authority could be required to take over the whole property, thereby minimising the trouble and inconvenience caused to the claimant. The tribunal was glad that in the present case the claimant was so protected and upheld the purchase notice as a valid notice in relation to the whole of the hereditament. The tribunal further directed that a notice to treat in respect of the whole hereditament was deemed to have been served by the authority on the claimant, the authority to pay the costs of the claimant on County Court scale 4 if not agreed and with discretion as to counsel's fees and a certificate for an expert witness fit to qualify.

(*Decision May 14, 1975*)

19

DISTURBANCE CLAIM. GOODWILL. TRIBUNAL'S "ROBUST" APPROACH SIMILAR TO THAT OF THE COURTS IN ASSESSING GENERAL DAMAGES.

The reference *Clibbett Limited* v. *Avon County Council* concerned the compensation following compulsory purchase of the leasehold interest in factory premises at Kingswood, Bristol, together with compensation for disturbance. The factory was concerned with the conversion of steel bars into nuts, bolts, screws, etc. and in 1973 the company concerned had a turnover of about £12,000. In 1971 a new lease for seven years was granted at a rent of £240 per annum and the parties had agreed that the claim should be treated on a total extinction basis. It was agreed, too, that the value of the lease was £275.

Most of the items of claim had been agreed between the parties but two remained in dispute. One was a minor one involving returned goods and the tribunal marginally amended the figure of claim, excluding the profit element from this small transaction. The second item was more considerable and it concerned the loss of goodwill, i.e. the loss of expected profits. Valuers for both parties had arrived at an adjusted net profit average over a period of years to which they applied a multiplier after allowing for proprietor's remuneration and interest on capital. The claimant's valuer supported a figure of £11,601 but the authority's valuer spoke to a valuation of £4,318. The tribunal (Mr. Douglas Frank, President) commented that useful though the respective valuers' calculations were he did not propose to determine each item in dispute, for how could he say, for example, what was the appropriate years' purchase when, on the evidence, he could choose any number between 1·5 and 10 without any evidence which of the figures he should choose other than the opinion of each of the valuers? He, therefore, proposed to adopt a robust approach similar to that used by the courts in assessing general damages and to award a sum which in his judgment, and in all the circumstances, was reasonable. On that basis he thought the right award was for £9,000 and taking into account other agreed and settled figures his total award was £12,605 plus surveyor's fees. The amount of the tribunal's award was in excess of the sealed offer and accordingly the acquiring authority was ordered to pay the claimant's costs on the High Court scale if not agreed.

(*Decision May 21, 1975*)

20

INTEREST SUBSISTING AT DATE OF NOTICE TO TREAT TO BE VALUED, AND BY REFERENCE TO PRICES PREVAILING WHEN NOTICE OF EXISTENCE OR OTHERWISE OF PROTECTED TENANCY.

The reference *Midland Bank Trust Company Limited* v. *London Borough of Lewisham* concerned a preliminary point of law as to whether in assessing compensation following compulsory purchase of a property in Lewisham the first and second floors should be treated as vacant or as being subject to a protected tenancy. In May 1971 the compulsory purchase order was confirmed and in September of that year the acquiring authority served on the owner of the freehold interest notice to treat. In the October the owner gave a notice of claim which included a note that there was a tenant of the first and second floors at an inclusive rent. The tenant was rehoused by the local authority in September 1972 and on that date the council took possession of the two floors. In December 1972 the owner died and in March 1973 the authority addressed a notice of entry to the deceased owner followed in August 1973 with a further notice to treat in 14 days to the owner's executors. In September 1973 the claimants submitted a claim for £18,000.

In December 1973 the borough solicitor advised the claimants by letter that the notice to treat in August 1973 had been served in error and should be disregarded and that the notice to treat served on the late owner in September 1971 had not been abandoned or withdrawn. Enclosed was another notice of entry related to the notice to treat dated September 1971 which was to become effective 14 days after December 1973. In March 1974 the authority entered into possession of the basement and ground floor.

Counsel for the claimants said that there were three possible dates for the valuation of the claimants' interest in the first and second floors and submitted that vacation by the tenant must have preceded entries by the council so that at entry the top floors were vacant. He submitted his contentions by reference to the Lands Tribunal's decision in *Bradford Property Trust* v. *Hertfordshire County Council* (1973) as being relevant. Whatever date was considered to be the correct date the valuation must be on the basis of vacant possession. On the other hand counsel for the council thought the acquiring authority should be deemed to have entered different parts of the property at different dates and, therefore, that each part must be considered separately.

The tribunal (Mr. Douglas Frank, President, and Mr. R. C. Walmsley) thought it did not matter which was the appropriate date because it seemed to them that the council could not enter into possession of the first and second floors until after they had been vacated by the tenant but if it should be relevant for other reasons they did not think that there was sufficient evidence before them that the council occupied on September 11, 1972 other than as licensees and probably, although they had no direct evidence of this, to ensure the premises did not become occupied again either by new tenants or by trespassers. They did not think the notice of entry in March 1973 would be of effect because it was addressed to the owner who had already died. In the tribunal's view the appropriate date of valuation was that pursuant to the notice of entry in December 1973. The only question then which had to be decided was whether the *Hertfordshire* case had been wrongly decided. The conclusion was that valuation as at the time of entry could only be a sensible exercise or principle if the interests were to be taken as they existed on that date. The *Hertfordshire* case was rightfully decided, from which it followed that the first and second floors of the subject property fell to be valued as vacant. Acquiring authority to pay the claimants their costs on the determination of the preliminary point of law on the High Court scale unless agreed.

(*Decision May 22, 1975*)

21

COMPENSATION FOR LAND IN AN AREA OF COMPREHENSIVE REDEVELOPMENT BASED ON REASONABLE PLANNING PERMISSION FOR RESIDENTIAL DEVELOPMENT.

The reference *Hawkins* v. *City of Birmingham District Council* concerned the amount of compensation payable for 30·6 acres of land at Woodgate Valley, four or five miles from the centre of Birmingham. As the subject land was in an area of comprehensive development s. 16(4) and s. 16(5 to 7) of the Land Compensation Act 1961 were relevant and the question to be decided by the Tribunal (Mr. Douglas Frank, President and Mr. W. H. Rees) was what planning permission might reasonably have been expected in the absence of the declaration of the land as an area of comprehensive development. Prior to the area being so declared some residential development had been carried out on two sides of the Valley but not in the base of the Valley. Having heard the evidence of the claimant's surveyor and by the Area Planning Officer as to the town planning history of the subject land and of adjoining and nearby lands, and their opinions, the tribunal came to the conclusion that planning permission might reasonably have been expected for residential development on the whole of the land apart from a small piece in the north. On the basis of agreed valuations subject to the tribunal's decision it followed that after a deduction for registered land charges the compensation payable was £866,037. To that was added the claimant's surveyor's fees. A sealed offer by the authority was less than the award, so it was ordered to pay the claimant his costs on the High Court scale if not agreed.

(*Decision June 4, 1975*)

22

COMPENSATION CLAIM. RENTAL VALUE UNDERESTIMATED. STABLE ACCOMMODATION NOT CONSIDERED WORTHLESS.

The reference *Wheeler* v. *Redditch Development Corporation* concerned the compensation payable for an end-of-terrace shop, since demolished, following compulsory purchase under the New Towns Act 1946. The claimant claimed £9,300 for the property, plus sums for disturbance and professional fees. The acquiring authority assessed the compensation at £7,750 for the property based on 12 years' purchase on a rental of £645. For the claimant it was contended that the rental value had been underestimated, that a somewhat higher years' purchase was appropriate and that certain stable accommodation was not worthless as the district valuer had alleged. The tribunal (Mr. Douglas Frank, President) thought the rental value to have been underestimated and that £700 per annum was the correct figure. The 12 years' purchase was thought by the tribunal to be appropriate. The stable was worth something, even if only a nominal sum of £50. Compensation determined at £8,540, plus surveyors' fees together with value added tax at 8 *per cent.* A sealed offer by the acquiring authority was less than the award. Costs against the authority on County Court scale 3 if not agreed.

(*Decision June 18, 1975*)

23

COMPARABLE DATA OF DISTRICT VALUER PREFERRED.

The reference *Brogden and Others* v. *Wigan Metropolitan Borough Council* concerned the compensation payable for the leasehold interest in three houses in Leigh, the subject of a clearance area compulsory purchase order, the agreed valuation date being November 5, 1973. The lease was for a residue of a 999 year lease from March 1892, subject to the payment of a ground rent of £6·75 per annum but with the benefit of a receivable ground rent of £2 per annum. The claimant's valuer submitted a valuation in accordance with the provisions of s. 59 of the Housing Act 1957, and the Land Compensation Acts, 1961 and 1963, in a sum of £1,090. This was supported by reference to two sales by auction of land in Leigh in 1973. The district valuer spoke to a valuation of £485 and this was supported by reference to 14 transactions which included three settlements with surveyors. The tribunal said that the claimant's valuer's two comparables were situated in very different areas but the majority of the sites referred to by the district valuer were in areas much more similar to that surrounding the reference site. The tribunal (Mr. W. H. Rees) preferred the district valuer's figure of £485. This was awarded, plus surveyor's fees and as the acquiring authority's sealed offer exceeded this award the claimant was ordered to pay the authority's costs of the reference on County Court scale 3 if not agreed.

(Decision June 23, 1975)

24

NO CLAIM ADMITTED FOR GOODWILL OR DISTURBANCE. TRIBUNAL APPLIES STATUTORY TESTS. FAIRNESS AND REASONABLENESS NOT RELEVANT STATUTORILY.

The reference *Smith* v. *Wakefield Metropolitan District Council* concerned the compensation for the freehold interest in a house at Pontefract, following the declaration of a clearance area under s. 43 of the Housing Act 1957. Part of the property comprised a lock-up shop with living accommodation above and the other part was in use as a preparation room for the fish and chip shop; it was in poor repair. The dwelling part was subject to a tenancy at an inclusive weekly rent of £1·20. The individual unit of ownership was not capable of redevelopment for residential purposes within the building bye-laws. For the acquiring authority the district valuer confirmed an agreed compensation of £120 plus a surveyor's fee, plus value added tax on the fee as he considered that the value added tax could not be recovered by the claimant. He had added nothing for goodwill and he did not consider that the claimant qualified under s. 61 of the Housing Act 1957. The claimant's valuer put the compensation for goodwill at £450, 1½ years' purchase of the year's profits for the last two years. Following cross-examination this was adjusted and in any case he agreed that only £120 compensation was payable if the claimant had no right to disturbance. The tribunal (Mr. W. H. Rees) concluded that s. 61 of the Housing Act 1957 did not apply and that the claimant had no right to compensation for disturbance in respect of the shop and dwelling and preferred the district valuer's view that at the relevant date the other subject of compensation was not being used for business purposes. The district valuer's compensation figure was approved, the tribunal finding it difficult to see why the claimant had contested the reference. The acquiring authority's unconditional offer exceeded the award so the claimant was ordered to pay the acquiring authority's costs of the reference on County Court scale 3 if not agreed.

(*Decision June 23, 1975*)

25

COMPENSATION CLAIM FOR DWELLING. WIDE DIVERGENCE BETWEEN VALUERS. TRIBUNAL ITSELF TAKES INTO ACCOUNT THE GENERAL SPECTRUM OF EVIDENCE, I.E., AGE, SITUATION, CONDITION, AREA, ETC.

The reference *Trustees of W. H. Flower* v. *Secretary of State for the Environment* concerned the compensation payable for the freehold interest in a property at Hinksey Hill, Oxfordshire, following compulsory acquisition for purposes connected with the construction of the Abingdon By-Pass. The district valuer supported a valuation in a sum of £17,500, and the claimants' valuer a sum of £35,000. A third valuer, called by the claimant supported a figure of £25,000, but the tribunal (Mr. Douglas Frank, President) did not find his evidence of any assistance. The tribunal declared that there could be no doubt that the opinion of expert witnesses based on their expertise and experience was not only evidence but valuable evidence, particularly in the kind of proceeding concerned, but when the tribunal found such an enormous divergence of opinion and when each had to be treated with equal respect and weight then those opinions ceased to be of value. The tribunal turned to the other evidence on which the valuers relied to support their opinions, sales of so called comparable properties, although in truth all of them varied substantially in various characteristics from the reference properties. Therefore it was necessary to take into account the general spectrum of evidence, i.e. age, situation, state of repair, method of drainage, areas, rating assessments, sale prices and so on. The tribunal concluded that the open market value was £20,500. This was the award, plus surveyor's fees. A sealed offer by the acquiring authority was for £20,000 inclusive of all heads of claim. Acquiring authority to pay the claimants a sum of £100 towards their costs.

(*Decision June 25, 1975*)

26

TWO MONTHS' BREAK IN RESIDENTIAL OCCUPATION SUFFICIENT TO DEFEAT CLAIM FOR OWNER-OCCUPIER'S SUPPLEMENT.

The reference *Cartin* v. *Hartlepool Borough Council* concerned the compensation payable following compulsory acquisition of a house at Hartlepool under Part 3 of the Housing Act 1957. The claimants, in addition to site value, claimed an owner-occupier's supplement under s. 68 of the Act and the fifth schedule. In an earlier decision the tribunal had decided six out of seven references in the same vicinity. The claimants in this seventh case contended that throughout the qualifying period the house had been wholly or partly occupied as a private dwelling. There had, however, been a period of delay after the vendor had quitted and before the claimants took up residence. The qualifying period was from April 6, 1971 to April 5, 1973. On December 19, 1972, the vendor ceased to reside at the house but left curtains, fitted carpet, gas fire, fitted table, stool, gas cooker, linoleum, sideboard, chest of drawers and a bicycle. The hope was that the buyer would take these items over. In February 1973 the claimants, with the vendor's permission, began to live in the house. This followed informal agreement about the price to be paid. Completion took place in April 1973. Between December 1972 and February 1973 the vendor visited the house and turned on the light at night to give the impression to vandals and squatters that the house was occupied. A void for rating purposes had been allowed during that same period. The tribunal (Mr. V. G. Wellings) said that the question was one of fact and degree for his decision. Occupation was a matter of fact and only existed when there was sufficient measure of control to prevent strangers from interfering. There was a break in residential occupation of approximately two months during the qualifying period. In the result the claimants were entitled to site value compensation only. The sum of £30 had been agreed so that was the award plus surveyors' fees and all proper legal costs incurred by the claimants prior to the date of the reference to the tribunal. Claimants to pay £10 towards the costs of the acquiring authority.

(*Decision July 2, 1975*)

27

GAP BETWEEN VACATION BY VENDORS AND OCCUPATION BY PURCHASERS FATAL TO CLAIM FOR OWNER-OCCUPIER'S SUPPLEMENT REQUIRING THAT THROUGHOUT QUALIFYING PERIOD THE HOUSE SHOULD BE WHOLLY OR PARTLY OCCUPIED AS A PRIVATE DWELLING.

There were six references in *Reeves and Others* v. *Hartlepool Borough Council*, on the question of compensation following compulsory acquisition under Part 3 of the Housing Act 1957. Each claimant sought an owner-occupier's supplement. After the vendor had quitted there was a period of delay before the purchaser took up residential occupation. In such circumstances could a claimant allege that "throughout the qualifying period the house was wholly or partly occupied as a private dwelling?". Section 68 of the Housing Act 1969 and its fifth schedule were in point. For the particular cases the qualifying period meant the period of two years ending with the relevant date, i.e. the date of declaring a clearance area. In each of the claims cases a rate void allowance had been claimed and paid.

Counsel for the claimants submitted that under the fifth schedule to the 1969 Act a house was to be regarded as occuped as a private dwelling in any period in which it was in fact empty (*a*) if it was empty pending sale and the vendor left with the intention of selling for use by the purchaser as a private dwelling or (*b*) if it was empty pending the purchaser's moving in; that being his intention. Appropriate case law was cited. For the acquiring authority it was said that the question in the first place was one of interpretation of the words in the fifth schedule. "Occupied as a private dwelling" did not bear any artificial meaning. Occupation did not begin until the claimants began to reside in their respective houses in a full sense. The schedule expressly contemplated that there might be an interval of time between cesser of residential occupation by a vendor and the beginning of residential occupation by a purchaser and that eventuality was expressly catered for in sub-paragraph (2) of paragraph 1 of the schedule. But no application had been made to the acquiring authority under that sub-paragraph.

The tribunal (Mr. V. G. Wellings) did not consider that Rent Act decisions were a useful or relevant guide. The word "occupied" had its ordinary meaning. The word "throughout" meant what it said. There must be no break in residential occupation. None of the claimants entitled to an owner-occupier's supplement. Agreed site value compensation was awarded, together with surveyors' fees and legal costs incurred prior to the references. On the question whether the tribunal could give guidance on an approach under sub-paragraph (2) of paragraph 1 of the fifth schedule it was pointed out that this was a matter solely for the acquiring authority, not open to review by the tribunal or the courts. Each claimant was ordered to pay £10 towards the costs of the acquiring authority.

(*Decision July 2, 1975*)

28

PLANNING RESTRICTIONS WOULD PREVENT DEVELOPMENT. SITE VALUE BASIS OF COMPENSATION ONLY.

The reference *Medhurst* v. *Leicester City Council* concerned the compensation payable following compulsory purchase under Part 3 of the Housing Act, 1957, of a dwelling in Leicester. The valuation on behalf of the acquiring authority was in a sum of £135, plus surveyor's fees and proper legal costs. The valuation for the claimant was in a sum of £819. This was based on the assumption that it would have been possible to build one house on the subject site. The acquiring authority did not agree. There was also disagreement on the amount of compensation. The planning authority had required new houses to be set back 35 feet from the centre of the carriage way. Another obstacle was a requirement about space between buildings. It could not be claimed, however, that such requirements had not been waived in certain cases, but there were no special circumstances in the present reference to justify any waiver. As between the two opposing valuers the tribunal (Mr. J. R. Laird) accepted the valuation on behalf of the acquiring authority and awarded a sum of £135 compensation, plus surveyor's fees and any legal costs incurred from the date of the notice to treat up to the date of notice of reference. The acquiring authority's sealed offer was for an amount the same as the award so the claimant was ordered to pay £40 costs to the acquiring authority.

(*Decision July 9, 1975*)

29

PURCHASE NOTICE. DECREASE IN VALUE DUE ENTIRELY TO SCHEME UNDERLYING THE ACQUISITION. CLAIMANT'S VALUATION APPROVED.

The reference *Morris and Jacombs Ltd.* v. *Birmingham District Council* concerned the purchase price payable in respect of 2·35 acres of land at Stirchley, Birmingham, following service of a purchase notice on the local authority under s. 129 of the Town and Country Planning Act 1962. Ten years ago the reference land stood as part of a larger area of about 20 acres used as non-statutory allotments and so allocated in the current development plan. The local authority wished the land to be made available for housing and obtained an appropriate release from the Minister. An outline planning permission was granted to a company in December 1965 for the development of the 20 acres for residential purposes, subject to the provision of about 3 acres of public open space. In January 1966 the present claimants submitted an application for the development of the whole of the 20 acres residentially. After discussions it was agreed that 1·60 acres should be allocated for public open space. This 1·60 acres formed part of the 2·35 acres in the present reference. What remained for determination was the compensation payable for the balance of ·75 acres. This comprised a strip of land 20 feet wide and 1,600 feet long, immediately abutting the back gardens of houses fronting a main road. On their January 1966 planning application the claimants were given permission to develop conditional on their providing an access road at the rear of the aforesaid dwellings fronting a main road. A further application in September 1966 the claimants lodged showed provision of this access road. In October 1966 the planning authority indicated that it would be necessary for the access road to be paved with a suitable hard impervious material. The access area still remained as a grass covered area at the time of the reference, with obstacles at each end as a barrier to vehicles. The area provided no access to anyone. An application by the claimants to develop the access area residentially was refused. The company served a purchase notice covering both the ·75 acres and the 1·60 acres, asserting that both had become incapable of reasonably beneficial use. A counter-notice was served by the authority. In due course the Minister confirmed the notice and directed that the authority be deemed to have served a notice to treat. Agreement was reached on the valuation date and on the open space value at £500. It was also agreed that the value of the ·75 acres of accessway if developed as part of the 20 acres might be taken as £15,000. This figure the claimants pursued, whereas the authority argued that the ·75 acres fell to be valued as a private service road on the basis of the confirmed s. 17 certificate. Clearly, said the tribunal (Mr. R. C. Walmsley), the open market value of the ·75 acres as at the date of the deemed notice to treat was its value as a private service road. On that basis the claimants asked for £4,000 and the authority contended for £500. Witnesses supporting these valuations did so on the assumption that the most likely purchaser would be one whose motive would be to derive a profit from the sale of access rights to individual frontagers. Neither valuation was supported by external evidence so the only course was for the tribunal to value the valuers. The claimants' valuer's opinion was thought by the tribunal to be the more reliable. Consideration was then given to s. 9 of the Land Compensation Act, 1961, providing that no account was to be taken of any advantage or disadvantage due to the carrying out of the scheme for which the property was compulsorily acquired. The tribunal said that in this case the scheme seemed readily identifiable. It was the provision of an access road. If developed as part of the claimants' 20 acres the accessway area had been agreed as worth £15,000. The tribunal found its value to be £4,000 as a private access road. Was the £11,000 decrease due entirely to the scheme underlying the acquisition? The circumstances left the tribunal in no doubt. The purchase price was determined in a sum of £15,500 including the open space. The authority's sealed offer was less than the award. The acquiring authority to pay the claimants their costs of the reference on the High Court scale, the claimants to pay the costs of the authority in respect of an adjournment at the claimants' request.

(*Decision July 21, 1975*)

30

RELIEF ROAD PROPOSALS. BLIGHT NOTICE CHALLENGED BY LOCAL AUTHORITY. CLAIMANT'S NOTICE VALID. NOTICE TO TREAT ASSUMED TO HAVE BEEN SERVED.

The reference *Avery* v. *Surrey County Council* concerned compensation following the serving of a blight notice by the owner of the freehold interest in a house in Weybridge, standing in ·40 acres of land. The notice was under the provisions of s. 193(1) of the Town and Country Planning Act 1971 requiring purchase by the authority on the grounds that reasonable endeavours had been made to sell the freehold but a sale was not possible except at a price substantially lower than that reasonably expected if the property was or was likely to be comprised in land in one of the descriptions in s. 192 of the 1971 Act. The authority served a counter-notice. The reason for the blight notice lay in the provision of a relief road to ease the town centre traffic problem and three alernative routes were under consideration. Uncertainty as to the selected route continued throughout the period from October 1973 to early 1975 during which time the claimant had tried to sell the house. At the time of the counter-notice no decision had been reached about the road scheme. Subsequently the authority made up its mind on a route directly affecting the subject property. The counter-notice fell to be considered under paragraph (*c*) of s. 194(2)—"that the authority proposed in the exercise of relevant powers to acquire a part of the hereditament but (unless compelled to do so by virtue of these provisions) do not propose to acquire any other part of that hereditament in the exercise of such powers". That had to be read with s. 202(2) of the 1971 Act. The tribunal (Mr. R. C. Walmsley) said that the issue to be resolved was whether or not the ·15 acres required for the road scheme could be taken from the ·40 acres without material detriment to the property. Following its inspection the tribunal found that there would be material detriment, the significant factors being the loss of a screen of trees and the bringing of traffic much nearer the house. The blight notice was declared to be valid. A notice to treat was deemed to have been served by the authority. Although currently occupied as a private dwelling there was permitted use as a guest house and a planning permission for conversion into three flats. The authority accepted that the claimant was entitled to present her case under one or other of these three and evidence was given accordingly. Having found that there would be material detriment to the property as a house the tribunal deemed it unnecessary to set out the evidence relating to the two alternative possible uses. The acquiring authority was ordered to pay the claimant's costs on County Court scale 4 if not agreed, with discretion as to counsel's fees and with certificate for increased fees to expert witness.

(*Decision July 22, 1975*)

31

CONFLICT BETWEEN VALUERS. EVIDENCE LEADS TRIBUNAL TO MAKE A DETERMINATION. PERIOD OF NOTICE TO QUARTERLY TENANT DECIDED IN FAVOUR OF ACQUIRING AUTHORITY.

The references *UDS Tailoring Ltd. and Alexandre Ltd. v. Cambridge City Council* concerned the assessment of compensation of leasehold interests in the centre of Cambridge. Agreement had been reached on the disturbance claim by UDS at £18,000. There was a wide difference between the valuers on compensation. For the company a total claim of £1,192,750 was supported. For the Corporation a figure of £405,000 was submitted. In both cases legal costs and surveyors' fees would be payable to the claimants. The valuers differed on the prices for zone A (20 feet deep) and, consequently, on zone B and the remainder. There was also a difference so far as upper floor space was concerned. Additionally they differed when it came to capitalising their respective estimated rental values. The authority's valuer capitalised the actual and his estimated reversionary rentals using one rate of interest for each property for both term and reversion. This approach was preferred by the tribunal (Mr. J. Stuart Daniel and Mr. J. R. Laird). There was also a difference in approach between the valuers on the way to deal with the head rent payable to the freeholders. The authority's valuer apportioned this rent between each of the reference properties and then deducted such apportioned amounts from the rents reserved under the respective leases and from the estimated rack rental values, thereafter capitalising the respective profit rents. This too was adopted by the tribunal. On the question of the correct zone A rental value there was a wide gap. For the claimants' valuer the figure of £27·50 per square foot was supported. The authority's valuer supported a figure of £12·50. The tribunal thought the answer could only be deduced from a correct analysis and study of the comparables given in evidence. This included lettings and negotiated settlements of compensation with experienced surveyors acting for claimants. The tribunal concluded that for zone A (20 ft. deep) the rental value per sq. ft. was £15, zone B (also 20 ft.) £7·50 and £3·75 p.s.f. in the case of the three small remainders. The tribunal also determined the values of ancillary accommodation at somewhat different figures. On the important question of the rate *per cent.* to be applied to the rental values the tribunal agreed that the four necessary questions for a valuer to answer were (1) should tax be reflected; (2) if so, by what method; (3) what was the over-all yield rate to be; and (4) what was the type of investment being sold. On the first item the tribunal agreed with the authority's valuer that there was no cause to reflect income tax in the present case because the particular property and the type of transaction did not require it, the bulk of the income being in the rents reserved or in the value of the property in hand. The second item, therefore, did not arise. In the light of the whole of the evidence the tribunal thought there was adequate support for the authority's valuer's figures of 6 *per cent.* for the shops, 7 *per cent.* for a Henekey's Bar and 9 *per cent.* for upper parts. This produced a total compensation figure of £494,107 apart from the £18,000 disturbance figure. To that total were to be added any legal costs from the date of the notice to treat up to the date of notice of reference and a surveyor's fee.

A question of law arose on one reference (the claim by Alexandre Ltd.). This was whether, for the purpose of assessing compensation, the company was entitled to six months' notice (as argued for the claimants) or only three months (as argued by the authority). The contending arguments were fully explored and the tribunal confirmed that only three months' notice was appropriate. The actual figure of compensation was marginally higher than that submitted on behalf of the authority. A point about interest on surveyor's fees was not pressed as both parties were evidently agreed that the tribunal had no jurisdiction in that respect. In one reference the sealed offer by the authority was less than the tribunal's award, in the other it exceeded it. The acquiring authority was to pay each claimant their costs in their particular reference up to the date of the relevant sealed offer. After that date the acquiring authority were to pay the claimants' costs where the sealed offer was less than the tribunal's award, and the claimants were to pay the acquiring authority's costs where the sealed offer exceeded the award made. All costs were to be on the High Court scale if not agreed.

(*Decision July 25, 1975*)

32

DIMINUTION IN VALUE ATTRIBUTABLE TO NEED TO PROTECT CIVIL AVIATION AUTHORITY'S RANGE STATION NOT TO BE IGNORED. CLAIMANTS NOT ENTITLED TO BE RECOUPED.

The reference *Packwood Poultry Products Ltd.* v. *Metropolitan Borough of Solihull* raised as a preliminary issue the legal basis of compensation for a deemed compulsory purchase arising under confirmed purchase notices relating to part of a former airfield near Kenilworth. There were three purchase notices, each related to a rectangular plot 500 ft. long by 60 ft. wide, each of these plots being the intended site of a chicken broiler house. In one case there was a double plot. All four sites lay within a radius of 750 ft. of an electronic signalling device known as a VOR station. This was near Elmdon Airport, Birmingham, and was part of a network of air navigation installations, providing signals for aircraft wherever bound. Following planning refusals intended to protect the station the four sites were sterile from a planning point of view. Questions raised by the claimants for determination were whether the existence of the VOR station was to be ignored for the purpose of assessing compensation under part IX of the Town and Country Planning Act 1971 and whether the grant of planning permission for erecting broiler houses was to be assumed by virtue of s. 112 of the Town and Country Planning Act 1971 for assessing compensation under the same part of the 1971 Act. The tribunal (Mr. V. G. Wellings) took note of the facts relating to the planning position, the arrangements for safeguarding the VOR station and certain rights and duties of the Civil Aviation Authority. The claimants argued that but for the need to protect the VOR station they would have obtained planning permission to erect broiler houses on the four sites. That diminution in compensation was to be ignored. The scheme underlying the acquisition was a scheme to enforce sterilisation of the subject land to protect the VOR station. The refusal of planning permission and the consequent deemed compulsory purchase took place at the behest of the Civil Aviation Authority. Alternatively s. 112 of the Town and Country Planning Act 1971 through s. 186(1) of that Act, applied, concerning deemed authority from the Secretary of State to a local authority following confirmation of a purchase notice. The acquiring authority disagreed about the relevance in the present instance of the *Pointe Gourde* principle. This was because there was no scheme underlying the acquisition, the principle could only apply where the land was necessarily required for the purpose of a scheme, the acquiring authority itself had no scheme, and the *Pointe Gourde* principle might not be applicable to deemed acquisitions. The tribunal was, with regret, unable to infer that the acquiring authority ever formulated or possessed anything which could be dignified by the title of scheme, undertaking or project with respect to the need to protect the VOR station. The alternative argument, based on s. 112 of the 1971 Act was rejected as it was contrary to reality. The tribunal decided that the diminution in value of the subject land which was attributable to the need to protect the VOR station was not to be ignored. The claimants were not entitled to be recouped in respect of the amount of that diminution. The grant of planning permission for broiler houses was not to be assumed by virtue of s. 112 of the Town and Country Planning Act 1971 and s. 15(1) of the Land Compensation Act, or at all. Claimants to pay the acquiring authority's costs on the High Court scale if not agreed.

(*Decision July 28, 1975*)

33

LICENCE TO USE CANAL, PREVIOUSLY ENJOYED AS OF RIGHT, A MATTER FOR COMPENSATION IF CASE IS MADE OUT.

The reference *Lord Brecon* v. *British Waterways Board* led to an interim decision on two fundamental submissions by the Board. The original right to use boats on a canal at Brecon referred specifically to pleasure boats. When that right had statutory authority, in 1793, boats propelled by mechanical means were unknown. The tribunal (Mr. Douglas Frank, President) had no doubt that the words in the statute of 1793 were unambiguous and that a pleasure boat meant a boat used for pleasure or constructed for the use for pleasure, however propelled. The second submission arose under subs 7 of s. 105 of the Transport Act 1968. This referred to the suffering of loss by reason of the extinguishment of private rights and the payment of compensation. The Board contended that loss meant financial loss and the claimant had not shown any loss in the sense of proving depreciation in the value of his property. In the tribunal's view loss included money's worth. The obligation to pay for a licence in place of a free right established such a loss. It seemed to the tribunal that a loss by reason of extinguishment meant the loss of the right to use the canal for pleasure purposes and there was nothing in the relevant Act which said, or at least the tribunal had not been directed to it, that the loss should be of a particular kind, or that it should be calculated in a particular way.

The tribunal did not decide if the claimant had made any financial loss. That was a matter for evidence. Matter adjourned to hear submissions. Liberty to apply for the calling of additional witnesses.

(*Decision July 29, 1975*)

34

UNDERGROUND TRAIN NOISE. NO COMPENSATION PAYABLE TO HOTEL.

The reference *Knott Hotels Company of London Ltd.* v. *London Transport Executive* concerned a claim for compensation in respect of the Westbury Hotel, London. It related to the use of the Victoria underground railway line. The south-bound tunnel runs under the hotel and the other is close to the corner of the hotel. There was a distance of 30 ft. between the top of the tunnel and the foundations of the hotel. Noise from trains could be heard in various parts of the building. It was contended that a total of 16 bedrooms were significantly affected, together with two public rooms in the basement. The claimants contended for the value of land taken and for injurious affection sums of £2,375 and £204,000 respectively. On the first day the tribunal (Mr. Douglas Frank, President, and Mr. W. H. Rees) raised the question of the statutory rights relied on for the claim. The claimants referred to s. 63 of the Lands Clauses Act 1845 and s. 27 of the British Transport Commission Act 1955. Additionally, s. 27 of the 1955 Act was relied upon by the compensating authority. The tribunal had given much thought to the question of its jurisdiction. Had it come to the conclusion that it had not, because the construction of the railway was *ultra vires* (which the tribunal believed) that would have immense significance far beyond the issues in the present case. There had been no argument, however, on jurisdiction, so the tribunal thought it right to proceed to determine the reference. The basis of the claim for land taken was that if the whole site was to be redeveloped at some future date a sub-basement could be constructed were it not for the tunnel. This was too remote a factor in the tribunal's view. On the noise factor the tribunal did not think it would interfere significantly with the basement rooms. So far as the affected bedrooms were concerned few people would be affected by train noise compared with other noises.

On the matter of compensation the claimants made no attempt to formulate a claim on the basis of loss of profits, although the tribunal gave them an opportunity of doing so. Such evidence as there was did not, in the tribunal's opinion, establish that the train noise caused loss of profits. The claim as formulated, based on a hypothetically reduced years' purchase was wholly unacceptable to the tribunal. No compensation payable. Claimants to pay the respondent' costs on the High Court scale, if not agreed, less £100.

(*Decision July 31, 1975*)

35

NO OPEN MARKET TRANSACTIONS AS EVIDENCE. SETTLEMENT EVIDENCE OFFERED. ACQUIRING AUTHORITY'S OFFER CONFIRMED.

The reference *Hodgson* v. *Eden District Council* concerned the compensation payable in respect of two houses at Penrith, compulsorily acquired under part 3 of the Housing Act 1957. One of the houses was let to a weekly tenant, re-housed by the acquiring authority, the other was vacant, having been subject to a closing order. The district valuer, for the authority, said that he had based his valuations on s. 59(2) of the Housing Act 1957, the compensation payable being the lesser of the value of the site cleared of buildings or the market value, assuming the area in which the property stood had not been declared a clearance area. His total for compensation was £230 plus £20 surveyor's fee. There were no open market transactions that would be helpful so he had had to rely on settlement evidence. The claimant had not been able to accept that there was a quite different basis of compensation between owner-occupiers and owners and was concerned about the apparently less favourable treatment being received. The tribunal (Mr. R. C. Walmsley) accepted the district valuer's figures and awarded compensation accordingly. The authority's sealed offer was the same as the tribunal's award so it was thought appropriate that the authority should pay the claimant's costs of the reference up to the date of the sealed offer, the claimant to pay the authority's costs as from that date; all such costs payable by the claimant compounded by the tribunal at £25.

(*Decision September 18, 1975*)

36

EVIDENCE OF SETTLEMENTS RATHER THAN SALES. DISTRICT VALUER'S EVIDENCE ACCEPTED IN ITS ENTIRETY.

The reference *New* v. *West Yorkshire Metropolitan County Council* concerned the compensation payable following compulsory purchase of land taken from the front garden of a bungalow in Wakefield under the Highways Act 1959. No particulars of claim had been lodged by the claimant. The figure of £528 (£3 per square yard of land taken from the front of the garden) was submitted at the hearing. No professional evidence was called by the claimant. Including a valuer's fee the district valuer supported a figure of £200 compensation. There was no direct evidence of actual sales but he supported his valuation by reference to a schedule of 31 settlements between 1967 and 1969 with other valuers representing clients. The tribunal (Mr. J. D. Russell-Davis) accepted the district valuer's evidence in its entirety. Two hundred pounds compensation awarded, inclusive of surveyor's fee, to which was to be added any legal costs from the date of the notice to treat up to the date of the reference. The authority's sealed offer was the same as the tribunal's award. Authority to pay the claimant's costs up to the date of the sealed offer, claimant to pay the authority's costs from that date, such costs to be on County Court scale 3 if not agreed.

(*Decision September 30, 1975*)

37

COMPENSATION BASED ON ACTUAL USE (REGULATED TENANCY) AT THE DATE OF THE NOTICE TO TREAT, NOT ON ANOTHER ESTABLISHED USE AS A WAREHOUSE.

The reference *Tranter* v. *City of Birmingham District Council* concerned the compensation payable following compulsory acquisition of premises in Aston, Birmingham, which had an established use as a warehouse, although no planning permission had been obtained. Both on the date of the notice to treat and the date of possession the premises were let on a regulated tenancy under the Rent Act 1968. The issue was whether the actual or established use applied for determining compensation. If the former a figure of £1,400 had been agreed. If the latter £3,850. Originally built as a public house the premises had been used as a warehouse over a long period, more recently by way of short lettings, the last of which was as a house and shop but subsequently occupied residentially in its entirety subject to a regulated rent, although without planning for residential use. But for this letting there would have been a market for the premises as a warehouse, the likely sale price for that use being £3,850. The acquiring authority contended that existing use at the date of notice to treat determined the compensation. The tribunal (Mr. V. G. Wellings) thought that s. 9 of the Land Compensation Act 1961 was concerned with valuation and not with the determination of the interest to be valued, and agreed with the authority that depreciation induced by the scheme should be ignored. Consequently the claimant was entitled to compensation in the sum of £1,400. The parties had agreed not to ask for costs so there was no costs award.

(*Decision September 30, 1975*)

38

NON-APPEARANCE OF CLAIMANT. OBJECTION TO BLIGHT NOTICE UPHELD.

The reference *Green* v. *Staffordshire Moorlands District Council* concerned the validity of the authority's objection to a blight notice under s. 193(1) of the Town and Country Planning Act 1971 as amended or extended by s. 68 of the Land Compensation Act 1973. No appearance was made by the claimants, even though the tribunal (Mr. W. H. Rees) delayed one hearing and adjourned another. He proceeded to determine the reference under rule 53 of the Lands Tribunal Rules 1975. Counsel for the authority reserved the right to challenge the blight notice on the grounds that the claimants had not made reasonable endeavours to sell their interest. For the authority it was confirmed that the property was in a designated industrial area on the approved town map. It did not appear to be in an action area. There was no local plan which related to the property and the authority did not propose to acquire it. Evidence accepted. Objection to blight notice upheld. Costs £50 awarded against the claimants.

(*Decision October 13, 1975*)

39

COMPENSATION. EVIDENCE OF COMPARABLES LEADS TRIBUNAL TO A FIGURE ALMOST MID-WAY BETWEEN CONTENDING CLAIMS.

The reference *Morley* v. *London Borough of Hackney* concerned the compensation payable in respect of the compulsory acquisition of a house in Hackney under part 3 of the Housing Act 1957. The subject property was regarded as an unfit dwelling but the Secretary of State had classified it as wholly well maintained. No well-maintained allowance fell to be made, however, because the claimant was entitled to an owner-occupier's supplement in addition to cleared site value. The house was one of a terrace statutorily listed as buildings of architectural and historic interest. The parties had agreed that the value fell to be determined as at the first day of the Lands Tribunal hearing, that the property was to be assumed not included in a compulsory purchase order, that none of the other properties included in the same Order was in a c.p.o., that aspects flowing from the Order were to be ignored, but that it should not be ignored that all the properties included in the Order were unfit for human habitation. For the claimant a compensation claim of £17,000 was pressed. For the acquiring authority a figure of £9,250. The parties agreed that the tribunal (Mr. R. C. Walmsley) should adopt for site value purposes a figure of £925, midway between their two valuations. Both valuation witnesses relied wholly on the evidence of comparables. Much of the locality was occupied by commercial and industrial properties, but a considerable part was being developed residentially. Not far away was the Angel Area, now an area of middle income families intent on applying a high standard of renovation to the Georgian and Victorian architecture. Another nearby area, the De Beauvoir area, was developing in the same way. These areas were relevant on the matter of comparables. Having heard the evidence and having made an extensive inspection the tribunal view was in agreement with the claimant's valuer about the likely bidder of the subject property. On the other hand the tribunal did not like his residual valuation. It was the tribunal's view that a purchaser would adopt the authority valuer's approach. On the evidence of the comparables the tribunal put the value of the subject house at £13,250, including the agreed site value. Additionally there would be a surveyor's fee and legal costs from the date of the notice to treat up to the date of the notice of reference. The sealed offer by the acquiring authority was less than the award, so the authority was ordered to pay the claimant's costs of the reference on the High Court scale if not agreed.

(*Decision October 27, 1975*)

40

ACQUIRED POPRERTIES SUBJECT TO TENANCIES. TENANTS RE-HOUSED BY ACQUIRING AUTHORITY. AFTER WHICH THE CLAIMANTS WERE IN POSSESSION UNTIL DEMOLITION. VACANT POSSESSION VALUE ALLOWED FOR COMPENSATION PURPOSES.

The reference *Buckingham Street Investments Ltd.* v. *Greater London Council* raised the question whether compensation fell to be assessed on the basis of a sale with vacant possession or subject to existing tenancies. Two houses in S.E. London were involved, the acquisition being for education purposes. The appropriate values were £3,000 for each property with vacant possession. With existing tenancies £1,500 each. Counsel for the claimants relied on a statement of agreed facts, namely, that possession was taken by the acquiring authority on the date demolition commenced. This was over four months after the tenants had vacated. However, the acquiring authority submitted evidence of padlocking and securing of the houses four to five months before demolition. This was accepted by the tribunal (Mr. V. G. Wellings). There was no evidence that the acquiring authority's attitude in respect of alternative accommodation for the tenants was other than persuasive. There was no evidence that eviction powers had been mentioned. The tenants had vacated their houses before the acquiring authority had taken possession, according to counsel for the claimants. Counsel for the acquiring authority submitted that the acquiring authority took possession of the subject houses on the date when the occupying tenants were re-housed. Arguments were presented to distinguish the circumstances from those in cited cases on behalf of the claimants. It was suggested that in the present case the process of obtaining possession had been a continuous one which started with re-housing of the tenants and ending with padlocking and securing the properties. When the tenants were re-housed they were dispossessed by the acquiring authority. The tribunal did not accept the authority's submissions. There was no evidence that when the tenants were re-housed the keys were handed to the acquiring authority. The proper inference was that upon re-housing and vacation by the tenants the legal possession of the properties vested in the claimants as owners. Where no one else was in possession then possession followed title. No servant or agent of the acquiring authority set foot in the properties prior to the dates on which the properties were padlocked and secured. Those were the dates on which they took possession. The correct basis on which to assess compensation was to value the freehold interest as being with vacant possession. £6,000 awarded, together with surveyors' fees and proper legal costs incurred prior to the date of the reference. Acquiring authority to pay claimants' their costs on the High Court scale if not agreed.

(*Decision November 12, 1975*)

41

LESSEE'S RIGHTS TO EXTENDED LEASE UNDER LANDLORD AND TENANT ACT 1954 TAKEN INTO ACCOUNT IN COMPENSATION AWARD FOR GOODWILL.

The reference *Traggett* v. *Surrey Heath Borough Council* concerned the compensation payable by reason of a confirmed blight notice affecting a shop at Camberley. By November 1972 the shop and surrounding area had become subject to planning blight attributable to published proposals to make the area a comprehensive development area. At that time the claimants served a blight notice under s. 193 of the Town and Country Planning Act 1971 and this had been accepted by the local authority. There was a wide gap on the question of compensation. The claimants sought £29,700 and the acquiring authority considered that £11,011 was the appropriate total compensation. The claimants offered no evidence on loss of earnings so the tribunal (Mr. V. G. Wellings) rejected that part of the claim. There was a dispute about the date of entry, the claimants contending for January 1, 1973. The claimants handed over the keys on that date and although they did not return considerable amount of stock remained for some months until they were sold. The tribunal, however, accepted evidence on behalf of the authority that the keys were not delivered to the authority until July 27, 1973. That was the material date for compensation purposes. The claimants also asserted that there had been a firm undertaking by the authority to re-locate displaced traders in the new shopping centre, but it was proved to the tribunal's satisfaction that the actual undertaking was that in the event of displacement the authority would use its best endeavours to assist in satisfactory re-location. That part of the claim was also rejected. The tribunal thought the claimants' position under Part II of the Landlord and Tenant Act 1954 to be more promising. Under s. 47 of the Land Compensation Act 1973 the right of a tenant to a new tenancy under the 1954 Act was to be taken into account in assessing compensation. The tribunal considered that it was entitled to draw the inference that a new tenancy would have been granted for a term of three years, which could reasonably have been expected to last that time in spite of redevelopment prospects. The district valuer contended that the value of leasehold interest, as in the present case, lay in the profit rent and no purchaser would pay anything extra for a profit rent which would have ceased to exist after the end of the extended lease term under the 1954 Act. The proper place to take security of tenure into account was under the head of compensation for goodwill. The district valuer's computation for compensation for losses on a forced sale was accepted. On goodwill the tribunal thought the claimants' accountant had submitted a novel method of calculation. This related to gross turnover growth rate over a three-year period and an adjustment of net profits. The district valuer first adjusted the net profit into the accounts for the three years, adding back proprietor's salary, amortisation and part insurance, also an adjustment against the claimants to take account of profit rent and interest on capital not shown in the accounts. He applied three years' purchase of the latest net profit, which allowed for an upward trend in business. The tribunal rejected the accountant's approach and accepted most of the district valuer's figures. However, he had allowed insufficiently for the growth potential of the business. A total award of £12,061 was made, together with surveyors' fees and proper legal costs before the date of the reference. The authority's sealed offer was for less than this award so the acquiring authority was ordered to pay the claimants' cost of the reference on County Court scale 4 if not agreed.

(*Decision November 12, 1975*)

42

LAST CLAIM FOR INJURIOUS AFFECTION CAUSED BY USE OF VICTORIA TUBE LINE SUCCESSFUL. RELEVANCE OF RATING ASSESSMENT REDUCTION FOR THE SAME REASON.

The reference *Bradd* v. *London Transport Executive* concerned a claim in respect of injurious affection to a house in Walthamstow. It was stated by the tribunal that the Victoria line ran under some 1,300 properties, of which about 900 were residential. Only four claims in respect of injurious affection by reason of noise and vibration had been made, one of which had subsequently been withdrawn. So far as a further two were concerned the tribunal had determined a nil figure of compensation. The present reference was on the last claim. The measure of injurious affection was agreed to be the difference, if any, between the price which the subject house would have commanded in the open market at the time the rail service began and the price if the line had never been constructed. Professional evidence was given about sales and expert opinions were tendered about the comparative prices with and without the line. The tribunal (Mr. R. C. Walmsley) was in agreement with much of what the valuer for the authority had said about changing values over the years and decided that the price the reference property would have commanded at the relevant time if the line had never been constructed was £3,000. On the question of noise the tribunal thought the level to be low but something which could not be switched off during 19 hours out of the 24. On vibration the tribunal did not think the structure was likely to be affected by the line. An exercise by the claimant to "test the market" did not carry any weight as evidence but as the tribunal had to consider matters away back in September 1968 when use of the line started the valuation officer for the area was present on subpoena. He testified about ratepayers' proposals at that time seeking reductions in the rating assessments on account of the existence of the Victoria line. On the valuation officer's advice reduction had been made. A reduction in the region of 12 *per cent.* had been thought appropriate by the valuation officer, an independent and impartial valuer. The tribunal thought him more likely to have interpreted the market correctly, at least in rental terms. The tribunal found the depreciated value due to the line to be £350 and the authority was ordered to pay that sum, plus a surveyor's fee, costs on County Court scale 3 if not agreed and with discretion as to solicitors' charges and counsel's fees.

(*Decision December 8, 1975*)

43

CLAIMANT ACCEPTS ADVICE AGAINST SELLING HIS INTERESTS. THEREBY UNABLE TO SHOW HIS INABILITY TO SELL EXCEPT ON DISADVANTAGEOUS TERMS. BLIGHT COUNTER-NOTICE EFFECTIVE.

The reference *Perkins* v. *West Wiltshire District Council* raised the question as to whether an objection by the local authority to a blight notice was well founded. The subject land was a level field of about 5·4 acres at Trowbridge. On the town map the land was shown as unallocated (i.e. white land) indicating that its existing use was to remain for the most part undisturbed. The draft review of the town map showed the land as a proposed public open space. In December 1971 the claimant submitted an application for residential development of the land but this was refused by the county council on the grounds that it was contrary to the town map, and the draft review, that the land was reserved for use as a public open space, that development of the land as requested would simply result in a further need for public open space and, in any case, there was no deficiency of land for residential development. An appeal against this refusal was later dismissed by the Secretary of State.

In January 1975 the claimant served a blight notice requiring the authority to purchase his interest but one of the grounds of the counter-notice was that the council did not propose to acquire any of the land in the exercise of any relevant powers. The other ground was that certain conditions of s. 193(1) of the Town and Country Planning Act 1971 were not fulfilled. So far as the council's alleged intentions were concerned there was correspondence indicating that there was no provision for the purchase of the land in the then current estimates and the senior development control officer indicated that he knew of no proposals in that direction. So far as planning was concerned the council had the objective of use as a public open space but when and how this was to be achieved remained to be determined. In the meantime it was suggested that the long-existing agricultural use could continue. It was contended that it was not necessary in order to achieve a public open space allocation that the authority should itself exercise statutory powers of acquisition. So far as the tribunal (Mr. R. C. Walmsley) was concerned, if that part had been the only ground to be considered, i.e. the authority's objection could not be sustained, the tribunal had not been satisfied, on that ground at least, that the case was well founded.

Evidence would be necessary of an inability on the part of the claimant to sell his interest only at a price substantially lower than that which might reasonably have been expected in normal circumstances. The claimant had approached certain surveyors who had advised him that it would be quite impossible to sell the land at a figure approaching residential development prices in view of the proposals by the local authority for use of the land as a public open space. What the claimant had done was to take professional advice as to the likely outcome if he were to *try* and sell his land for residential development. But that, the tribunal pointed out, was not what the statute required. The requirement was that the claimant had made reasonable endeavours to sell. He had to have put his interest in the market and he must have tried to sell it just as it was. After dealing with some of the obvious disadvantages attaching to the claimant's interest the tribunal said that the simple fact was that the claimant had been advised against making endeavours to sell, he accepted that advice, and that acceptance precluded him from invoking the provisions of s. 193. Therefore, on that second ground it had not been shown to the tribunal's satisfaction that the authority's objection was not well founded and the authority's objection was upheld. The claimant was ordered to pay the costs of the authority on County Court scale 4 if not agreed.

(*Decision December 11, 1975*)

44

PURCHASE NOTICE. CERTIFICATE OF APPROPRIATE ALTERNATIVE DEVELOPMENT FOR RESIDENTIAL USE HELD NOT TO BE GOOD ONLY FOR THE PARTICULAR ACQUISITION. TWO LOCAL AUTHORITIES INTERESTED IN ACQUISITION OF SEPARATE PARTS. TWO VALUATIONS HELD TO BE REQUIRED.

The reference *Hoveringham Gravels Limited* v. *Chiltern District Council and Buckinghamshire County Council* concerned a long narrow enclosure of land of just short of 2½ acres not far from the centre of Chesham,

Buckinghamshire. The land formed part of a larger area of disused land, in all some 17 acres, of which about 15 acres carried planning permission for the extraction of sand and gravel. When the claimants purchased the 17 acres it was shown in the town map as metropolitan and local green belt, a zoning still in force. The claimants took the land with a burden of a tenancy to a firm owning a garage, showrooms and workshop covering about $\frac{1}{4}$ acre. Unfortunately the use involved was unauthorised from a planning point of view. The claimants subsequently applied to the county council for planning permission for the $2\frac{1}{2}$ acres for six pairs of semi-detached houses and garages. This was refused and the Minister dismissed the claimants' appeal on green belt grounds.

The claimants then sought to open negotiations with the district council for the sale to the council of the land in question for use as a public open space. The district council were willing to negotiate but declined to accept residential development as the basis for compensation. The claimants then applied to the county council for a certificate of appropriate alternative development under s. 17 of the Land Compensation Act 1961 specifying residential development at a density of six houses to the acre. The county council issued a negative certificate but on appeal the Minister allowed the claimants' appeal by issuing a new certificate indicating that planning permission might reasonably have been expected for residential development at the stated density but subject to access being arranged from a service road within the site.

There then followed two further planning applications, two refusals by the county council and two appeals to the Minister which were dismissed. Eventually the claimants served on the district council a purchase notice under s. 180 of the Town and Country Planning Act 1971 for the whole of the land involved. The council expressed unwillingness to comply with the purchase notice. In their view the county council should be substituted as the acquiring authority because the purchase notice arose as a direct result of the county council's exercise of their functions since the paramount reason for the Minister refusing planning permission was the intention of the county council as highway authority the widening and improving of a road so that a large part of the land would have been needed for that scheme. It would be manifestly wrong for the burden of land purchase to be imposed on the district council ratepayers. Moreover it was the policy of the county council to preserve and enhance the green belt so that the financial burden of carrying out that policy should lie with the county council. But for the possibility of obtaining financial assistance the district council would never have contemplated purchasing the land for a public open space because of the existence of a conditional certificate of appropriate alternative development for residential use. Although the question of obtaining financial assistance was being pursued no such help was, as yet, assured. Finally, having regard to the probable ultimate use of the land the Secretary of State should consider substituting the county council as purchasing authority.

The Secretary of State had offered an opportunity to the parties concerned to make representations at a hearing he had arranged and the district council replied that they did not wish to be heard further nor did the county council. The Secretary of State's decision was to require the county council to purchase the smaller part of the land, the frontage land and the district council to purchase the larger plot of back land. It was further directed that separate notices to treat should have been deemed to have been served by both councils on the date of his decision, March 13, 1973. Compensation negotiations commenced but the district council asserted that the certificate of appropriate alternative development given in June 1970 did not apply to the back land and that in the absence of a valid certificate the basis of compensation must be one appropriate to the green belt. The claimants gave notice of reference to the Lands Tribunal in respect of this situation but notice of reference in respect of the front land was not given until August 1974. In February 1974 the county council had issued a s. 17 certificate that if it were not proposed to acquire the front land then planning permission might reasonably have been expected to be granted for residential development. Certain conditions were laid down. In November 1974 the county council purported to issue a similar certificate in respect of the back land also subject to conditions but that certificate was given out of time and had no effect. After examining the statutory position governing s. 17 certificates the tribunal (Mr. Douglas Frank, President and Mr. J. R. Laird) found nothing in the statutes nor in the certificate to support the proposition that such a certificate was good only for the acquisition for which it was granted. Moreover, they did not consider that the acquiring authority's intention could be relevant. They did not understand how the certificate could relate only to a particular interest in the land concerned.

On the method of valuation the claimants submitted that one interest was being acquired so that the correct method of assessing compensation was one valuation followed by apportionment. For the district council it was contended that one must value what had happened, i.e. acquisitions by two different local authorities of two adjacent but different pieces of land. The sum of the values of the two areas was not necessarily the value of the whole and, therefore, the sale price of the whole was an invalid approach. The front land and the back land must be valued separately.

On the actual valuations, the tribunal said that in view of the evidence they thought that a prospective purchaser of the back land would have a strong expectation that residential planning permission would be granted, but he would have to make allowance for risks and also take into account that he would either have to wait until road works were completed so that access could be gained to the backland or he would have to buy a means of access over the front land. The tribunal thought that the claimants' valuer had over valued the land and put his valuations on one side. Effectively, the only valuation before the tribunal was that of the county valuer in a sum of £21,915 for the front land accepted and agreed by the claimants. That sum was awarded plus surveyor's fee and legal costs properly incurred from the date of the deemed notice to treat to the date of the notice of reference. The sealed offer of compensation by the acquiring authority exceeded the award so the authority was ordered to pay the claimants' their costs up to the date of the sealed offer and the claimants would pay the costs of the acquiring authority from that date, both on the High Court scale unless agreed. So far as the back land was concerned, again the county valuer's figure was adopted, i.e. £27,500 but this was discounted by 50 *per cent.* to allow for the risk of not securing planning permission and more particularly for the difficulties of access. Thus the award was £13,750 plus surveyor's fee and legal costs from the date of the deemed notice to treat to the date of the reference. The acquiring authority would pay the claimants' cost of the reference on the High Court scale unless agreed.

(*Decision December 18, 1975*)

LAW OF PROPERTY

LIST OF CASES REPORTED

SUBJECT MATTER OF CASES

1

COVENANT REGARDING SALE OF ALCOHOLIC LIQUORS IN GENERAL STORE DISCHARGED. OBJECTORS NOT ARGUING THAT THEY HAD THE BENEFIT OF COVENANT.

The application *Re Tickner* under s. 84 of the Law of Property Act, 1925, as amended, concerned an establishment in Cowley, Oxford, described by the applicant freeholders as a small supermarket. Their wish was the discharge of a covenant so they could include off-sales of alcoholic liquors from the shop. None of the five objectors had the benefit of the covenant so on that ground alone the application succeeded. But the tribunal, at the applicants' request heard the evidence on the merits of the application. The tribunal (Mr. Douglas Frank, President) could not see what possible harm would be caused by such sales and there had been sufficient changes in the neighbourhood to render the covenant obsolete. Covenant discharged.

(*Decision January 8, 1975*)

2

RESTRICTIONS MODIFIED WHERE APPLICANTS AND OBJECTORS AGREE TERMS IN WRITING.

The application *Re Marsh* concerned land at Berkhamstead and as the applicants and objectors had agreed upon terms in settlement in writing, the tribunal (Mr. V. G. Wellings), being satisfied that it had power to modify the restrictions exercised its discretion and modified the restriction to permit the erection on the application land of a house and double garage. No order as to costs.

(*Decision January 14, 1975*)

3

RESTRICTION TO THREE DWELLINGS MODIFIED TO PERMIT SIXTY-ONE TO BE BUILT ON TERMS AGREED BETWEEN OBJECTORS AND APPLICANTS.

The application *Re Graham-Smith* concerned land at Forvie, Cambridge, where there was a restriction on just under 6 acres to three dwellings together with ancillary accommodation. The applicants sought to build 61 dwellings on the land. There was no question but that the objectors concerned were entitled to the benefit of the restriction, but certain other persons who had opposed the application had not given the Registrar of the Lands Tribunal the necessary documentary evidence. Therefore, the tribunal (Mr. J. Stuart Daniel) concluded that they were not to be admitted to oppose. In any case they did not seek to do so at the hearing. The terms of a written agreement between the objectors and the applicants included the payment of a sum of money, the conveyance of a narrow strip of land to the objectors and the erection of a fence. In spite of this agreement the applicants preferred to obtain an order from the tribunal. As all disputes under the Law of Property Act had in the present case been concluded by compromise or otherwise the tribunal saw no reason why it should not exercise its discretion in granting the application. No order as to costs.

(*Decision January 30, 1975*)

4

RESTRICTIVE COVENANT MODIFIED. OBJECTIONS WITHDRAWN OR NOT ADMITTED WITH ONE EXCEPTION, TO WHOM COSTS WERE AWARDED.

The application *Re Collenette* concerned land at Harrow where all but one married couple had withdrawn their objections and the tribunal (Mr. V. G. Wellings) ordered that the application be amended to enable the applicant to rely on s. 84(1)(*b*) of the Law of Property Act, 1925. One other objector was not admitted as such. The agreed modification of a restrictive covenant was endorsed, and there was no order as to costs except that the applicant should by consent pay £100 towards the costs of one other married couple admitted as objectors.

(*Decision February 4, 1975*)

5

COVENANT DISCHARGED. PARTIES' AGREEMENT.

The application *Re Exors. J. A. Bowen* concerned land at Upton-on-Severn, but the applicant and the objector had come to terms. Notwithstanding publicity only the one objector had come forward. Leave was given to amend the application so that reliance could be on s. 84(1)(*b*) of the 1925 Act. Restriction discharged. No compensation and no costs.

(*Decision February 12, 1975*)

6

APPLICATION INVOLVING SMALL BLOCK OF FLATS REJECTED. PLOTS LIMITED TO A SINGLE DWELLING.

The application *Re Vallance and Hughes Ltd.* concerned land at Llandudno and the modification of restrictive covenants to permit the erection of four flats in two blocks. Two plots on an estate were involved, each being limited to development to one house. Two of the applicant's witnesses virtually conceded that there had been no change in the character of the neighbourhood. On the other hand the tribunal (Mr. Douglas Frank,

President) noted it was common ground that there would be ample demand for a house or houses on the subject land. Therefore, he could not accept that the covenants should be deemed obsolete. The proposed development would be different in character, the density on the plots would be double that permitted under the covenant and in the tribunal's judgment that development would be injurious to the persons entitled to the benefit of the covenants. It would have been reasonable to have erected a single dwelling on each plot. County Court scale costs awarded to objectors entitled to the benefit of the restriction.

(*Decision February 26, 1975*)

7

APPLICATION TO MODIFY RESTRICTIVE COVENANT. PRELIMINARY HEARING TO DETERMINE WHICH OBJECTORS WERE TO BE ADMITTED.

The application *Re Baron Sons Ltd.* concerned about half an acre of land in Northampton, the applicants, as owners, wishing to build three-storey flats whereas a restriction expressly provided that a block of flats was not to be deemed a private dwelling, to which, among other purposes, the land was to be confined. Owners of 35 dwellings in the vicinity objected to the application and the registrar of the Lands Tribunal ordered that the question of their entitlement to oppose the application should be determined at a preliminary hearing before the tribunal. The tribunal (Mr. Douglas Frank, President) reached the conclusion that the only question which merited investigation was whether which, if any, of the objectors was an assign of the land to which the benefit of the covenant was annexed. One owner was able to produce conveyances which established that the benefit of the covenant had been expressly assigned to him. The tribunal was of the opinion that words in the covenant brought in two other objectors. The tribunal directed that these three objectors should be admitted to oppose the application. Costs of the preliminary hearing were reserved for decision at the substantive hearing.

(*Decision March 4, 1975*)

8

PROPOSED DEVELOPMENT, IF RESTRICTION MODIFIED, WOULD BE INTRUSIVE AND OUT OF CHARACTER. APPLICATION DISMISSED.

The application *Re Gillenden Development Co. and Cowcher* under s. 84 of the Law of Property Act, 1925, as amended, sought a modification of restrictive covenants on land at Cobham, Surrey, limiting development to one house per plot, whereas the applicants each wished to build six houses, planning permission having been obtained. When the covenant was imposed the area was rural and undeveloped but a lot of development had since taken place. One applicant intended to demolish a large dilapidated house which had been unoccupied for some years. The other also had it in mind to demolish a property to permit development. Both involved road works. The two objectors were retired people who enjoyed their gardens. The tribunal (Mr. Douglas Frank, President) considered the form of development proposed to be out of character and intrusive even if in keeping with much of the surrounding area. Noise, traffic increase, children, parties and garden machinery would be features affecting the objectors. The restrictions did confer substantial advantages and were of substantial value to the objectors, the need for more houses did not in this instance over-ride the objections, money could not be an adequate compensation and a restriction having such advantages could not possibly be deemed obsolete. Applications dismissed. Costs awarded against the applicants. *(Decision March 7, 1975)*

9

DISCHARGE AND MODIFICATION OF COVENANTS, RESTRICTING DEVELOPMENT TO PERMIT RESIDENTIAL USE, TO ALLOW THE BUILDING OF A MOSLEM PRAYER HALL.

The application *Re Trustees of the Wimbledon Mosque* sought the discharge of three restrictive covenants and the modification of a fourth so as to permit the erection and use of a Moslem Prayer Hall on land in Wimbledon, for which planning permission had been obtained. The area was predominantly residential although there was some commercial and industrial use in the locality. The restrictions limited development to dwellings and the owners of 49 properties objected, but the applicants did not admit any of them as entitled to the benefit of the covenants. Only three appeared but were unable to satisfy the tribunal (Mr. Douglas Frank, President) that they were so entitled. The tribunal was satisfied that the site as it was was injurious to the amenities, the proposed use was reasonable, it would cause no injury to the amenities, the building proposed would improve the visual amenities, if there were any persons entitled to the benefit of the covenant then impeding the proposed use would confer no benefit on them, the development was in the public interest and there would be no damage for which a compensation claim could be founded. Applications granted.

(Decision March 12, 1975)

10

DISMISSAL OF APPLICATION FOR THE DISCHARGE OR MODIFICATION OF RESTRICTIONS TO ENABLE APPLICANTS TO ERECT A BLOCK OF FLATS.

Restrictions on the development of land in Cambridge were the subject of the application *Re Trustees of Marcus Bradford.* On about one acre of land there was a substantial Victorian house which had been unoccupied since 1972. Demolition was proposed and the building of a three storey block of flats, 30 in all, with spaces for 55 cars. The application land was affected by a building scheme and restrictions limited building heights to 12 feet and nothing but houses and offices appurtenant to the houses. There was also a minimum value provision so far as the houses were concerned. Only on specific sections would any shop, warehouse, factory or building be allowed. There had already been some contravening developments. Seventeen people objected to the application, their title to the benefit of the restrictions was admitted, but only 11 appeared at the hearing. Much development had taken place, involving government offices, bank offices, university departments, flats and other uses within the area of the scheme and much similar development outside the area of the building scheme. The large house to be demolished was not, the tribunal agreed, suitable as a private residence, extra traffic would not in itself give the objectors cause for concern, the restrictions so far as one specific property was concerned were not obsolete and overlooking would be minimal. The architect of the proposed development said it would be possible to build up to ten houses on the land. The owner of the above specific property would face a block of flats instead of the more open view of the Victorian house and in any case would prefer a view of houses rather than the block of flats. The applicants suggested that having regard to the many changes that had taken place the restrictions were obsolete. The tribunal (Mr. V. G. Wellings) did not agree. One objector, it was pointed out, had herself been in breach of the restrictions, but the tribunal was not influenced by technical and trivial breaches rather than real and serious ones. The application failed, with costs in respect of the specific objector against the applicants on County Court scale 4 if not agreed.

(*Decision March 17, 1975*)

11

MODIFICATION OF COVENANTS SUBJECT TO COMPENSATION. LIMITS ON AND SITING OF DEVELOPMENT AND OBLIGATION FOR ROADWORKS.

The application *Re Kershaw and Clempert* under the Law of Property Act, 1925, concerned the modification of restrictive covenants on land in Poynton, Cheshire, the main effect of the covenants being to require that the two areas of land concerned should be used only as an open space. The applicants sought modification to enable them to build two bungalows on one plot and a single bungalow on the other.

Four objectors were entitled to the benefit of the covenants, others who might have had entitlement had not appeared nor had they in any way pursued their objections so they were not admitted.

The application was under para. (*aa*) of s. 84(1) of the Law of Property Act, 1925, as amended, i.e. that the modification of the restrictions, in impeding the use as proposed, would not deprive the objectors of any benefit of any practical or substantial value or advantage to them. The land on which it was proposed to build two bungalows was completely unused and the land on which a single bungalow was proposed was used as rough pasture. The applications were only in outline, no details of design and layout of the buildings being involved so the tribunal (Mr. Douglas Frank, President) said that so far as a positioning of the bungalows was concerned, he had to assume the worst from the point of view of each of the objectors.

There was no doubt that during the period of construction some occupiers would suffer considerably from builders' noise, construction of the driveway and general disturbance; sufficient to cause considerable disadvantage for as long as it lasted, for about a year, and thereafter, although there would be some inconvenience, there would be an increased number of vehicles. The most important question was what weight should be given to the period of intensive inconvenience. The tribunal thought it right to look at the matter as a short term of intensive interference but not substantial in relation to the long term enjoyment of the property.

The tribunal decided that the covenants should be modified but subject to appropriate conditions and on the question of compensation, the tribunal's approach was what sum would make up for any loss suffered in consequence of the modification, i.e. what would the owners as reasonable people have accepted in friendly negotiations? The modifications which were imposed by the decision provided for a sum of £750 compensation to one owner in respect of each development, i.e. unused and rough pasture land. It was also made a condition that this should be paid before the end of 1975 and there were other restrictions about height, situation and completion of certain roadworks before development was commenced. The above compensation applied to one objector and three others got sums of £250, £500 and £750 with somewhat similar conditions. The applicants were ordered to pay the objectors costs on the High Court scale if not agreed.

(*Decision April 16, 1975*)

12

APPLICATION TO MODIFY COVENANT PROHIBITING ERECTION OF FLATS FAILS, MAINLY ON DENSITY OF DEVELOPMENT.

The application *Re Baron Sons Limited* concerned the modification of a restrictive covenant on land in Northampton so that 27 flats, not exceeding three storeys in height, could be built, whereas the covenant expressly provided that a block of flats was a tenement house and not to be deemed a private dwellinghouse. Four owners opposed the application. The net density of the existing properties was of the order of six to seven houses per acre.

The subject land at the time of the imposition of the covenant was used in connection with aircraft manufacture and until quite recently there was a large aircraft hanger on the land. The application was made under paras. (*a*) and (*aa*) of s. 84(1) of the Law of Property Act 1925. The applicants conceded that there had been no change in the character of the neighbourhood since the covenant was imposed and the tribunal (Mr. Douglas Frank, President) was unable to understand why from that point of view the covenant should be deemed obsolete. Moreover, the tribunal could not see why the intended doubling of the population of the area should affect the covenant. Nor could it see why the building of a new school could be regarded as detrimental to the neighbourhood and on the question of a proposed road, the tribunal could not see that a proposal in 1975 to build a road ten years hence made a covenant obsolete in 1975. The fact that there was a need for flats in Northampton generally did not make the covenant lack value or become obsolete so far as the benefits it conferred on those entitled to those benefits under the covenant were concerned.

The application failed under para. (*a*). However, it did seem, having regard to all the facts, that the use of the land for construction of flats was a reasonable one but as against the existing density the proposed density was for 54 dwellings per acre. There would undoubtedly be a lot more traffic and noise of all kinds and sounds of habitation would multiply. The application failed because the covenant, in impeding the proposed use of land, did secure to the persons entitled to the benefit of the covenant, practical benefits of substantial advantage. Application dismissed, applicants to pay the costs of the objectors on the High Court scale if not agreed.

(*Decision April 22, 1975*)

13

COVENANT, ALREADY DISREGARDED FOR OVER 20 YEARS, FORMALLY DISCHARGED IN THE ABSENCE OF OBJECTIONS.

The application *Re Dawes* concerned land in Brighton and the discharge of a restrictive covenant imposed in 1885. Had the tribunal (Mr. Douglas Frank, President) had more information the discharge might have been achieved without a hearing since the premises had been in use as offices for at least 20 years, contrary to the covenant. Nobody seemed to be in a position to enforce it and at no time had there been any challenge to that office use and notwithstanding the usual publicity, there had been no objection to the present application. The tribunal ordered the complete discharge of the covenant.

(*Decision April 24, 1975*)

14

COVENANT PROHIBITING OTHER THAN DOMESTIC USE UPHELD ON APPLICATION TO SECURE FAIRLY GENERAL PROFESSIONAL USE. APPLICATION SPECIFICALLY FOR DENTAL SURGERY USE LIKELY TO BE ACCEPTED.

The application *Re Harries* concerned a property in Newton Abbot, Devon, and involved three covenants imposed by a conveyance in 1906. The restrictions required written consent of the covenantee or his agents in respect of additions or alterations, prohibition of use for the sale of spiritous liquors and offensive, obnoxious or dangerous trades and to use the premises only as a private dwelling except where written consent had been given. The applicants sought limitation of the restrictions to external alterations and by excepting from the restrictions on user the use of the premises as an office or surgery in connection with the practice of a doctor, a dentist, solicitor, accountant or similar profession. Estate trustees had objected and the tribunal (Mr. E. C. Strathon) was satisfied that they would be injured if the restrictions were to be modified as requested. The estate was zoned primarily for residential use and the tribunal was of the opinion that it was a use which should continue to be protected.

The application failed and was dismissed but the tribunal, with a view to the possibility of avoiding further proceedings, said that if the modifications asked for had been for the use of the affected property as a dental surgery only, then on the evidence the tribunal would have been prepared to exercise jurisdiction so to modify the covenants. The applicants were ordered to pay the objectors' costs on County Court scale 4 if not agreed.

(*Decision April 30, 1975*)

15

BREACHES OF COVENANTS. FLATS UNSUITED TO AREA. APPLICANTS' CONDUCT PREJUDICIAL TO CASE FOR FAVOURABLE CONSIDERATION. APPLICATIONS DISMISSED.

The applications *Re Nesawood Properties Ltd.* and *Boltmore Properties Ltd.* concerned two adjoining pieces of land in Stanmore, Middlesex, and the applications were by inter-related companies under s. 84 of the Law of Property Act, 1925, as amended. The modification sought in the first application was for the construction on site A of a parking area with not more than two flats over. The use of such parking area to be in conjunction with the two flats and also an appreciable number of private dwellings to be erected on site B.

Site B, the subject of the second application concerned permission for the erection of not more than three detached dwellings and a two and three storied block of 25 flats with two penthouse flats over. The original restrictions limited development to one detached house at a specified minimum cost. There was also a restriction of use to that of a private residence and a restriction on associated land so that it was not used for purposes other than that of a garden or recreation ground. The grounds on which reliance was placed related to paras. (*a*) and (*aa*) of s. 84(1) of the 1925 Act. There were 15 objectors. Most of them claimed compensation in the event of the restrictions being modified but it was agreed that any question of compensation should be deferred if necessary until after the decision on the main question of modification. There was some query about two objectors but all the rest were admitted to be entitled to the benefit of the restrictions, although in the case of some the benefit applied only to parts of the gardens of these objectors. A considerable amount of legal argument proceeded on the admissibility of two other objectors and after examining extensive case law the tribunal (Mr. V. G. Wellings) directed that they were to be admitted.

The tribunal referred to the history of Stanmore from the time it was a village, then went on to consider recent changes including potential ones, examined the proposed development of the two sites and noting that the development would provide accommodation for about 130 people. Notice was also taken of the fact that the applicants themselves had breached the covenants but a writ had been issued against both of them claiming appropriate declarations, negative injunctions and a mandatory injunction to demolish a house in the course of erection. Considerations relating to the public interest included evidence from the local authority's controller of planning who considered that the proposed development would be of benefit to the community provided that an existing tree screen was retained as far as possible and that the enjoyment of existing premises was not impeded. It appeared that except in one case the proposed development would cause an average diminution in property values of about 5 *per cent.* and on behalf of the applicants it was contended that for the purposes of s. 84(1)(*a*) the term "neighbourhood" related to an area of about three square miles. However, the tribunal thought the area which best fitted the description of the "neighbourhood" was the square lying north of a line drawn through a particular thoroughfare, much more limited. After hearing argument the tribunal thought the case failed under para. (*aa*) because the consideration which in its opinion outweighed all others was that the effect of mass which the proposed flats would present to certain owners would be a poor substitute for the pleasant rural outlook which the properties enjoyed. On the contention by the applicants that the restrictions, in impeding the proposed development, were contrary to the public interest, it was, in the view of the tribunal, not tenable and the tribunal had heard no evidence which would justify the view that money would be an adequate compensation for the loss or disadvantage which persons entitled to the benefit of the restrictions would suffer through modification. It appeared to the tribunal that the applicants' case under para. (*a*) failed unless they were entitled to pray in aid the changes on the sites which they had unlawfully and wrongfully brought about. The applicants had been, in the tribunal's judgment, most seriously, deliberately and cynically in breach of covenant and it was right that the tribunal should take no account of the changes on the sites which the applicants themselves had occasioned. The restriction as it concerned density could not be said to be obsolete. Finally, if the tribunal had been in favour of the applicants it would have felt reluctant to exercise its discretion in their favour because it appeared that the development in so far as it consisted of flats was quite unsuited to the area and that the applicants, by their conduct had disentitled themselves to the favourable consideration which in other circumstances they might have expected to have received. Applications dismissed. Applicants to pay the objectors their costs on the High Court scale unless agreed.

(*Decision May 7, 1975*)

16

MONEY COMPENSATION DETERMINED IN RESPECT OF APPLICATION TO MODIFY RESTRICTIVE COVENANT. OTHER ARCHITECTURAL AND STRUCTURAL CONDITIONS IMPOSED.

The application *Re Dransfield* under s. 84 of the Law of Property Act, 1925, as amended, sought modification of a restrictive covenant limiting the use of the subject land to the erection of a single dwelling. The applicants built a house on land affected by the covenant but wished to build a second house within the garden of their property, having obtained outline planning permission for that purpose. A Mr. Cook objected to the application, which was based on paras. (*a*), (*aa*) and (*c*) of s. 84. Both the applicants and the objector called expert witnesses and the only significant areas of disagreement related to the extent of what should be properly called the neighbourhood and the amenity effect of carrying out the proposed development. The tribunal (Mr. J. H. Emlyn Jones) did not consider he would be justified in holding that the restriction ought to be deemed obsolete and was satisfied that the proposed modification would injure the objector, something confirmed by a witness for the applicants. On the other hand it was not disputed that the continued existence of the covenant impeded some reasonable user of the land. The question remaining was, therefore, whether the restriction, in impeding the building of a second dwelling, did or did not secure to the objector practical benefits of a substantial value or advantage for which money would be adequate compensation. The tribunal considered it was a case where adequate compensation could be made in money terms. The covenant would be modified to permit the building of a second private dwelling and carport but subject to conditions. Restrictions on height, matching materials and the payment of £1,000 to the objector within six months of the tribunal's decision. Applicants to pay the objector his costs on County Court scale 4 if not agreed and with discretion as to counsel's fees and certificate for expert witness fit to qualify.

(*Decision June 9, 1975*)

17

TRIBUNAL CONSIDERS DEVELOPMENT PROPOSALS MIGHT BE MODIFIED. SEVEN HOUSES INSTEAD OF TEN. TIME LIMIT FOR AGREEMENT AND FOR COMPENSATION IF APPLICANTS PROCEED.

The application *Re F. Patten Ltd.* concerned land at Westcliff-on-Sea where it was intended, given the necessary modification of a restrictive covenant, to build ten houses and ten garages. The restriction was for one house on any plot. Six objectors appeared. The application site was carved out of two pieces of land. The larger consisted of parts of the back gardens of certain houses. The smaller parts of gardens of other houses. The applicants had previously sought complete discharge of the restrictive covenant so that they could build 18 houses on the site. The present application was based on grounds in s. 84(1)(*a*), (*aa*), (*b*) and (*c*) of the Law of Property Act, 1925. A witness for the applicants thought that if ten houses were built on the affected site there would be only a minimal difference in density and the development would be harmonious. He produced a schedule of 13 planning permissions relating to the subject site. It was, he thought, better to concentrate on good layout and quality. The current trend was towards higher density, smaller gardens and better accommodation.

The tribunal (Mr. J. Stuart Daniel) explained that before he had written his decision there became available the judgment of the Master of the Rolls in the case of *SJC Construction Company* v. *Sutton LBC*, a case where the Court of Appeal had upheld the Lands Tribunal in fixing compensation on the basis of finding the realisable development value and splitting it equally between the developers and the objectors. Such a method was thought to be fair and sensible and involving no error of law. The tribunal in the present application circulated copies of the judgment to the parties. Subsequently certain owners had withdrawn or had provisionally accepted a cash consideration. On the question of the development value of the site, and on the assumption that the modification would be allowed it was submitted on behalf of the applicants that the development value was £36,000 excluding compensation to objectors. There would be little profit in the project if the number of houses permitted was reduced below ten. With eight houses the project would be just about viable provided the compensation was not too severe. The tribunal noted that all the objectors really wished the covenants to be preserved and enforced. The tribunal was not satisfied that the restrictions would be deemed to be obsolete. Nor was it satisfied that the proposed modification would not injure the persons benefiting. The question was whether the applicants should be allowed to build more than two houses, and if so on what terms. There was no doubt about selling and the houses would help meet a shortage. The proposed user was reasonable, the covenants impeded that user, but if the application was a matter of all or nothing the tribunal could not be satisfied that impeding the proposed use was contrary to the public interest. The applicants' proposal would be overcrowded and unpleasant for those living near to it. It was not contrary to the public interest to refuse to impose it on those people. Impeding the proposed use did secure to the objectors practical benefits of substantial value or advantage. Some of the buildings would be, visually, an affront. If the application was to be regarded as all or nothing the tribunal was not at all satisfied that it was made out either on para (*a*) or (*b*) and the question of money compensation did not arise. The tribunal was certainly not prepared to modify the restriction so as to permit eight houses. Serious loss of amenity could be avoided if the three houses on the western side of the proposed development were omitted. The tribunal was prepared to grant a modification permitting seven houses and if the applicants elected to accept such a restriction the tribunal also fixed the money compensation payable to the objectors. The applicants should make up their minds within the period up to the September 30, 1975. If, on or before that date, the applicants notify the Registrar that they accept the proposed modification the tribunal undertook to give a short final decision. Compensation would be payable not later than 28 days from the date of the final decision. Applicants in any event to pay each of the objectors who appeared at the three hearings involved £30 costs.

(*Decision June 25, 1975*)

18

DANGEROUS EYESORE OF A BUILDING. RESTRICTIONS MODIFIED TO PERMIT AN EXTENSION WHICH WOULD OTHERWISE TRANSGRESS BOTH BUILDING LINE AND USER, BUT WOULD STRENGTHEN THE BUILDING.

The application *Re The Third Ravensbourne* (*Charitable*) *Housing Association Ltd*. concerned the modification of restrictions affecting land in south-east London. These restrictions kept any development well behind the road boundaries and prohibited trade, business or manufacture. The house on the land was very dilapidated, had attracted a dangerous structure notice and, later, a closing order from the local authority. It was unfit for human habitation and was not capable of being made fit at reasonable cost and, according to the terms of the closing order, it was inexpedient to make a demolition order having regard to the effect of demolition on other houses or buildings. The applicants wished to build an extension to restore stability and to provide extra living accommodation by conversion into two small flats. They had received planning permission for that. The owner-occupiers of ten neighbouring properties objected and appeared at the hearing. The development proposed would be the thin end of a wedge encouraging further relaxations so that in the end the restrictions became obsolete. The tribunal

(Mr. V. G. Wellings) said that something had to be done about this dangerous eyesore. The proposals by the applicants provided a sensible solution to a difficult problem. In its discretion the tribunal granted the modification sought. No order as to compensation. Each party to bear their own costs.

(*Decision July 7, 1975*)

19

REASONABLE USE OF LAND PROPOSED WHERE BUILDING RESTRICTION APPLIED. SUBJECT TO SAFEGUARDS RESTRICTION MODIFIED TO PERMIT THE DEVELOPMENT SOUGHT. ARGUMENT ABOUT DANGEROUS PRECEDENT NOT ACCEPTED.

The application *Re Finch* under s. 84 of the Law of Property Act 1925, concerned the modification of a restrictive covenant against the erection of a second house on land even though planning permission had been granted. The site of the proposed development was part of the garden of a vicarage. There was a neighbouring area of land, also affected by the covenant, presently used as a school playing field, owned by the county council. The objector to the application thought the development would be an objectionable intrusion but, more importantly, if the application were to be granted, the county council would rely on it as a precedent. The tribunal (Mr. Douglas Frank, President), thought the proposed development to be a reasonable use of the land. The erection of a house on the subject land would not have any material effect provided that certain trees remained. The granting of the application could not possibly be advanced with any degree of seriousness as a precedent for development of the playing fields. The application succeeded subject to two safeguards. One was that the restriction continued so far as the proposed house was concerned, i.e. any additional development beyond the proposed house and the other was intended to preserve the trees, other than those on the actual building site. The applicant was ordered to pay the objector's costs on County Court scale 3 if not agreed.

(*Decision October 1, 1975*)

20

INTERIM DECISION ON POSSIBLE DEVELOPMENT SHORT OF THAT PLANNED. OPPORTUNITY NOT ACCEPTED SO ORIGINAL APPLICATION REFUSED.

The application *Re F. Patten Limited* under the Law of Property Act, 1925, concerned land at Westcliff-on-Sea. The tribunal (Mr. J. Stuart Daniel) had given an interim decision in which he had offered a modification of certain covenants affecting the land. This would have enabled the applicants to build seven houses but it was doubtful if that would be acceptable and for that reason the tribunal left the matter open, making it clear that if the arrangement was not accepted then the application would be rejected. In due course it was stated by the applicants that the modification was not acceptable so the tribunal's final decision was to refuse the application.

(*Decision December 15, 1975*)

21

NOT A CASE WHERE A MUTUAL BARGAIN SHOULD BE UPSET. COVENANT UPHELD.

The application *Re Hurley* concerned land at Salcombe, Devon, and the discharge or modification of a restrictive covenant was sought so that the applicants could construct an extension to a cottage, planning permission having been obtained. The covenant prohibited the erection of any building without written consent or the alteration of the external plan or elevation without written consent.

The applicants had rearranged the accommodation whereby three small bedrooms had been constructed, together with a lounge/dining room and a bathroom and w.c. plus kitchen. As a consequence the rooms were small but in any case the property was used only as a holiday home. The applicants wished to construct a larger bathroom and a larger kitchen. In their view the neighbourhood had changed because of the sub-division of the parent property into three separate dwellings, the character of the village had been changed by reason of developments since the covenants were imposed and there had been an increase in density of development. They also thought the restriction to be contrary to the public interest because the proper provision of facilities at the cottage in question was prevented.

The tribunal (Mr. Douglas Frank, President) was satisfied that there had been no material change in either the parent property or the neighbourhood, nor had there been changes in other circumstances. No doubt the proposed use of the property was reasonable but were the benefits of the covenant of substantial value or advantage to the objectors? The question of public interest did not arise and in any case it had not been established. The proposed extension would be small and could not be more than a minor irritation. Money would be an adequate compensation for any loss or disadvantage. However, the applicants bought the land only 16 years ago with full knowledge of the covenant. They chose to convert the property to bring about the very standard of accommodation of which they now complained. They did so knowing that the vendor had retained the right to withhold consent to any extensions and nothing had occurred in the meantime, so that the case for modifying the covenant was as strong on the day it was imposed as it was today. This was not the kind of case where the Lands Tribunal should upset a bargain made between parties. Application dismissed, applicants to pay the objectors their costs on the High Court scale if not agreed.

(*Decision December 22, 1975*)

LEASEHOLD REFORM

LIST OF CASES REPORTED

SUBJECT MATTER OF CASES

1

FREEHOLD VALUE TO TENANT. FACTORS RELATING TO SITE VALUE AS PROPORTION OF ENTIRETY VALUE. RATE OF RETURN FOR DETERMINING AND CAPITALISING S. 15 RENT.

The reference *Nash* v. *Castell-y-Mynach Estate* called for a determination of the price to be paid for the freehold interest of a dwelling near Pontyclun, south Glamorgan, by the resident lessees under s. 9 of the Leasehold Reform Act 1967 as amended. The lessees' interest was for the residue of a 99 year lease from December 1875 at a ground rent of £2 per annum. At the date the lessees served notice of their desire to acquire the freehold the lease had about 1½ years unxpired. The valuer for the lessees supported a freehold value of £1,905. The valuer for the landlords supported a figure of £7,500. The valuers disagreed on the site value, the rate of return to arrive at a s. 15 rent and the rate of return for capitalising the s. 15 rent. On site value the lessees' valuer thought that the site value proportion of his entirety value was 30 *per cent*. This was, he submitted, in line with previous Lands Tribunal decisions. The landlords' valuer said he had looked at the property, assumed that the house was not there and offered evidence of sales of single building plots within a distance of about eight miles of the subject property. The tribunal (Mr. R. C. Walmsley) pointed out that it was only when the subject house was nearing the end of its economic life that the required site value was helpfully to be ascertained by reference to the prices of sites sold for development or redevelopment. That valuer's comparables were not helpful. The more dependable approach was that of the tenants' valuer, whose first step in ascertaining the entirety value was a consideration of prices being paid for other comparable properties. However, the comparables in this instance provided only meagre evidence but it was sufficient to support the landlord's valuer's entirety value of £15,000, less £1,000 to cover the cost of modernising the water supply. In ascertaining the site value as a proportion of the entirety value it was necessary first to identify the most likely type of purchaser and then to identify those attributes for which such a purchaser would be looking. The subject property was only about 15 minutes distance by road from the centre of Cardiff. That pointed to the most likely purchaser being someone who works in Cardiff but preferring a country home. To such a purchaser the tribunal thought the attributes of a site in the open country would be at least as important as the bricks and mortar standing on the site. This indicated a site value of £7,000. As to what rate of return on that value would represent the s. 15 rent the landlord's valuer had used the 7 *per cent.* table, whereas the valuer for the tenant had used the 12 *per cent.* table. The tribunal emphasised that the first step was to decide what s. 15 rent could be reasonably expected. It was no use a landlord "requiring" 12 *per cent.* if, from a tenant's point of view, that produced a rent which was unacceptably high. Recalling the Dulwich case (*Carthew and Others* v. *Estates Governors of Alleyn's College of God's Gift*) the tribunal said that the implications of s. 15 of the 1967 Act had been exhaustively explored in that case where it was found on the evidence that 6 *per cent.* was right for houses in Dulwich. The tribunal found on the evidence in the present case that 7 *per cent.* was right. This produced a s. 15 rent of £490. Again, when capitalising the s. 15 rent the tenants' valuer used the 12 *per cent.* table, whereas the valuer for the landlord used the 7 *per cent.* table. The former supported his rate of return by reference to open market sales of freehold ground rents in Newport and Cardiff, the latter had used what was the customarily used figure in Cardiff although he admitted that if he had been acting for an intending investor-purchaser his valuation would have been at a figure showing a return to the purchaser of 10 *per cent.* or even more. In the light of the evidence the tribunal found that any purchaser other than the tenants of the property would have required an 11 *per cent.* return. Until the Court of Appeal decision in *Official Custodian of Charities and Others* v. *Goldridge* it was a common practice among valuers to adopt differential rates of return because an investor-purchaser would expect a greater return on his money than the freeholder would get on the granting of a lease under the terms of s. 15. Since that decision valuers, according to the landlord's valuer, assumed the same rate of return at both stages of the calculation. The Court of Appeal in *Gallagher Estates Ltd.* v. *Walker* directed the tribunal to look for dependable evidence primarily to the "land market" and to the "money market" only as a factor. Open market transactions were the best evidence in compulsory acquisition cases, the tribunal thought, and then, cautiously, to evidence of settlements. Bearing in mind the exclusion of the tenant's bid under s. 9 of the 1967 Act by virtue of s. 82 of the Housing Act 1969 directly comparable open market transactions were not available so the "land market" comparables had taken the form of prices which had been agreed for other freeholds under the 1967 Act.

The tribunal stated that the valuation exercise under s. 9 of the Leasehold Reform Act 1967 was not only hypothetical, it was also artificial. No landlord in the open market would contemplate granting a lease under the terms postulated by s. 15, nor would any well advised tenant wish to take such a lease. With a jurisdiction of that nature consistency of application of the statutory formula must be of quite exceptional importance. The tribunal's decisions, as reviewed by the Court of Appeal, will have been used as the basis of settling many thousands of cases which have never reached the tribunal. On the evidence in the present cases the tribunal was satisfied that there was an established "land market" in Cardiff, based directly on tribunal decisions. It would, said the tribunal, be inapt now to reject the valuation technique of that "land market" on the grounds of evidence drawn solely from the "money market". A purchase price of £6,325 for the freehold was determined. The tenants' sealed offer was for less than this so they were ordered to pay the landlord's costs of the reference on the High Court scale if not agreed.

(*Decision March 4, 1975*)

2

TRIBUNAL SETTLES DISPUTE ON COSTS FOLLOWING MUTUAL AGREEMENT ON PRICE FOR FREEHOLD.

The reference *Addison* v. *London Borough of Hackney* concerned a property in Clapton, East London, and the amount which the tenants should pay for the freehold interest of their dwelling, the landlords being the local authority. When the case had been called the tribunal (Mr. E. C. Strathon) had been told that he would not be troubled with the question of the amount of the purchase price since the landlords had accepted an unconditional offer of £750 by the tenants. The issue concerned costs and counsel for the landlords submitted that had the tenants accepted an offer of £760 made by the landlords a year earlier the reference would have been unnecessary.

In all the circumstances the tribunal decided that the tenants should pay the landlords their costs of the reference up to and including February 1975 (the date on which the tenants had submitted an unconditional offer) and the landlords would pay the costs of the tenants as from that date and to include the tenants' surveyor, such costs to be on County Court scale 4 unless agreed.

(*Decision April 15, 1975*)

3

EVIDENCE OF "LAND MARKET" OF SETTLEMENTS POINTS TO 8 *PER CENT*. BEING APPROPRIATE FOR S. 15 RENT AND FOR CAPITALISING THAT RENT.

The reference *Briddon* v. *Field* concerned the amount to be paid by the tenants for the freehold interest in a house in Lenton, Nottingham. The lessee's interest was held for the residue of a term of 99 years from March 1898 at a ground rent of £7·50 per annum. The relevant date for determination of the price was June 14, 1974, when the lessee had served notice of her desire to purchase the freehold. At that time the lease had 23 years unexpired. Valuations indicated that the tenants should pay only £170 but the valuation on behalf of the landlord indicated £450. This discrepancy arose because of considerable difference between the percentage yield between the two valuers for capitalising the ground rent, one seeking to support 12 *per cent.* and the other an appreciably lower figure.

The tribunal (Mr. E. C. Strathon) said that reliable evidence of the "land market" was not to be sought in the sales of long distance reversions but was more probably to be found in settlements of comparable transactions under the provisions of the Leasehold Reform Act 1967. The landlord's valuer had shown that throughout all his negotiations a rate of 6 *per cent.* for capitalising the ground rent had been shown to be acceptable and had been accepted by the tribunal in numerous other references. In the present reference the tribunal accepted that it was more appropriate than a rate of 12 *per cent.* sought by the contending valuer. The landlord's valuer had produced alternative valuations, one being related to the entirety value of the reference property. He had applied 8 *per cent.* years' purchase in perpetuity deferred 23 years, to his modern ground rent and this was preferred by the tribunal to the 12 *per cent.* applied by the tenant's valuer. However, the tribunal thought that the 8 *per cent.* should be applied both to the site value in order to arrive at the s. 15 rent and also to capitalising that rent. In the result a figure of £350 emerged and that was the price determined for the freehold. A sealed offer by the tenant was less than that award and the tribunal determined that the tenant should pay the landlord's costs of the reference on County Court scale 3 if not agreed.

(*Decision April 30, 1975*)

4

EFFECT OF TRIBUNAL'S DECISION IN *DELAFORCE* v. *EVANS 1970* WHERE ACCOUNT WAS TAKEN OF AN "ANXIETY TO SETTLE" FACTOR BY TENANTS.

The reference *Guiver* v. *Francine Properties Ltd.* concerned the price to be paid under the Leasehold Reform Act 1967 for the freehold interest of a dwelling in Barnet. The lessee's interest was for the residue of a 99 year term from March 1933 at a ground rent of £9·45 per annum. The lease had about 59 years to run when the tenant served notice of his desire to have the freehold, in March 1973, this being the relevant date for value purposes. The valuation for the tenant was in the sum of £225 whereas for the landlord a figure of £350 was supported. There was evidence of settlements and the average going price for the enfranchisement of similar houses was agreed to be £350. The issue really was what deduction if any fell to be made for the effect of *Delaforce* v. *Evans 1970* where there was an adjustment from the price ascertained on land market evidence to take account of the deemed anxiety by purchasing tenants to settle rather than face the expense, delay and uncertainty involved in tribunal proceedings.

The valuer for the tenant had allowed £125 from his £350 for this factor and the tribunal (Mr. R. C. Walmsley) recognised and accepted that if the practice of the tribunal was blindly to follow its previous decisions then such a figure might be justified but the tribunal's practice had always been to reach decisions on the evidence and arguments in particular cases but, especially with any new jurisdiction, considering each fresh case against the background of earlier decisions to obviate possible inconsistencies. After examining the circumstances in the case of *Finkel* v. *Simon and Others 1973* it was clearer why the figure of £125 had been settled in that case but in the present case the evidence was different. For the tenant the opinion was offered and accepted that an enfranchising tenant might not increase the value of his ownership by even as much as the cost of enfranchisement, because the value of a typical house in the locality could be put at between £12,250 and £12,500 leasehold in March 1973 and its freehold value at about £12,750. Thus, a tenant who purchased his freehold at £350 might increase the value of his ownership by as much as £500 but on the other hand he might find it increased by only £250.

Looking at the facts in the present case the tribunal perceived little, if any, evidence of tenant's anxiety. In addition the tribunal thought the effect of the *Delaforce* decision might be a reason underlying different treatment of the costs of enfranchisement. In some of the cases landlords had been obtaining £350 with the tenant also paying such costs as were provided for in s. 9(4) of the Leasehold Reform Act 1967 but in other cases the landlord had to find such costs out of the purchase price. In the present case the section applied requiring the tenant to bear the costs in addition to paying the purchase price. The tribunal fixed a purchase price of £325 which in effect, allowed a *Delaforce* deduction of only £25. The sealed offer by the tenant was less than the amount of the award so the tenant was ordered to pay the landlords the cost of the reference on County Court scale 3 unless agreed.

(*Decision May 5, 1975*)

5

VALUE OF FREEHOLD INTEREST. TRIBUNAL ACCEPTS EVIDENCE DISCLOSING HIGHER PERCENTAGE FOR DEFERMENT ELEMENT THAN THAT APPLIED WHEN CONVERTING SITE VALUE TO EQUIVALENT GROUND RENTAL VALUE. USE OR REJECTION OF "ADVERSE DIFFERENTIAL" A QUESTION OF EVIDENCE.

The reference *Lead* v. *J. & L. Estates Ltd.* concerned the price to be paid for the freehold interest in a house in Edgware, calculated in accordance with the provisions of s. 9 of the Leasehold Reform Act 1967 as amended by s. 82 of the Housing Act 1969. The tenant occupied the premises under a 99 year lease from September 1934 at a ground rent of £8 per annum. The relevant date for determining the freehold value was August 22, 1972, the date on which the tenant served notice on the landlords. The landlords neither appeared nor were they represented at the hearing. No documents had been submitted either. A recently qualified surveyor appeared for the tenant as his principal was away ill. He spoke to a valuation of £105 for the freehold interest. He took 10 *per cent.* to capitalise the rent reserved under the lease for the unexpired term of 61 years. He derived the standing house value from evidenc of sales of similar freehold properties in the locality. His 40 *per cent.* of that to represent the site value was a matter of opinion but backed up by earlier Lands Tribunal decisions. He then took 8 *per cent.* of the site value to arrive at the s. 15 rent. This he capitalised in perpetuity deferred 61 years at 9 *per cent.* This valuation was of course unchallenged in the absence of the landlords. The tribunal (Mr. J. H. Emlyn Jones) noted that the surveyor had adopted a higher rate *per cent.* at the last stage of his valuation than that taken in arriving at the s. 15 rent. That difference had been referred to as the "adverse differential" and in those terms was disapproved by the Court of Appeal. After questioning the surveyor the tribunal accepted his evidence. Then the tribunal examined the statutory provisions under s. 9(1) and ss. 14 and 15 of the Leasehold Reform Act 1967. The rent which the surveyor arrived at for the purposes of s. 15(2) was £432 per annum, 8 *per cent.* of the site value of £5,400. That represented the annual return which an owner would expect from the demise of the site under a lease for a term of 50 years with a rent review at the option of the landlord after 25 years. The next stage was to calculate what price the freehold interest, subject to such a lease, might be expected to realise in the open market subject to the provisions of s. 9. For present purposes the tribunal accepted that approach of capitalising the rental value in perpetuity. The ultimate reversion to the full value after 111 years was too remote to have any effect on the value, and the 25 year review could quite properly be reflected in the choice of interest rates. After referring to certain passages in judgements in *Official Custodian of Charities and Others* v. *Goldridge* (1973) the tribunal asked itself whether it was precluded as a matter of law from accepting the evidence of the surveyor. It was not thought so. After examining further extracts from the judgments the tribunal said it seemed clear that the use or rejection of the "adverse differential" was not to be taken as a matter of law or of principle regardless of the evidence. The tribunal looked again at the surveyor's evidence, which was summarised as follows. A house is worth more in the open market if it can be sold with vacant possession rather than with a tenant in occupation. Where a tenant occupies under a long lease neither the landlord nor the tenant are in a position to dispose of the property with vacant possession. The tenant can offer vacant possession subject to payment of a ground rent for a limited period. The landlord is able to sell the right to receive the ground rent with the reversion to the freehold. Therefore, freehold vacant possession value can be realised only by a merger of the two interests. From the landlord's point of view the sitting tenant would pay more than any other purchaser for the freehold, because he could realise the "marriage " value, which is found in the market. Where the tenant is not immediately able or willing to buy the freehold the premises are nevertheless worth more than a price based on rent income. This is because as the lease nears its end the need for the tenant to safeguard his possession becomes more pressing. In such circumstances the investment value assumes the character of a growth stock producing the prospect of capital growth in addition to income partly on the expectation of the reversion itself and also because of the possibility of a sale at a later date to the sitting tenant. These were factors operating in the real world and were properly to be taken into account in considering a ground rent payable under a lease which the landlord is bound to grant by virtue of s. 15 of the Act. The next stage was to determine what price should be paid for the freehold encumbered by such a lease. The rent is thus established but the purchaser now finds that the freehold interest lacks the same characteristics as at the time the current vendor granted the lease. This is because of the statutory assumption in s. 9 of the Act that the tenant and his family residing in the house are not buying or seeking to buy. The notional capital profit realisable on a sale to the tenant has been lost. The investment value has, therefore, fallen and this can be best expressed by the valuer in adopting a lower multiplier of of the rent, i.e. a higher return on the investment. In the opinion of the surveyor in the present case if 8 *per cent.* was correct at stage two of the valuation then 9 *per cent.* was correct at stage three. The tribunal accepted this evidence. It was, in any case, the only evidence before the tribunal. Freehold interest assessed at £105. The tenant's sealed offer exceeded the sum determined. Landlords to pay the tenant the costs of the reference on County Court scale 3 if not agreed.

(*Decision November 13, 1975*)

RATING

LIST OF CASES REPORTED

SUBJECT MATTER OF CASES

1

DISABILITIES. DISTINCTION BETWEEN THOSE AFFECTING RATING VALUES AND THOSE WHICH DO NOT. LACK OF RENTAL EVIDENCE. VALUATION OFFICER'S DUTY STILL TO BE CARRIED OUT.

The appeal *Barrett* v. *White* (*Valuation Officer*) concerned a house and garage in Dulwich where a court had reduced the gross value from £810 to £740. This reduction had been made on the valuation officer's suggestion because a former gas-fired central heating system had been replaced by electric night storage heating and there were certain disabilities.

The ratepayer contended that the valuation officer had no evidence of rents which were relevant to the appeal property but it was confirmed that the valuation officer had served on the ratepayer a notice referring to returns for two named houses and when that information had gone to the ratepayer he was reminded that he was entitled only to refer to the returns of a similar number of hereditaments.

It appeared that in the whole of the London Borough of Southwark there had apparently been only two returns disclosing rents for good-class houses in a good residential area.

The tribunal (Mr. R. C. Walmsley) recognised and accepted that what the valuation officer had to do was to extrapolate by the use of his professional judgment the rental evidence of smaller houses in inferior areas so that he could formulate a consistent pattern for the valuation of larger and better houses. He accepted the valuation officer's professional opinion since there was no evidence in rebuttal that the tone of value adopted for houses such as the appeal property was not pitched above the level of the available rental evidence.

The tribunal divided matters submitted as relevant by the ratepayer into those which might affect gross value and those which did not. In the former category stood matters related to a nearby school, physical factors concerning the property, a somewhat close adjoining garage and the loss of garden due to a room extension. Those which the tribunal did not think affected gross value included matters concerned with pop concerts at Crystal Palace, overlooking neighbours' dogs and the sight of dustbins. The allowance conceded by the valuation officer was quite adequate for accepted disabilities.

Appeal dismissed. £10 costs against the ratepayer.

(*Decision January 10, 1975*)

2

IMPROVEMENTS. VALUATION OFFICER'S DUTY. CHANGES BEFORE, ON OR AFTER APRIL 1, 1974. ANOMALIES. REDUCTION ON ACCOUNT OF CAR REPAIRING ACTIVITIES.

There were two appeals in *Rosen* v. *Pickard* (*Valuation Officer*) affecting two dwellings near Wandsworth Common. The appellant ratepayer lived in one and his mother lived in the other. In both cases a valuation court had confirmed the gross values at £535 on the basis of the original ratepayers' proposals.

Late in March 1974 the valuation officer, following an inspection relevant to ratepayers' proposals, had discovered a need to revise the assessments because central heating had been installed and conversions had been made so that there were additional bathrooms. These improvements had not been reflected, of course, in the original valuation list entry. Not surprisingly the ratepayer was unhappy, particularly as there were to his knowledge other cases in the area where no changes had been made on account of the same improvements. The valuation officer regretted the effect of changes made before, on or after, April 1, 1974, but he had no option in the present case since clearly the changes had taken place before that relevant date.

The tribunal (Mr. R. C. Walmsley) was given a great deal of evidence relating to rents and assessments in the locality and he was satisfied that the gross value complained about was not pitched above the available rental evidence. On the question of revising other assessments, the valuation officer regretted that it was impossible in an area with 120,000 hereditaments to inspect every one but a small team was going through the district with a view to making proposals where necessary. On the question of disabilities one of the two houses suffered, in the view of the tribunal, from a substantial nuisance at the next door property from which car repair work was carried out, the work being done mainly in the street itself and there were cars in various stages of disrepair both in the street and in the front garden of this adjoining property. In this case the tribunal thought that the valuation officer's allowance of £45 for this disability was inadequate and determined a gross value of £535. In the other case there was no justification for any such deduction and the second gross value of £595 was confirmed.

The contention of the valuation officer that the assessments determined by the valuation court were not excessive was upheld and the appeals were dismissed. £10 costs awarded against the ratepayer in respect of each appeal.

(*Decision January 10, 1975*)

3

HIGH DENSITY DEVELOPMENT. NO REDUCTION ON ACCOUNT OF "OVERLOOKING" FACTOR.

The appeal *Brundish* v. *Bailey* (*Valuation Officer*) concerned a bungalow at Lytham, Lancashire, and was on an estate of about 600 newly erected dwellings. These comprised bungalows, chalets and houses. The appeal property carried a gross value of £305 and this had been confirmed by a valuation court. The ratepayer complained about being overlooked from a chalet and from another house.

The general facts were not in dispute and the sole question was whether a hypothetical tenant coming fresh to the scene would or would not reduce his rental bid. In the light of its inspection, the tribunal (Mr. W. H. Rees) thought that in view of the high density of development on the estate there would be no difference in rental bids. Appeal dismissed, £5 costs against the ratepayer.

(*Decision January 13, 1975*)

4

VALUATION COURT'S ALLOWANCE FOR TRAFFIC AT ROAD JUNCTION INCREASED.

The appeal *Clague* v. *Chadwell* (*Valuation Officer*) concerned a semi-detached house at Ditchling where the ratepayer complained about increased traffic involving excessive noise, dirt and danger, reference being made to four major accidents, in some of which the appeal property had been involved. A valuation court had reduced the gross value from £450 to £430 and the issue before the tribunal was the effect of the traffic, the valuation officer agreeing that there should be a reduction of £20 against the ratepayer's view that it should be for £90. The decision related the traffic factors and although there was now some restriction on heavy vehicles this was not the case at the date of the proposal and the ratepayer's evidence disclosed that he was particularly affected by traffic at weekends and in the evenings. Northbound traffic had to give way to traffic on another route so vehicles accelerated when travelling away from a position in front of his house after slowing down. His front wall had been damaged on more than one occasion and even his car had been damaged beyond repair when hit by a passing vehicle.

The valuation officer thought the ratepayer's claim for relief to be unrealistic and he told the tribunal (Mr. W. H. Rees) that out of some 100 houses on the main road he had received only 12 proposals from occupiers and he referred to five decisions of the tribunal relating to traffic disturbance, but as to that the tribunal said it would derive little assistance from these since each one depended on the particular facts. In the present appeal the tribunal considered the £20 allowance too small and increased this to £35, fixing the gross value at £415, allowing the appeal and awarding £5 costs against the valuation officer.

(*Decision January 13, 1975*)

5

UNSUCCESSFUL ARGUMENT BASED ON COMPARATIVE INCREASES BETWEEN OLD AND NEW VALUATION LISTS.

The appeal *Morris* v. *Reed* (*Valuation Officer*) concerned shop premises at King's Lynn. The valuation list description for a gross value of £1,100 was "shop, house and premises" but a valuation court had reduced the gross value to £1,080 and had amended the list entry to shop and premises, since the whole of the upper part of the premises was now used for business storage in connection with the shop.

The ratepayer did not think that he was in a good trading position since it was no longer on a bus route but his main ground of complaint was that his assessment had been increased between revaluations by a much higher percentage than other shops in the locality. Moreover, a named shop he regarded as an eyesore and he suffered some obstruction on his right of way to a garage. The valuation officer supported his unit prices by the analysis of rents paid for seven shops in the neighbourhood.

The tribunal thought the trading position of the appellant's shop common to all the premises in the area and stated that the respondent valuation officer in a well presented and documented case had supported his valuation to the tribunal's entire satisfaction by reference to rental evidence and such evidence over-rode any arguments based on relationships between two valuation lists.

Appeal dismissed. £25 costs awarded against the ratepayer.

(*Decision January 13, 1975*)

6

ACTUAL RENT PAID, SUPPORTED BY OTHER RENTAL AND ASSESSMENT EVIDENCE, JUSTIFIED DISMISSAL OF APPEAL.

The appeal *Phillips* v. *Smedley* (*Valuation Officer*) concerned offices and a flat at Higham Ferrers, Northamptonshire. The property was assessed at £310 gross value and this had been confirmed by a valuation court. The ratepayer leased the premises for four years from January 1971 at a rent of £284 per annum, the tenant paying rates and being responsible for internal repairs and decorations. The premises were over a grocer's shop in the centre of the town and in his evidence confirmed that he had paid a premium and he had also spent £200 on decorations and a further £100 in adapting a kitchen to a bedroom. Cross-examined by the valuation officer he said that he had exercised an option to continue his lease for another four years but the new rent had not yet been agreed.

The valuation officer supported his assessment, not only by reference to the rent paid for the appeal property appropriately adjusted by 5 *per cent.* for inflation for each of the two years from 1971-1973, a rate of increase consistently used throughout the valuation list, but also by a further 5 *per cent.* for the occupier's repairs obligation. No adjustment had been made for the expenditure by the tenant nor for the premium. His level of assessments was supported by reference to a recently fixed rent for a first-floor flat over a bank and by reference to other assessments. The valuation officer thought the ratepayer's approach to be vague and arbitrary whereas the tribunal (Mr. W. H. Rees) found it obscure and indirect, preferring the valuation officer's approach by reference to rent and other assessments.

Appeal dismissed. £10 costs awarded against the ratepayer.

(*Decision January 13, 1975*)

7

APPELLANT'S OWN COMPARISONS CONFIRM FAIRNESS OF OWN ASSESSMENT.

The appeal *Robinson* v. *Kent* (*Valuation Officer*) concerned a bungalow and garage in Ipswich with a gross value of £453. A valuation court had reduced this figure to £425 mainly because of an error in measurement disclosed at the valuation court. The ratepayer considered that his bungalow should more properly be described as a chalet rather than being described in the valuation list either as a house or as a bungalow, the choice of which appeared to depend on the ratio of the areas of the ground floor to the first floor. The valuation officer submitted that the list description did not affect the value. However, the ratepayer did not persuade the tribunal (Mr. W. H. Rees) that the valuation court had been wrong in declining to amend the valuation list description.

The valuation officer submitted details of open market rents for nine properties in or near the borough of Ipswich and these supported the assessments of the properties and the general level of assessments throughout the borough. The ratepayer admitted in cross-examination that in the open market a rent equivalent to the gross value would be obtained but no one could afford to pay it. He also complained of property conversions which depreciated the value of his dwelling. The ratepayer drew comparisons between his own and 16 other properties in Ipswich but looking at the evidence the tribunal concluded that it supported the gross value on the appeal property rather than indicating a lower value. The ratepayer had failed to prove his case. Appeal dismissed. £10 costs against the ratepayer.

(*Decision January 13, 1975*)

8

NEARBY DEVELOPMENT IN PLACE OF OPEN VIEW CONSIDERED NOT TO AFFECT RENTAL VALUE.

The appeal *Smith* v. *Morton* (*Valuation Officer*) concerned a bungalow and garage in Aughton, Lancashire, assessed at £415 gross value, a figure confirmed by a valuation court but the ratepayer sought a reduction because what had been a fairly open view had been replaced with the rear view of property far below the standard in his own road.

The tribunal (Mr. W. H. Rees) said that the rear of houses of which the ratepayer complained were a little over 100 yards away and most of the intervening space comprised unused land which was formerly agricultural but now overgrown. The valuation officer said his valuation had been made with the knowledge that the properties in question were there and no addition had been made previously for the open aspect. He pointed out the circumstances under the rating hypothesis and he was convinced that the hypothetical tenant coming fresh to the scene would take the site as he found it. The tribunal preferred this approach and dismissed the appeal, awarding £5 costs against the ratepayer.

(*Decision January 13, 1975*)

9

CONDITION OF ROAD USED TO ENTER AND LEAVE HOUSING ESTATE JUSTIFIES ONLY SMALL REDUCTION FOR CERTAIN HOUSES FRONTING THE ROAD.

The appeal *Nuttall* (*Valuation Officer*) v. *Miller and Others* related to 32 appeals on an estate in Bryn near Ashton-in-Makerfield. The estate had been developed in two parts, the westerly part comprising some 250 privately owned houses and the easterly part comprising about 300 local authority houses. The subjects of the appeal related to the private section of the estate and the issue raised throughout was the effect of the condition of the estate roads.

It was complained that although the roads had all been completed they were not all in a satisfactory condition and one particular carriageway caused anxiety as it was a natural entrance and exit route for the whole estate and was, therefore, a matter of concern to all the residents.

It appeared that two development companies had been involved and had entered into agreements with the local authority under s. 40 of the Highways Act 1959. The residents could not put pressure on these firms to remedy matters and could only put pressure on the local authority so to do. One way of achieving action was to set about getting their rating assessments reduced. A valuation court had reduced the gross value of each of the appeal properties by £20, being of the opinion that a hypothetical tenant would lower his rental bid in the light of the conditions. The valuation officer appealed and sought restoration of the gross values in all cases.

The valuation officer thought that two questions had to be decided. Was the fact that an approach road to a house happened to be unadopted any reason for reducing an assessment and was the condition of the approach road in such a state as to warrant an assessment reduction? It appeared that the phrasing of the ratepayer's proposals had referred to the making up of the roads but during the proceedings it was said that there never was any question so far as the ratepayers were concerned in raising the question of a road being unadopted. It was simply the physical condition that bothered them and the only question to be resolved in the view of the tribunal (Mr. R. C. Walmsley) was whether or not the deplorable condition of one particular thoroughfare, i.e. the road used mainly to enter or leave the estate, would cause a prospective tenant to reduce his rental bid for any or all of the appeal houses. The conclusion was that apart from those houses actually in the middle section of that thoroughfare the conditions would be regarded by prospective tenants as little more than a source of considerable irritation. As a pedestrian he would be largely unaffected by carriageway conditions and as a motorist he could make detours without adding greatly to the length of his journeys.

The tribunal determined that all gross values should be reinstated as the valuation officer had claimed, i.e. £20 in each case except for 13 dwellings in the middle of the thoroughfare used for entrance and exit purposes where an increase of £15 was appropriate. There was no order as to costs.

(*Decision January 14, 1975*)

10

REDUCTION ON ACCOUNT OF REFUSE TIP. HIGH FENCES ERECTED BY TENANTS NOT CONSIDERED TO BE A LANDLORD'S RESPONSIBILITY UNDER THE DEFINITION OF GROSS VALUE.

The appeal *Billington and Others* v. *Grice* (*Valuation Officer*) concerned bungalows at Whiston, Merseyside. There were five properties involved and the subject of concern by the ratepayers was the use of some open land adjoining their properties. The tribunal thought it right to refer to the material circumstances not only at the relevant date, June 1973, but also as at 1971/72 when the valuation officer was deciding on the tone of assessment for the new valuation list. The locality contained about 350 post-war dwellings and in 1971/72 and thereafter had immediately to the south a chemical works which emitted a fine white dust and involved a fall-out as far north as the appeal bungalows. Nearby was a small public open space but the appeal bungalows in 1971/72 backed on to a worked-out claypit of some 28 acres. However, by June 1973 this former claypit had been taken over as a local authority tip for household and industrial refuse and the tribunal (Mr. R. C. Walmsley) found on the evidence that in addition to authorised tipping there was also much fly-tipping, fires were frequently started by vandals and involved acrid smells and a great deal of smoke. There had been a dramatic increase in flies and insects and there was rat infestation. Moreover, the refuse itself was unsightly and gave off a nauseating smell. Machines operating on the tip were noisy and because of the number of vehicles going to and from the tip, parts of the area had become a pedestrian hazard.

So far as the gross values of £255 for each of the appeal bungalows were concerned the tribunal was satisfied that such figures were not pitched above the tone of assessment for similar dwellings in the same locality and this tone had now been established, partly as a result of test cases and partly through agreements reached with ratepayers. The ratepayers in the present appeals agreed that but for the refuse tip they would not object to their assessments. Undoubtedly, the proximity and use of the tip was a rental disability for the five bungalows which abutted the land immediately surrounding the tip.

To help themselves the tenants had erected high fences but not at the date of the proposal. In any case the valuation officer submitted that the landlord should be regarded as willing to provide such fences for prospective tenants but the tribunal disagreed, stating that in determining the reasonably expected rent it was well established that the property was always the actual property and that the hereditament was to be valued *rebus sic stantibus* save that, in general terms, items of disrepair were deemed to have been remedied. In the present case neither light fencing nor shrubs would have served any good purpose and no year to year tenant could reasonably be expected to erect a substantial 7 ft. high fence without making a compensating reduction in his rental bid. In June 1973 not only were the bungalows unscreened but the tipping operations had only a few weeks earlier been carried out just beyond their back gardens. Taking all the circumstances into account the tribunal considered that the allowances in terms of gross value at the relevant date should be £30 for one, £25 for another and £20 for each of the three remaining bungalows. The appeals were allowed and the valuation officer was ordered to pay each of the ratepayers £3 costs.

(*Decision January 14, 1975*)

11

PROXIMITY TO PLACES OF WORK A FACTOR INFLUENCING THE HYPOTHETICAL TENANT. OTHER MINOR DISABILITIES UNPROVEN OR REJECTED.

A valuation court had confirmed a gross value of £450 on a house and garage in Gosport, the subject of the appeal *Bradley* v. *Barnes* (*Valuation Officer*) but the ratepayer thought his assessment compared unfavourably with other similar but better situated properties. He referred also to an inefficient central heating system but had not provided the tribunal with a written report by a qualified person that the defects were inherent and could not reasonably have been put right by the hypothetical landlord; given that evidence the matter could be reconsidered. On the damage by vandals and nuisance by children as well as access to and prices in local shops, these were complaints common to the area generally and could not be taken into account any more than inconsiderate parking by delivery vans. The main ground of appeal was question of comparison with seven other properties but in better districts.

The valuation officer thought the proximity of naval establishments and industries attracted managerial and skilled labour into the better district but there was little rental evidence apart from three cases and he cited 11 other properties in support of his argument on the appeal property. He also put in a schedule showing a similar analysis of the ratepayer's comparables.

The tribunal (Mr J. D. Russell-Davis) thought the appeal property to be a pleasant contemporary house and in a locality which was a little stark when contrasted with the more mature better class locality where his comparables were. However, the tribunal believed that the hypothetical tenant of the appeal property would put against that the consideration of proximity to places of work. The tribunal was convinced that the appeal hereditament would command in terms of gross value a rent of not less than £450. Appeal dismissed. £25 costs awarded against the ratepayer which was not questioned by the ratepayer. The tribunal was satisfied that the cost of preparation of the respondent's case, documentation and other expenses could be quantified at not less than £25.

(*Decision January 15, 1975*)

12

SMALL ASSESSMENT REDUCTION CENTRAL LONDON OFFICES. NO PUBLIC AUTHORITY CONDEMNATION OF ALLEGEDLY WEAK FLOOR MEMBERS. VALUATION OFFICER'S ADDITION FOR ANCILLARY SPACE APPROVED.

The appeal *Mayer & Partners* v. *Veness* (*Valuation Officer*) concerned offices in Bloomsbury, London, where a valuation list description of offices, flat and premises carried a gross value of £2,100. A valuation court, when confirming the gross value, had altered the description to offices and premises because what had one time been a caretaker's flat was no longer so used. However, the ratepayers maintained that the third floor space was unsuitable for use as offices because of physical shortcomings and a poor approach. They claimed that the accommodation did not comply with London building regulations covering office use. The space was merely storage space and they sought a reduction of the gross value to £1,475. The ratepayers had a lease for five years from March 1970 at a rent of £1,500 per annum, the tenants being liable for rates and internal repairs and for 2/5ths of the cost of repairs and insurance of the building and of the maintenance of the common parts.

The valuation officer had only limited rental evidence but he calculated initially that the actual rent under the lease was equivalent to a rent of £1,800 in terms of gross value. The second and third floors of a nearby suite, similar but slightly larger, were let in September 1970 at a rent equivalent to £3,425. Finally he cited rents of four other nearby office suites. Office rents, he claimed, had risen sharply between 1970 and 1972 but he could not explain the vast difference between two neighbouring suite rents. Nevertheless he was satisfied that his gross value of £2,100 was not excessive.

The tribunal (Mr Douglas Frank, President) considered that so far as the second floor of the appeal premises was concerned a gross value of £1,280 should be determined. In considering the third floor accommodation a qualified structural engineer gave evidence about the floor strength but admitted that at the date of the proposal there had been no intervention by the district surveyor nor had any restrictions been placed on the use of the floor. This witness conceded that the floor could be used for some limited office purpose. The valuation officer argued that the use for storage was ancillary to the main office use and he had reduced the rate per square metre to reflect the disadvantages.

The tribunal thought the valuation officer was right in his claim about the third floor being considered as ancillary to the office use, and that he had sufficiently recognised in his valuation the limited use of the third floor. A gross value of £730 was applicable to that floor. This gave a total gross value of £2,010 which the tribunal rounded down to £2,000. To that extent the appeal was allowed. There had been a call for an adjournment but the tribunal did not think that had been justified or that the appellants' case would have been prejudiced by certain small differences of detail. Therefore, each party was ordered to pay its own costs of the adjournment and with that exception costs were awarded against the valuation officer on County Court scale 4 if not agreed.

(*Decision January 15, 1975*)

13

VALUATION COURT ACCEPTS RECOMMENDED REDUCTION FOR UNSPECIFIED DISABILITIES AFTER MAKING ITS OWN CHECK VALUATION. TRIBUNAL CONFIRMS IT.

The valuation officer had suggested to a valuation court that the assessment of a house and garage near Leek, Staffordshire, should be reduced to £514 gross value but the ratepayer in *Turner* v. *Bott* (*Valuation Officer*) appealed, claiming that the court had overlooked or ignored some lack of impartiality by the valuation officer. There had been some lack of identification of disabilities included within the allowance of 22½ *per cent.* but the court had checked by making its own valuation and expressed satisfaction that the end figure proposed by the valuation officer must be supported as not being excessive.

The ratepayer had referred to certain comparables but the tribunal (Mr. Douglas Frank, President) thought that these comparables fully supported the gross value of the appeal property and thought that the allowance for disabilities was perhaps generous. Appeal dismissed. There had been nothing to suggest any lack of impartiality on the part of the valuation officer. In the absence of special circumstances the valuation officer sought £30 costs, a sum which the tribunal thought not only reasonable but considerably less than would have been awarded on taxation. Ratepayer to pay £30 costs to the valuation officer.

(*Decision January 15, 1975*)

14

UNSUCCESSFUL RATEPAYER NOT LANDED WITH COSTS. VALUATION OFFICER INCREASES ASSESSMENTS OF COMPARABLES.

The appeal *Craggill* v. *Herd* (*Valuation Officer*) concerned a house and garage in Whitley Bay assessed at £336 gross value, a figure confirmed by a valuation court. The appeal property was in fact a semi-detached bungalow with two rooms in the roof space but with a bathroom on the ground floor. Space was taken up by staircases. The ratepayer relied on the assessments of three dwellings in the same road but following his examination of those properties the valuation officer concluded that they were under-assessed and he had made proposals to increase their gross values. He depended on rental evidence but the tribunal (Mr. Douglas Frank, President) did not find that evidence really assisted him. Therefore, he was left with another schedule presented by the valuation officer indicating the assessments of comparable dwellings.

The tribunal was satisfied that this was the best evidence available and established that the appeal property was not over-assessed. Appeal dismissed. On the question of costs, the ratepayer claimed that his appeal was justified for he had shown over-assessment on the basis of comparisons, something effectively conceded by the valuation officer. The valuation officer recognised that there was substance in this argument and asked for only £10 costs. However, the tribunal thought that once it had been accepted that the ratepayer had been justified in appealing then the case became exceptional and the right course was to make no order as to costs.

(*Decision January 22, 1975*)

15

NO COSTS AGAINST UNSUCCESFUL RATEPAYER CLAIMING RELIEF FROM THE ANOMALOUS PROVISIONS GOVERNING MINOR ALTERATIONS AND CENTRAL HEATING INSTALLATIONS.

The appeal *Pickering* v. *Barrow* (*Valuation Officer*) concerned a house and garage in Whitley Bay and involved a point of law under s. 21 of the Local Government Act 1974, the issue being whether the gross value of the appeal property should be reduced by the amount attributable to the installation of central heating before April 1, 1974, a value of £26. The ratepayer pointed out that without such a reduction he would have paid something like £200 rates more than a comparable hereditament in which central heating was installed after April 1, 1974, this sum covering the estimated period before the next rating revaluation could take account of improvements to the comparable property.

The tribunal (Mr. Douglas Frank, President) considered in detail the appropriate statutory provisions and much though he sympathised with the ratepayer and fully appreciated the force of his argument on the grounds of equity, there was nothing that could be done about it since Parliament had so decreed. Accordingly the appeal was dismissed.

The tribunal had not found it necessary to call the valuation officer who had asked for £25 towards his costs on the ground that he had had to prepare plans and other documents. However, the valuation officer was fully aware from the valuation court proceedings that the sole question was one of construction of a legal provision and there were only minor facts which might have been in issue. It was quite unnecessary for the documents to be prepared and the tribunal saw no reason why the ratepayer should be called upon to help pay for them. The valuation officer had appeared in person so the question of costs did not arise. There was no order as to costs.

(*Decision January 22, 1975*)

16

PERCENTAGE ADDITION FOR HOUSE ADAPTED FOR OCCUPATION IN PARTS QUERIED, BUT NOT CHALLENGED BY RATEPAYER.

The appeal *Leadley* v. *Keith* (*Valuation Officer*) concerned a house in Bedford in which the owner lived but let out single furnished rooms on the first and second floors. In the new valuation list the premises were described as "House, Adapted for Occupation in Parts" and assessed at £700 gross value. A valuation court had reduced this figure to £670 at the suggestion of the valuation officer. The ratepayer claimed that the dwelling had not been adapated for occupation in parts. The valuation officer cited 12 comparables and explained his approach in the case of dwellings in single occupation, those so arranged that they could be occupied in parts (e.g. extra bathroom, extra kitchen, fire escape, etc.) and a boarding house. His schedule indicated firm percentage increases to gross values of the first named to reflect the appreciated annual value for the other two groups. In the case of the appeal property a 17 *per cent.* addition had been made. This was not queried by the ratepayer and in the absence of any evidence from him the tribunal (Mr. J. R. Laird) was unable to say that the percentage was wrong. It was also unable to find that the valuation court had come to a wrong decision. Appeal dismissed. Costs £15 against the ratepayer.

(*Decision January 23, 1975*)

17

UNSUCCESSFUL RATEPAYER'S CLAIM FOR THE SAME ASSESSMENT ON HIS END TERRACE COUNCIL HOUSE AS FOR INNER TERRACE HOUSES.

The tenant of a Bedford council house was the appellant in *Savage* v. *Keith* (*Valuation Officer*). It was an end house of a terrace of ten and carried an extra gross value of £15 because it was an end terrace house. This differential was reduced, at the valuation officer's suggestion, to £5 by a valuation court, the resultant gross value being £225. This adjustment was because the appeal dwelling did not have a side entrance, as had been assumed. The ratepayer did not consider that in this instance any differential was called for. People had thrown all sorts of rubbish over his wall. Children climbed it. The open space adjoining his house encouraged such behaviour. The valuation officer thought his suggested reduction amply met the ratepayer's case. There had been very few ratepayers' proposals on council houses. The tribunal (Mr. J. R. Laird) had inspected the area and could find no evidence that the appeal property was in any way unique so far as disabilities were concerned. The tribunal had not been satisfied by the ratepayer that the valuation court had come to a wrong decision. Appeal dismissed. Costs £10 against the ratepayer.

(*Decision January 23, 1975*)

18

TRAFFIC AND UNEVEN STREET SURFACE NOT FACTORS JUSTIFYING AN ASSESSMENT REDUCTION.

In the appeal *Jarman* v. *Heywood* (*Valuation Officer*) the ratepayer claimed that the street, which was paved with stone setts, had an uneven surface and that traffic past his house caused vibration and noise. He wanted his old list gross value of £95 reduced by £20 on that account. The valuation officer did not consider that the uneven surface would influence the hypothetical tenant. The tribunal (Mr. W. H. Rees) preferred the valuation officer's evidence, dismissed the appeal and awarded £10 costs against the ratepayer.

(*Decision January 27, 1975*)

19

WORKS ON NEW BRIDGE NOT REGARDED BY TRIBUNAL AS WARRANTING A REDUCED ASSESSMENT.

The ratepayer in *Seddon* v. *Taylor* (*Valuation Officer*) agreed that but for certain public works being carried out close by he would not have sought a reduced rating assessment. His house in Liverpool was assessed at £235 gross value. The activity to which he referred involved the building of a new bridge to carry a road over the Leeds and Liverpool canal, together with approach roads. He sought a 50 *per cent.* reduction on account of excessive noise, dirt and pollution over a substantial period of 12 months. The valuation officer submitted details of comparable houses disclosing a consistent pattern of assessment. He considered the disability to be small and submitted that the hypothetical tenant coming fresh to the scene would notice that the works were well advanced and would not reduce his rental bid. The tribunal (Mr. W. H. Rees) was swayed by the distance from the works and the presence of buildings in between. Appeal dismissed. Costs £10 against the ratepayer.

(*Decision January 27, 1975*)

20

LACK OF BATHROOM AND ATTENDANT BENEFITS HELD NOT TO WARRANT REDUCED ASSESSMENT OF OLD FASHIONED DWELLING.

The appeal *Watson* v. *Sture* (*Valuation Officer*) concerned a terrace house in Bowness-on-Windermere. The ratepayer sought a reduction because of the lack of such facilities as hot water pipes and bathroom, the state of disrepair and outlook. A valuation court had reduced the gross value from £138 to £133. The valuation officer submitted some rental evidence but had rejected controlled rents, including that of the appeal property. The tribunal (Mr. W. H. Rees) preferred the valuation officer's well presented and documented evidence and dismissed the appeal. Costs £5 against the ratepayer.

(*Decision January 27, 1975*)

21

FACTORY NOISE AND NUISANCE, AND AIRPORT TRAFFIC, HELD TO WARANT SMALL ASSESSMENT REDUCTION.

In the appeal *Tubman* v. *Leighton* (*Valuation Officer*) concerning a house at Stockon-on-Tees it was agreed by the parties that in the event of the tribunal (Mr. Douglas Frank, President) rejecting the ratepayer's contentions for a reduction on the grounds of certain disabilities a gross value of £295 was correct. Five grounds of appeal were presented. Foundry noise, smoke, etc., noise from bulk tankers delivering at a factory, nuisance from training flights at Teesside airport, use of a nearby disused railway track as a walkway and the adverse effect on amenities of a trunk road. On the first and second ground the tribunal thought a reduction of £5 to be appropriate, a further £5 reduction on the third, but considered that the hypothetical tenant would not be affected in his bid so far as the remaining matters were concerned. Gross value £285 determined. No costs awarded.

(*Decision January 29, 1975*)

22

ELECTRICITY BOARD'S OFFICES USED WHOLLY OR MAINLY AS SUCH AND NOT ON OPERATIONAL LAND, HELD TO BE SEPARATELY RATEABLE.

The appeal *Goodwin* (*Valuation Officer*) v. *London Borough of Waltham Forest and the London Electricity Board* concerned the rateability of certain offices in a building occupied by the London Electricity Board. The building contained, in addition to the offices, showrooms and stores, the building itself standing within the curtilage of a depot. The valuation officer had been advised by the Ministry of Technology that the offices were not situated on operational land. Thereupon, he made a proposal to delete an existing entry in the valuation list and substituting an entry showing a gross value of £9,600 in respect of showroom, offices and premises. No objection was lodged. However, later on the Board made a proposal that the showroom should be entered as a separate hereditament and that the office premises should be deleted from the list. Subsequently the valuation officer made a proposal to assess the premises in two parts—£3,000 gross value for the showroom, stores and premises, and £6,600 gross value for the offices and premises. The Board objected. In due course a valuation court determined only one entry, that of the showroom and premises at £3,000 gross value. The rating authority and the valuation officer both appealed to the Lands Tribunal. In the proceedings the rating authority took no part. If the offices were to be assessed at all the parties were agreed on a gross value of £6,500.

The valuation officer contended that office premiss occupied by an electricity board which were not situated on operational land were liable to be rated. The Board contended that office premises occupied by an electricity board and not situated on operational land, were only excepted by s. 34(2)(*c*) of the General Rate Act 1967, from the general exemption conferred by s. 34(1) if the office premises were a hereditament as provided in s. 32(2) and as defined by s. 115(1) and by authority. They further contended that the office premises forming part of the larger building were part of the depot and were not capable of being separately let, were not therefore a hereditament, and accordingly were not liable to be rated under s. 34(2)(*c*) of the Act. It was quite inconceivable that the office part of the premises would be separately let. If that part of the premises became surplus to requirements it would remain empty on security grounds. The offices did not form a hereditament in rating law because they could not be separately occupied, reliance being placed on the definition of hereditament in s. 115(1) and judgments of the courts. The valuation officer submitted that both the showrooms and the offices should properly be entered separately in the valuation list as artificial hereditaments created by s. 34 of the Act. The tribunal (Mr. Douglas Frank, President and Mr. J. H. Emlyn Jones) noted that the Board claimed that because they would not agree to let off part of their premises that part could, therefore, not be considered as a separate hereditament. That was misconceived. There was nothing unusual in the letting of property subject to special access arrangements. Unless it was possible to establish the proposition that no occupier of the depot and showroom would be willing to consider letting it was not possible to say that the office premises were incapable of separate letting. The tribunal came to the conclusion that even under what had been referred to as the "normal rules" the office premises were "a hereditament used wholly or mainly as an office or for office purposes" and that was enough to allow the appeal. In deference to the arguments put up by counsel the tribunal went on to consider the definition of hereditament, particularly since there appeared to be some inconsistency between the conclusions arrived at in *West Midlands Electricity Board* v. *Hereford City Council and Eastwood* (*Valuation Officer*) and *Eastern Electricity Board* v. *Smith* (*Valuation Officer*), in 1971 and 1974 respectively. After considering certain passages in judgments in *Gilbert* v. *Hickinbottom* the tribunal came to the conclusion that in considering the meaning of the word in rating law it was better to employ a commonsense assessment of the features of the case than to seek to have recourse to some standard formula. The office premises were to be treated as a hereditament for the purposes of s. 34 whether or not they were capable of becoming the subject of separate occupation. It probably followed from the tribunal's decision that a determination by the Minister that office premises were not on operational land was conclusive as to their rateability, provided the offices were used wholly or mainly as an office or for office purposes. Appeal allowed. Costs against the Board on the High Court scale if not agreed.

(*Decision February 3, 1975*)

23

MANAGER OF A PROPERTY, AS DISTINCT FROM PERSON RECEIVING RENTS BENEFICIALLY, NOT A RATEPAYER. RATEPAYER IN AN ALIEN RATING AREA NOT AN "AGGRIEVED PERSON". NOR IS HE AGGRIEVED AS A PRECEPT PAYER OR TAXPAYER.

The appeal *Arsenal Football Club Ltd.* v. *Smith* (*Valuation Officer*) *and Ende* concerned a preliminary issue to determine whether a proposal by the respondent was bad in law and void in that he was not "a person aggrieved" within the meaning of s.69(1) of the General Rate Act 1967. He had claimed to be aggrieved by the value and the description in the valuation list of the Arsenal football ground. The rateable value was £9,250 and the description was "Football Grounds, stands and offices". The hereditament was in Islington, but the respondent lived in Hackney. However, he was at all material times the manager of a property within the London Borough of Islington. This was a property in multiple occupation but his name appeared in the rate book as the person liable to pay rates on the property. He sought in his proposal "a more comprehensive description" of the hereditament and a rateable value of £60,000. When asked the grounds on which he claimed to be an aggrieved person he referred to his being a ratepayer in his rating area and in his precepting area. He also referred to his being a taxpayer, thereby being concerned about government grants. He also claimed to be aggrieved as a person managing real property from which rents of rated occupiers issued. The valuation officer objected to the proposal. Subsequently a valuation court accepted Mr. Ende as an aggrieved person and amended the rateable value, justifying the decision by reference to the inclusion of his name in the rate book, that he was resident within the same precepting area and that he lived near enough to the appeal premises to be affected by parking and match disturbance.

At one stage the club unsuccessfully sought a declaration from a Divisional Court that Mr. Ende was not an aggrieved person. The club was referred to the normal rating appeal procedure.

The tribunal (Mr. Douglas Frank, President and Mr. V. G. Wellings) noted in the course of the proceedings that it was concerned with the respondent's status as a ratepayer and as a taxpayer.

The club contended that the reference to the person who receives the rents of the parts of a dwelling in multiple occupation within s. 24 of the General Rate Act 1967 was to the person who received them beneficially and not merely as an agent and this view was endorsed by the tribunal. The respondent, therefore, was at no time a ratepayer in the London Borough of Islington.

In case the tribunal proved to be wrong on this point consideration was given to a related question. Did the fact that a person was a ratepayer in itself suffice, without regard to other considerations, to constitute him a person aggrieved if there was any error, unfairness or lack of equivalence in the valuation list? Consideration was given to judgments in *Grainger* v. *Liverpool Corporation (1954)* and *Regina* v. *Paddington Valuation Officer (1966)* concerning the Peachey Property Corporation, but counsel for the club argued that observations in the latter case did not mean that any ratepayer, a mere busybody, such as respondent was, could, without regard to the circumstances, come forward and allege that he was a person aggrieved, some demonstrable effect on the pocket, rights or interests of a proposer must exist and the question whether a person was aggrieved was one of fact. The tribunal agreed. Also examined was the question if the respondent was a ratepayer was he, on the facts, aggrieved by the club's underassessment? Expert evidence showed that the effect of an increase in the assessment as proposed would have been minimal so far as the rate poundage was concerned. The tribunal could not see, on the assumption that the club was underassessed, that the respondent had suffered any grievance personally or otherwise. On the question whether or not he could be aggrieved as a precept payer or taxpayer the tribunal agreed that a ratepayer in a rating area alien to the one involved could not be an aggrieved person and also that a grievance suffered by a precept payer or taxpayer was too remote.

The respondent's proposal was invalid and the local valuation court had no jurisdiction in the matter. Costs on the High Court scale were awarded to the club, 40 *per cent.* to be paid by the valuation officer and 60 *per cent.* by the other respondent.

(*Decision February 5, 1975*)

24

TRIBUNAL CONFIRMS VALUATION COURT'S REDUCTION ON ACCOUNT OF TRAFFIC AND OVERLOOKING, AND ITS REFUSAL TO HAVE REGARD TO PERCENTAGE INCREASES TO THE 1963 VALUATION LIST ENTRIES.

The appeal *Patey* v. *Millwood* (*Valuation Officer*) concerned a house and garage in Folkestone. The highway on which the property was situate became a trunk road and there had been development of a large residential estate, some of the houses considerably overlooking the side and rear of the appeal property. In 1971 a valuation court had reduced the gross value of the property from £250 to £231 on account of the road and the development. This was accepted by the valuation officer but subsequently an increase of £5 was proposed by the valuation officer following minor improvements. The gross value in the new list was £604 but a valuation court reduced this to £570 on account of traffic and overlooking. The ratepayer contended that the whole character of the immediate locality had changed and sought further relief. The tribunal (Mr. J. R. Laird) noted that the house was set back some 130 feet from the front boundary fence, thus being afforded some protection from the traffic and on the question of the relevance of the percentage increase above the 1963 assessment, a strong point made by the ratepayer, the tribunal agreed with the valuation court that it was not the correct approach in the present appeal. On the sufficiency of the relief given by the valuation court the tribunal had not been satisfied by the ratepayer that the court's decision was wrong. Appeal dismissed. Costs £20 against the ratepayer.

(*Decision February 19, 1975*)

25

ADJOINING WASTE GROUND AND HISTORY OF BURGLARY AND VANDALISM NOT LIKELY TO INFLUENCE THE HYPOTHETICAL TENANT'S RENTAL BID.

A property in Birmingham, assessed at £352 gross value, was the subject of the appeal *Gilkes* v. *Jordan* (*Valuation Officer*). A valuation court had reduced this by £2. The ratepayer claimed that by reason of the situation of his house it was vulnerable to attacks of burglars and damage by hooligans.

The valuation officer produced details of rents of six houses which satisfied the tribunal (Mr. J. H. Emlyn Jones) that the basic gross value of the appeal property was justified. The existence of waste ground at the side of the house would not, to many people, represent any particular disability, but even if it was a distinguishing feature any depreciatory effect was offset by the open view at the rear of the property. Burglaries and vandalism were, unfortunately, sad facts of life in localities on the edge of large cities and the tribunal did not consider that they caused any reduction in rental values. Appeal dismissed. No order as to costs.

(*Decision February 25, 1975*)

26

GROSS VALUE REDUCTION ON ACCOUNT OF AWKWARD SMALL THIRD BEDROOM.

The appeal *Slatter* v. *Taylor* (*Valuation Officer*) concerned a house and garage in Malvern. Following structural alterations and additions the gross value of £361 was to be increased to £405. The ratepayer contended for a figure of £385 but called no expert evidence in support. The tribunal (Mr. V. G. Wellings) was satisfied from the opinion of the valuation officer, from comparables and its own inspection that the assessment was correct save in one respect. The property suffered one special disadvantage. The third bedroom, measuring approximately 8 ft. by 7 ft. was so arranged that it was not possible to instal a normal sized bed and furniture. The tribunal reduced the gross value by £10. Costs £10 awarded against the valuation officer.

(*Decision February 25, 1975*)

27

SMALL REDUCTION OFFERED BY VALUATION OFFICER ACCEPTED BY TRIBUNAL. NO SUBSTANCE IN RATEPAYER'S MISCONCEIVED ALLEGATIONS AGAINST VALUATION OFFICER.

A valuation court had confirmed the gross value of £330 on a bungalow and garage in Horndeal, Hampshire, but the ratepayer in the appeal

Bieganek v. *Savage* (*Valuation Officer*) supported his grounds for a reduction by reference to measurements, incorrectness regarding accommodation, false evidence, lack of evidence on other bungalows, misuse of a recreational green, failure to explain assessment method, failure to produce rental returns and an excessive assessment anyway. The valuation officer had offered a small reduction of £5 gross value before the hearing and again offered it at the hearing.

The valuation officer said that rented dwellings in the area were few and rented bungalows scarce. He had found eight bungalows where rents had been fixed between 1964 and 1969. He also relied on a schedule of assessments of 24 bungalows and a house all on the estate and these included the bungalows cited by the ratepayer. After examining the rental evidence the tribunal (Mr. E. C. Strathon) concluded that the amended gross value suggested by the valuation officer was fair and reasonable. Appeal allowed to that extent. As the offer had been made to the ratepayer during the month before the hearing the ratepayer was ordered to pay £10 costs to the valuation officer. The tribunal also investigated other complaints by the ratepayer but noted that a crucial letter from the valuation officer had not been seen by the ratepayer because delivery had been refused.

(*Decision February 28, 1975*)

28

BUSINESS USE IN ADJOINING HOUSE HELD TO WARRANT TEMPORARY REDUCTION PENDING CLARIFICATION BY PLANNING AUTHORITY.

The appeal *Dunn* v. *Cousins* (*Valuation Officer*) concerned a house and garage in Fareham, Hampshire. A valuation court had reduced the gross value from £450 to £430. The ratepayer thought this to be insufficient. His grounds related to the loss, through development, of a view, inadequate fencing necessitating additional fencing which fostered friction between neighbours and the carrying on of a painting and decorating business from the adjoining house. The valuation officer conceded that he had been unaware of this business. The tribunal (Mr. E. C. Strathon) did not find the rental evidence helpful. The valuation officer considered that the effect of the business use on the annual value of the appeal property to be adequately reflected in the valuation court's reduction. In his view planning controls were the task of the local authority. The tribunal concluded that the hypothetical tenant contemplated by the valuation officer to be one who would be fully informed and who would expect the use problem to be dealt with, and would also expect to negotiate a reduced rent ending the realisation of further abatement of the nuisance. Gross value fixed at £415. Costs £10 against the valuation officer.

(*Decision February 28, 1975*)

29

REDUCED GROSS VALUE ON ACCOUNT OF UNSIGHTLY GARAGE ON APPEAL PREMISES.

A house and garage in Henley-on-Thames assessed at £465 gross value was the subject of the appeal *Robinson* v. *Mundy* (*Valuation Officer*). The ratepayer had sought a reduction to £450, but the valuation officer had made a proposal to increase the figure to £475 to match the assessments of three adjoining houses. At the valuation court the ratepayer was not successful but the valuation officer's proposal was accepted. The ratepayer thought that on revaluation he had suffered a disproportionate increase. Additionally, his garage was sited in front of the house and as such it was unsightly, the glazed entrance lobby was of poor quality and the central heating installation did not extend to the entrance lobby, cloakroom, landing or bathroom. Additionally, a chimney outlet on the adjoining house was at a low level, there had been increased traffic in the neighbourhood and the garage reduced natural light and air circulation. All these disabilities he quantified at £25 gross value. The ratepayer tendered ten comparables and the valuation officer a schedule of nine rented houses. He stated that in respect of 4,249 dwellings in the town only 274 proposals or objections had been received, of which 217 had been withdrawn. He also relied on five comparables.

The tribunal (Mr. E. C. Strathon) was impressed by the evidence of acceptance of the general level of assessments and apart from the garage was not prepared to make any reductions in respect of the ratepayer's other points. But the garage was obtrusive and ill planned in relation to the house. The gross value should be reduced by £10 on that account. Appeal in respect of the ratepayer's proposal dismissed. Appeal in respect of the valuation officer's proposal allowed. No costs awarded but valuation officer to pay the fees incurred in respect of the ratepayer's appeal, a sum of £2·50.

(*Decision February 28, 1975*)

30

DWELLING ACCOMMODATION SO POOR AS TO BE DISREGARDED. APPRECIABLE REDUCTION GIVEN.

The appeal *Cruise* v. *Lang* (*Valuation Officer*) concerned a shop, house and premises in Camberley, assessed at £725 gross value, but reduced, on the valuation officer's recommendation, to £635 by a valuation court, a reduction related to the unhelpfulness of available rental evidence in its application to the appeal property and to the fact that the living rooms were "very basic". It was an old property in an area which had tended to lose trade to premises in a new town centre. Structurally, there was some dampness, no bathroom, an outside w.c., no hot water system and little natural light in the living room. Allowance had been made by the valuation officer but not in respect of the damp and its consequences. The principles laid down in *Wexler* v. *Playle* (*Valuation Officer*) *were called* in aid but the tribunal (Mr. R. C. Walmsley) thought the valuation officer had misunderstood the *ratio* of that decision. In that instance the disrepair was of a temporary nature, easily remediable, but with the appeal premises the extent of the defect took it outside such a category. The tribunal visualised the property being let on the rating hypothesis at a rent related to its value as a lock-up shop only. The reasonably expected rent in gross value terms would be £525 per annum. Appeal allowed. Gross value determined at £525. Costs £10 against the valuation officer.

(*Decision March 4, 1975*)

31

HEAVY LORRIES NEGOTIATING SHARP BEND AFFECTING OTHER PROPERTIES TOO. NO REDUCTION.

In the appeal *Humphrey* v. *Verrinder* (*Valuation Officer*) a valuation court had confirmed the gross value of a house and garage in Datchet at £483. The house was one of an estate of 49 dwellings. The ratepayer's main complaint was the presence and use of a vehicle depot some 250 yards away. Very large vehicles were involved in complicated turns just near the site of the appeal property. Other dwellings were equally affected. The vehicle depot had been there for at least 15 years and the valuation court members had made their own inspection prior to making up their minds. The tribunal (Mr. R. C. Walmsley) stated that the onus was on the ratepayer to show that the court's decision was wrong but had failed to do so. Appeal dismissed. Costs £10 against the ratepayer.

(*Decision March 4, 1975*)

32

DETACHED OR SEMI-DETACHED. LINKAGE BY FLANKING GARAGE. SMALL ALLOWANCE MADE.

The appeal *McDonald* v. *Chamberlain* (*Valuation Officer*) concerned a house and garage at Wickford, Essex, assessed at £390 gross value, a figure confirmed by a valuation court. The appeal property was one of an estate of 31 dwellings. The ratepayer complained about being charged rates as a detached property, whereas it was considered that the property was semi-detached. The tribunal (Mr. R. C. Walmsley) noted the siting of properties and the different designs involving distinct siting of houses, walkways and garages. The appeal property had a walkway on one side, outside its flanking garage, but it was flanked on the other side by the garage of the next door house. The valuation officer thought a 5 *per cent.* increase to gross value justified in the case of a detached house compared with a semi-detached house. The tribunal regarded the appeal house as detached with some of the characteristics of a semi-detached house. The linkage factor prompted the tribunal to fix a gross value of £382. The valuation officer cited an earlier decision of the same tribunal but it was pointed out that this illustrated that the tribunal reached its decisions on the facts and evidence in each particular case. Appeal allowed. Costs £8 against the valuation officer.

(*Decision March 4, 1975*)

33

REVALUATION TREATMENT OF BUNGALOWS ALLEGED TO BE MORE FAVOURABLE. RENTAL EVIDENCE CHALLENGED. ASSESSMENTS CONFIRMED.

The four appeals *Bishop and Others* v. *Auton* (*Valuation Officer*) concerned houses in Dorchester assessed at different gross values all of which had been confirmed by a valuation court. It was claimed that whereas on the general revaluation house gross values had been increased up to three times the multiplier for bungalows had been only $2\frac{1}{4}$ times. The valuation officer relied on five rents referred to by one of the appellants and he also submitted a schedule of 13 properties. As the ratepayer had failed to persuade the tribunal (Mr. W. H. Rees) that the valuation court had come to a wrong decision the appeals were dismissed. Costs £15 against each ratepayer.

(*Decision March 7, 1975*)

34

DEVELOPMENT INSTEAD OF OPEN SPACE. AMENITY FACTORS INSUBSTANTIAL. NO REDUCTION.

In the appeal *Boast* v. *Buck* (*Valuation Officer*) the ratepayer proposed a reduction in assessment because of building development which had reduced the general amenity of the area, development which had not been envisaged. A valuation court had confirmed a gross value of £325. The ratepayer was unhappy that members of the court had not made their visit at times he had indicated—weekends and weekday evenings—as the crucial periods when adverse evidence was to be seen, i.e. vehicles, parking, fumes and dogs. Close to the appeal property was an area of about 4 acres with a frontage to the River Medway, open land which had been used recreationally. It was on this land that development had taken place. The valuation officer testified that no addition had been made to reflect any benefit derived from the original open space. The tribunal (Mr. W. H. Rees) agreed with the valuation officer and that the matters of complaint were not sufficiently substantial to affect the gross value. Appeal dismissed. Costs £25 against the ratepayer.

(*Decision March 7, 1975*)

35

STONE MASONRY WORKS NEARBY. VALUATION COURT'S REDUCTION CONSIDERED TO BE ADEQUATE.

The appeal *Carr* v. *Young* (*Valuation Officer*) concerned a house in Portland, Dorset, assessed at £190 gross value. The ratepayer had sought a reduction to reflect a rateable value of £100, complaining about the noise, dust and rats from a large masonry works. A valuation court had determined a gross value of £160. The house was an inner terrace unit in a block of four. The locality generally, according to the ratepayer, suffered from adverse conditions. Rubbish dumps, worked out stone quarries, dirty roadways due to industrial traffic, two prisons, dockyard tip and so on. The valuation officer did not disagree but considered the valuation court's allowance adequately reflected their existence. The tribunal (Mr. W. H. Rees) agreed. Appeal dismissed. Costs £25 against the ratepayer.

(*Decision March 7, 1975*)

36

VALUATION COURT DEDUCTION FOR WEEKEND COTTAGE LACKING MANY AMENITIES NOT PROVED WRONG.

The appeal *Gee* v. *Young* (*Valuation Officer*) concerned a house at Wareham, Dorset, assessed at £205 gross value which the ratepayer sought to be amended to continue to reflect the value as an agricultural dwelling. A valuation court had fixed a gross value of £130, considering that insufficient allowance had been made for an isolated position and the distance of the property from a tarmacadam road. The property included 2½ acres of land and the ratepayer occupied it as a weekend cottage. He complained about paying for services, sewerage and police, he did not receive. The valuation officer had no relevant rental evidence but presented details of other properties. The tribunal (Mr. W. H. Rees) having inspected the property could find nothing to justify a reduction. Appeal dismissed. Costs £25 against the ratepayer.

(*Decision March 7, 1975*)

37

ALLOWANCE FOR SITUATION OFFERED BEFORE AND DURING APPEAL HEARING CONFIRMED.

The appeal *McVicar* v. *Covell* (*Valuation Officer*) concerned a house in Carshalton where a valuation court had confirmed a gross value of £370. The ratepayer sought a reduction on account of situation and on the relativity between old and new valuation lists. He submitted a schedule of

29 assessments to illustrate this but gave no satisfactory reply to the tribunal (Mr. W. H. Rees) on the question why he, the ratepayer, expected increases between the two lists to be the same. The ratepayer also criticised the valuation officer's comparables but the tribunal accepted the evidence of the valuation officer and said that its own inspection confirmed that the ratepayer's house was to be preferred to others to which he had referred. However, the valuation officer had offered both before and during the hearing a reduction in gross value of £20. The tribunal accepted this and reduced the gross value to £350. Appeal allowed to that extent. No costs award.

(*Decision March 7, 1975*)

38

DISADVANTAGES OF SKEWED ROOMS? DISUSED RAILWAY EMBANKMENT AND POOR STREET LIGHTING JUSTIFY ALLOWANCE SLIGHTLY EXCEEDING ADDITION FOR BEING END TERRACE PROPERTY.

In the appeal *Murphy* v. *Young* (*Valuation Officer*) a valuation court had confirmed a gross value of £170 on an end terrace house in Weymouth. The house lay against a disused railway embankment which was used as a playground by children and as a dumping ground for rubbish. The structural condition of the dwelling was poor, although the ratepayer had made some improvements notwithstanding the refusal of an improvement grant from the local authority. The valuation officer submitted details of nine houses, evidence which was not challenged by the ratepayer. He also testified that because of the various disabilities he had not made the customary addition for an end terrace house. The tribunal (Mr. W. H. Rees) did not think the two balanced and reduced the gross value to £165. Costs £5 against the valuation officer.

(*Decision March 7, 1975*)

39

OUTER WALL MEASUREMENTS QUESTIONED. INADEQUATE RENTAL EVIDENCE CRITICISED. ASSESSMENT CONFIRMED.

A valuation court had confirmed a gross value of £291 in respect of a bungalow and garage in Scunthorpe, but the ratepayer in the appeal *Richardson* v. *Peck* (*Valuation Officer*) did not think his property had been properly valued because outside measurements had been used. He was also unhappy that the valuation officer had not used at least six rents to give him supporting evidence. The ratepayer presented a list of 117 bungalows, but gave no evidence as to size, situation, etc. The valuation officer said there were 1,524 houses and bungalows in the area, only 43 proposals had been made by ratepayers, of which 26 had been settled by agreement or had been withdrawn, leaving only 17 outstanding. This showed that the valuation list had been accepted. The tribunal (Mr. W. H. Rees) said he much preferred the valuation officer's evidence, which had not been seriously challenged. Appeal dismissed. Costs £25 against the ratepayer.

(*Decision March 7, 1975*)

40

ACTUAL RENT AS EVIDENCE FOR ASSESSMENT OF LAND USED AS RIVERSIDE MOORING.

The appeal *Stanbridge* v. *Spittle* (*Valuation Officer*) concerned land used as a mooring for a houseboat near Weybridge. It carried a net annual and rateable value of £80. The land was rented by the ratepayer from the National Trust at a rent of 4p per week per foot of frontage, an annual payment of £83·20. The ratepayer was concerned that nearby bungalows and houses were assessed at figures which made his assessment quite unreasonable. This argument was not accepted by the valuation officer on the grounds that such properties were not comparable and if the plot boundaries of such dwellings were extended to the riverside they would have to be revalued. The tribunal (Mr. J. H. Emlyn Jones) said it was clear that the mere right to a mooring was not rateable unless it was clearly linked with the occupation of land. The valuation officer regarded the annual payment made by the ratepayer as the best evidence of the net annual value under s. 19(3) of the General Rate Act 1967. The tribunal did not find any evidence of any actual liability for repairs so far as the lessors were concerned. The annual value of the appeal hereditament was, in the tribunal's opinion, clearly established by the rent payments which not only the appellant but the occupiers of other houseboats were clearly prepared to pay. Appeal dismissed. Costs £10 against the ratepayer.

(*Decision March 17, 1975*)

41

NO REDUCTION ON ACCOUNT OF TRAFFIC VOLUME.

The appeals in *Dunn and Another* v. *Ridgeon* (*Valuation Officer*) concerned two houses and garages in Harrow, assessed at £490 and £460 gross value. The ratepayers sought reductions on the grounds of heavy traffic conditions, resulting in noise, vibration, dust, fumes, etc., so that values were depressed. A valuation court had not thought the traffic to be so abnormal or excessive as to influence the hypothetical tenant. However, the ratepayers sought reductions to £453 and £434 respectively. The valuation officer, in a well-documented case, submitted a schedule of actual rents from ten comparable dwellings and two fair rents. He also put in a statement of traffic statistics. The tribunal (Mr. J. D. Russell-Davis) had visited the locality and had noticed that the traffic was free flowing. There had been a number of appeals before the tribunal on much the same grounds and on similar facts. Generally, the tribunal noted, the pattern of evidence had been the same, that rents were not lower in main roads of the type in question unless there were particularly adverse circumstances. The appellants had failed to prove their case. Appeals dismissed. Costs £25 against the ratepayers in a sum of £12·50 each.

(*Decision March 19, 1975*)

42

SIMILAR HOUSES IN ANOTHER PART OF THE VALUATION AREA JUSTIFIABLY ASSESSED AT LOWER GROSS VALUES.

The appeal *Kempsell* v. *Clee* (*Valuation Officer*) concerned a house and garage at Hucclecote, Glos., where a valuation court had confirmed a gross value of £324. The ratepayer complained about a ditch running along the bottom of his garden, but the tribunal (Mr. R. C. Walmsley) agreed with the valuation officer that the nuisance was insignificant. The ratepayer's more substantial complaint related to the lower level of assessment of similar houses in another part of the rating area. These had been erected by the same builder but carried a gross value £15 lower than the appeal property. The tribunal thought the two localities to be quite different and in the case of the other area there was a high proportion of local authority dwellings so that quite distinct rental influences might be expected to operate in the two localities. The best evidence was that provided by the settled assessments of similar houses in the same locality as the appeal property. The difference of £15 gross value was, the tribunal found, the outcome of a conscious and deliberate exercise of valuation expertise. Appeal dismissed. Costs £20 against the ratepayer.

(*Decision March 20, 1975*)

43

SMALL ADJUSTMENTS FOR CUPBOARD SPACE UNDER SLOPING ROOF AND NARROW, SOMEWHAT AWKWARD GARAGE.

The appeal *Sladen* v. *Corser* (*Valuation Officer*) concerned a surgery, house, garage and premises in Cheltenham, assessed at £670, but reduced by a valuation court to £650. The ratepayer thought both the professional dwelling parts of the property to have been overassessed. In addition he drew attention to an office building and to traffic density. A further point he made was that there was a certain amount of floor space upstairs where the steeply pitched roof ran down to floor level and which had been enclosed to form cupboarding. The tribunal (Mr. R. C. Walmsley) questioned an addition of £20 to the gross value for this space and thought the figure of £10 suggested by the ratepayer to be preferred. Additionally a small reduction by the valuation officer to the garage value allowed by the valuation court accounted for a further £5 off the gross value. Appeal allowed. Gross value of £635 determined. Costs £20 against the valuation officer.

(*Decision March 20, 1975*)

44

NO REDUCTION ON ACCOUNT OF ROAD TRAFFIC AND RAILWAY.

The appeal *Brown* v. *Masters* (*Valuation Officer*) concerned a house in Addiscombe, Croydon, assessed at £290 gross value. The ratepayer complained about heavy traffic at the front and a railway at the back of his property. It appeared that heavy traffic had used the road in question as a short cut, even if, as the tribunal noted, in no great numbers. The valuation officer did not agree with the ratepayer that the rental value of the house would be affected by either of the factors leading to the appeal. The tribunal (Mr. R. C. Walmsley) did not consider that the gross value of the appeal property was above the level of rents actually passing in the locality. The valuation officer had selected ten comparables out of a large number of properties where there was rental evidence. Appeal dismissd. Costs £15 against the ratepayer.

(*Decision April 7, 1975*)

45

VALUATION COURT'S REDUCTION, ON ACCOUNT OF NEGLECTED COPSE, REGARDED AS AN AMENITY, HALVED.

The appeal *Dewar* (*Valuation Officer*) v. *Cross and Another* concerned four houses in Tonbridge in respect of which reductions were sought on account of the loss of amenity in regard to a piece of land overlooked by the dwellings. A valuation court had made reductions of £20 gross value in each case but the valuation officer sought restoration of the original figures. The land, a copse, had been unkempt in 1967 and used as a rubbish dump. Residents had got together and with the owner's consent had levelled the ground and sown parts with grass seed. Thereafter they had kept the land tidy. In 1973 the owner had felled about three-quarters of the trees and the land had become somewhat unkempt. The valuation officer pointed out that no additional value had been placed on the properties on account of the copse and the removal of trees would not have depreciated the value. He supported the assessments in the new valuation list by reference to the assessments of 13 other houses in the neighbourhood, evidence which was not challenged and claimed that he had no evidence of any loss in capital values due to the tree felling. However, the ratepayers argued that the houses were assessed for rating when the copse was considered to be an asset so there should be a reduction when it became an untidy tangle of weeds. The tribunal (Mr. W. H. Rees) thought some allowance appropriate in view of the state of the copse at the relevant date and determined reductions of £10 gross value in each case. Appeals allowed to that extent. No costs awarded.

(*Decision April 8, 1975*)

46

ASSESSMENT REDUCED ON ACCOUNT OF NUISANCES ARISING FROM BUS STOP.

In the appeal *Gomez* v. *Page* (*Valuation Officer*) concerning a house in Benfleet, Essex, assessed at £445 gross value, it was agreed that a deduction should be made on account of a bus stop outside the appeal property, the dispute being about the amount of that deduction. The ratepayer sought £15, the valuation officer contended for £5. There was no question about litter, damage and other inconveniences and reference was made to earlier decisions of the tribunal. The evidence suggested to the tribunal (Mr. W. H. Rees) that the proper deduction was £10. Appeal allowed. Costs £32·60 against the valuation officer.

(*Decision April 8, 1975*)

47

VALUATION OFFICER'S OFFER OF REDUCTION ACCEPTED BY VALUATION COURT. APPROVED AS ADEQUATELY REPRESENTING LOSS OF AMENITY DUE TO NEARBY RAILWAY AND DEPOT.

The appeal *Johnson* v. *Robinson* (*Valuation Officer*) concerned a house in S.E. London, assessed at £515 gross value. A valuation court had reduced this by £10 on account of the loss of amenity at the rear of the premises where there was a railway line and a cable depot. This reduction had been suggested by the valuation officer. The ratepayer had submitted evidence of a trend in rents but the valuation court believed that his statistics contained controlled rents and fair rents which they considered should be disregarded in arriving at gross value for rating purposes. The ratepayer had also mentioned six floodlights in the depot set about 30 ft. above ground which shone directly into his house. He presented evidence in support of his contention for a reduction on the basis of the retail price index. The valuation officer supported his gross value of £505 by reference to the open market rents of 16 terrace houses within reasonable reach of the appeal property and also to the assessments of six other houses in the same terrace. Additionally, he referred to the assessments of five other houses in the near locality. He considered that an allowance for position should be made on three counts—the appeal house faced the rear of other houses, it backed on to the railway and the effect of the cable depot. Taken in isolation none of these would have justified a reduction. The appeal was dismissed as the allowance for the disabilities was adequate. Costs £25 against the ratepayer.

(*Decision April 8, 1975*)

48

VALUATION OFFICER'S ALLOWANCES FOR UN-MADE ROAD AND CESSPOOL DRAINAGE ADEQUATE.

The appeal *Pursell* v. *Alexander* (*Valuation Officer*) concerned a house in Hockley, Essex, which on revaluation carried a gross value of £495 thought by the ratepayer to be excessive. A valuation court on the recommendation of the valuation officer had reduced this figure to £400 but the ratepayer complained about the revaluation increase generally that the property had been revalued without sufficient knowledge of local circumstances and although a reduction had been made on account of un-made roads and lack of main drainage, no reduction had been made for the loss of amenities and the extra costs arising through the lack of these services.

The valuation officer's recommendation was partly based on the discovery of an error in dimensions. It was stressed that due to the state of the roads there was extra wear and tear on cars, official cesspool emptying was confined to one free service a year and in addition, it had to be done two or three times a year at cost to the occupiers. The valuation officer supported his gross value of £400 by reference to seven rents in the locality covering tenancies between 1965-1970. In addition he submitted a detailed analysis on the assessments of ten houses in the area, four being in the same road.

The tribunal (Mr. W. H. Rees) was entirely satisfied that the £400 could fairly be described as modest even when account was taken of the disadvantages. Appeal dismissed. £25 costs against the ratepayer.

(*Decision April 8, 1975*)

49

UNSUCCESSFUL APPEAL BASED ON NEW LIST INCREASE, NEARBY ESTATE DEVELOPMENT AND LACK OF MAIN DRAINAGE.

The appeal *Dickinson* v. *Darlington* (*Valuation Officer*) concerned a bungalow near Flint assessed in the new valuation list at £122 gross value. A court had reduced this to £112 on the valuation officer's suggestion because a room intended to be a bathroom still lacked the necessary plumbing. The ratepayer was concerned about the relative increase following revaluation and referred to the loss of an open view through the development of a new building estate in the immediate neighbourhood, some 50 houses having been built with more to come and that there was an obligation to pay a sewarage rate even though he had his own septic tank drainage system. The tribunal (Mr. J. R. Laird) noted that this septic tank system was functioning satisfactorily and agreed with the valuation officer that no assessment reduction was appropriate, reference being made to a House of Commons statement about statutory relief being related to the actual charge for sewerage services.

So far as the estate development was concerned, the tribunal also agreed with the valuation officer that in the light of the distance involved it was unlikely that the rental value of the appeal property would be depreciated.

Finally it was pointed out that comparisons between old and new lists could not be effective since the time factor involved made effective comparisons impossible.

The tribunal was satisfied that a gross value of £112 was neither incorrect nor excessive as the property stood at present. Appeal dismissed, costs £25 against the ratepayer.

(*Decision April 9, 1975*)

50

RENTAL EVIDENCE OF LATE 60'S AND EARLY 70'S NOT TO BE DISREGARDED. SUBSTANTIAL ASSESSMENT REDUCTIONS ON LONDON FLATS.

The appeal *Langley and Others* v. *Ware* (*Valuation Officer*) concerned flats in S.W. London. Ten flats were involved and for the ratepayers there were two main arguments. One was that available rental evidence justified reductions, the comparative assessments of other flats, over-shadowing by tall buildings, noise from an underground railway and the general standard of planning and fittings of older blocks of flats compared with more modern ones.

The valuation officer considered that the rents payable on the flats were unreliable. There had been no recent lettings and the rental levels related to the late 60's and were in the valuation officer's view below the true market value. The tribunal (Mr. J. H. Emlyn Jones) said that he agreed to some extent with the ratepayers that the flats cited as comparables were rather better than those of the appeal flats but he thought that the differences had tended to be over-estimated. There was a considerable amount of rental evidence contained in the valuation officer's schedule and direct evidence was available in respect of seven of the flats. Now although it was true that the dates of these rents were some years before the relevant valuation date the tribunal saw no reason why they should be disregarded and the analysis which the tribunal itself made indicated that during the late 60's and early 70's there was an annual increase in the value of flats of between 10 *per cent.*-15 *per cent.* This assisted the tribunal to make its own determination since it was quite unable to accept that figures derived from this evidence were below the true market value as suggested by the valuation officer.

All the appeals were allowed, gross value reductions ranging from £30-£150 being made. The valuation officer was ordered to pay £10 costs to each of the appellants.

(*Decision April 14, 1975*)

51

USE OF PART OF GARAGE AND ITS SHAPE JUSTIFIES ASSESSMENT REDUCTION. BUNGALOW ASSESSMENTS CLAIMED TO BE EXCESSIVE ON REVALUATION. COMPARISON WITH HOUSE ASSESSMENTS REJECTED.

The appeal *Stanley* v. *Nightingale* (*Valuation Officer*) concerned a bungalow and garage at Brackley, Northamptonshire, following confirmation of a gross value of £460 by a valuation court. The ratepayer thought his assessment to be higher than those of comparable properties bearing in mind accommodation and amenities and that the new assessment of his property was not uniform in relation to the old valuation list assessments. The ratepayer referred to assessments of seven bungalows and eight houses and his investigations led to the conclusion that bungalow assessments were proportionately excessive compared to those of houses and, therefore, if the basis of assessment of bungalows was the same as for his own then the basis was incorrect and bungalow assessments generally could not be relied upon as comparables. The ratepayer, therefore, placed more reliance on houses as comparables.

The valuation officer relied on the assessments of six bungalows in the same village and on the question of a difference in the level of assessments between bungalows and houses which had been concluded, from evidence over a wide area, that bungalows warranted higher assessments than houses of broadly similar construction, a difference of about 12½ *per cent.* being justified. He also stated that out of a total of 103,000 hereditaments only 3,850 proposals had been received and he thought such a weight of acceptance of the valuation list established the tone of that list.

The tribunal (Mr. E. C. Strathon) found the ratepayer's contention regarding the usefulness of old list assessment to be of no help and on the comparables found that the basic gross value of the appeal bungalow was supported by the bungalow comparables on which the valuation officer had relied and they were to be preferred to the house comparables cited by the appellant.

There was one remaining point and that concerned the garage which, although larger than average, had an awkward shape and part of it was used as a passageway to the back of the bungalow. This restricted its normal use. On that account the gross value was reduced by £7, the appeal was allowed, a gross value of £453 was determined and in view of the circumstances there was no order as to costs.

(Decision April 14, 1975)

52

ACCOMMODATION IN OLD RENTED COTTAGE WARRANTS GREATER REDUCTION THAN THAT MADE BY VALUATION COURT.

The appeal *Watkins* v. *Stringer* (*Valuation Officer*) concerned a cottage near Daventry where a valuation court had reduced the gross value from £100 to £90. The cottage was in a small village and at one time had been declared unfit for human habitation but a purchaser planned its rehabilitation at a cost of £400.

The ratepayer attempted comparisons with three cottages, in the same village, but the tribunal (Mr. E. C. Strathon) did not find these of any assistance. On the other hand the valuation officer produced rental evidence of cottages over a much wider area ranging from 11-17 miles and the tribunal was satisfied that the assessments of those comparables were supported by rental evidence. The valuation officer complained there were no comparable cottages in the same village and he relied also on the assessments of six cottages disposed about the county within a radius of about 10-12 miles. Although from far afield the tribunal accepted that basic values had been established by the comparables but there were certain structural features including a landing scantily furnished for use as a poorly shaped sitting area which was not describable as a bedroom and on that account, plus a small value attributed to some outbuildings led the tribunal to reduce the gross value further to £80. Appeal allowed. £10 costs against the valuation officer.

(Decision April 14, 1975)

53

NO REDUCTION ON ACCOUNT OF STREET PARKING AND CONDITION OF RIGHT OF WAY.

The appeal *Cartwright* v. *Thornton* (*Valuation Officer*) concerned a terraced house in Ilford, the gross value of £300 having been upheld by a valuation court. The ratepayer sought a reduction on account of the inconvenience through car parking and the condition of a private right of way near the appeal property.

The valuation officer referred to an earlier decision of the Lands Tribunal to which the ratepayer's attention had been called and in his opinion the rent under s. 19 of the General Rate Act 1967 would not be reduced on account of either of the matters mentioned. The tribunal (Mr. J. R. Laird) accepted the valuation officer's evidence and his submissions and dismissed the appeal, awarding £25 costs against the ratepayer.

(*Decision April 25, 1975*)

54

VALUATION COURT'S REDUCTIONS ON ACCOUNT OF TRAFFIC NUISANCE REJECTED. GROSS VALUES RESTORED ON APPEAL.

In the appeal *Horsey* (*Valuation Officer*) v. *Jordan and Others* the assessments of 27 houses at St. Mary Cray were in dispute. All the houses formed part of a residential estate but in due course part of a works area in the locality was leased to a firm of transport contractors which ran a fleet of 21 heavy lorries, 15 of which were large vehicles of 9-11 tons unladen weight and as much as 32 tons gross. When returning to their base the vehicles, with few exceptions, took a route right through a residential estate so that whereas at one stage the appeal houses were virtually traffic free they were now in very different circumstances. The assessments were thought to be too high because of this loss of amenity, damage had been caused to properties, road surfaces were deteriorating and the standard of the locality was greatly lowered. A valuation court reduced the gross values in all cases by £25 and it was against this decision that the valuation officer appealed, seeking restoration of the original figures, his case being that the traffic complained about was too sparse to influence rental values and prospective tenants coming fresh on the scene would not regard the traffic as a rental disability.

The tribunal (Mr. R. C. Walmsley) considered quite a number of earlier Lands Tribunal decisions relevant to the circumstances in the present appeal where reference had been made to persons being indifferent to a certain amount of noise, that noise would be tolerated up to a considerable point before dislike could be reflected in money terms, that traffic up to a certain level did not affect rental values although out of the ordinary traffic volume might do so. A great deal of evidence by way of a census of traffic was considered and the tribunal stated that it had to envisage in respect of each of the appeal properties a prospective tenant arriving, finding a house vacant and to let, and considering what rental bid to make. He would attach weight to the use of the estate road by heavy vehicles but on other matters relating to property damage, road surface defects and the deterioration of the surroundings, it was not likely that the rental bid would be influenced adversely. The question was whether the rent reasonably to be expected on this particular estate was less than for similar houses on other cited traffic routes in the same area. The tribunal thought not. The assessments should be restored. Appeals allowed. There was no order as to costs.

The valuation officer, as was customary when appearing in person as an appellant rather than as a respondent, declared that in the event of the appeals being successful costs would not be sought even though the preparation of the appeals involved an immense amount of documentation.

(*Decision April 25, 1975*)

55

VALUATION OFFICER'S PROFFERED REDUCTION ON SHOP PREMISES ENDORSED BY TRIBUNAL.

In the appeal *Lindley* v. *Bromidge* (*Valuation Officer*) shop premises in Manchester, carrying a gross value of £800, were accorded a reduction by a valuation court to £775. The premises comprised one of a cluster of five shops and the ratepayer complained about the revaluation increase, that the assessment in the new list was out of line with the cost of living index increase and he was not satisfied about certain procedures at the valuation court stage. The tribunal (Mr. R. C. Walmsley) considered there was nothing in those grounds to assist the tribunal. Additional complaints related to a layby and the proximity of council houses.

The valuation officer did not seek to defend the valuation court decision but only a gross value of £700, a reduced figure clearly made known to the ratepayer in advance of the proceedings.

The tribunal allowed the appeal to the extent conceded by the valuation officer and determined a gross value of £700. No costs were awarded in the light of the information imparted to the ratepayer before the hearing.

(*Decision April 25, 1975*)

56

TRIBUNAL UNABLE TO DISMISS FROM ITS MIND A RENT OFFICER'S CERTIFICATE OF FAIR RENT. RATEPAYER'S PROPOSALS TO INCREASE HOUSE ASSESSMENT ALLOWED.

The appeal *McElrea* v. *Gilmore* (*Valuation Officer*) concerned what had been a house in Portslade. A valuation court had determined a gross value of £195 following a proposal by the ratepayer that the gross value of that figure should be increased to £240. The tribunal (Mr. Douglas Frank, President) was unaware of the reasons for this unusual course but did not enquire into them and, in any case, the dwelling had been demolished for road widening purposes so that the tribunal did the best it could with photographs and a visit to the site so that a fair picture of the property and its location could be formed.

The property was one of a small terrace fronting on to a heavily trafficked trunk road and had been close to traffic lights. It had had a very attractive front elevation, so much so that it had been listed as a building of historical or architectural interest by the planning authority and it was understood that the front elevation was to be reinstated elsewhere. The interior of the house had been modernised and the local valuation court had found that the appellant in no way supported his proposal to increase the gross value despite the fact that his failure so to do was emphasised on four occasions during the court's hearing of the proposal.

The ratepayer had presented the valuation officer with a long list of other properties and although the valuation officer had not been bound so to do he had incorporated all of them in a schedule of relevant information but the tribunal stated that it would be addressing itself not so much to those hereditaments but rather to the schedule upon which the valuation officer relied. This had been divided into three parts covering rent comparables, three valuation court decisions and an additional comparable. So far as the first named was concerned the tribunal mentioned that in May 1971 a rent officer had issued a certificate of fair rent under the Rent Act 1968 in a sum of £286 per annum inclusive of rates. On the same day another certificate was issued for adjoining premises but neither of these certificates had been registered because neither of the houses had been let. Therefore, the valuation officer was quite unaware of those certificates until they were produced by the ratepayer at the hearing itself.

So far as the certificate of fair rent was concerned the tribunal conceded that these had been determined ex-parte, so to speak, and that there had been no tenants. Had there been tenants there was the possibility of a contest resulting possibly in the rent officer's determination being challenged and reduced on appeal to the rent assessment committee.

The tribunal did not agree with the valuation officer in dismissing the attractive elevation of the property by saying that this would not enhance the rent. The tribunal thought people would pay more, and often substantially more, for an attractive looking house.

The tribunal could not dismiss from its mind the certificate of fair rent and was prepared to accept that it might have been reduced to some extent on appeal but it could not dismiss it out of hand as the valuation officer had done, as really he was bound to do, if he was to maintain his own case. At the end of the day in a difficult case the tribunal concluded that the hypothetical tenant would have paid not less than £240 a year on the statutory formula. This being the amount proposed by the appellant the appeal was allowed and the gross value so fixed. The tribunal said there was no doubt that the valuation officer and his staff had acted with the utmost good faith and in allowing the appeal wished it to be made clear that there was no implication of any criticism of the valuation officer or his staff. There was not a jot nor a tittle of evidence to support observations and accusations of conspiracy on the part of the valuation officer's staff. Costs against the valuation officer of £10.

(*Decision April 25, 1975*)

57

ASSESSMENTS OF FLATS PROVIDED BY PRIVATE DEVELOPERS PREFERRED AS EVIDENCE TO RENTS PAID FOR HOUSING SOCIETY FLATS. ASSESSMENTS OF LATTER REDUCED.

The appeals *Wood and Others* v. *Garvie* (*Valuation Officer*) concerned flats in Chorlton-cum-Hardy, Manchester, the nine ratepayers concerned appealing against a valuation court decision confirming their assessment. Their flats formed part of a fully developed residential suburb of Manchester and the case for the ratepayers took the form essentially of a challenge to the valuation officer's general approach.

The valuation officer presented considerable evidence dealing with the history of development in the locality and, among other things, mentioned that in addition to private developers there had been considerable development by voluntary non-profitmaking bodies, i.e. housing associations and housing societies. Non-profit bodies had built to let and as a result there had been an abundance of rental evidence available for the purpose of the 1973 revaluation. By 1972 some 89 *per cent.* of the purpose-built flats were rented and only 11 *per cent.* were unoccupied.

The valuation officer claimed that there was a close affinity between the rents being paid by tenants of private developers and rents being paid under non-profitmaking bodies.

The tribunal (Mr. R. C. Walmsley) said that the case for the valuation officer would appear to be unassailable but for one factor. This factor was the assumption by him, confirmed under cross-examination, that he had regarded the rents payable for the flats concerned as being ordinary rents and that he had accepted them as providing dependable evidence of market rental value for the purpose of arriving at a gross value. For the ratepayers it was claimed that they did not regard themselves as being tenants of their properties but rather as co-owners. The rent payable was akin to mortgage repayment instalments payable by an owner-occupier because at the end of a 40 year period the rent for each flat would revert to an amount representing simply a sharing of the costs of maintenance. The tribunal accepted this viewpoint claiming that rents payable by occupiers of a cost and rent development, although paid under an agreement of tenancy, seemed more like annual payments by purchasers buying on a fixed term mortgage whose payments included instalment repayments of the debt in addition to interest on that debt.

At the block of flats concerned rents were determined or agreed by a collection of individuals in their capacity as landlords but to be paid by themselves in their capacity as tenants. That was a far cry from "ordinary rents" negotiated at armslength. There was a known disparity between the annual amount a seeker after residential accommodation was prepared to find to meet a purchase price and the amount he would expect to pay by way of rent. The reasons for this included the general effect of statutory intervention in the field of rents and the fact that annual payments by a purchaser normally included some element of capital repayment.

In addition there was the matter of tax relief on mortgage interest. In the light of this and that the valuation officer claimed to have found a close affinity between private rents and rent payments under non-profit bodies it was necessary to scrutinise this claim. From an examination of a schedule of properties covering privately built housing society and housing association developments in the same area the tribunal failed to detect that close affinity and concluded, too, that the assessment of flats in non-profit developments did not provide dependable evidence of rental value for gross value purposes. As to what should be used as a yardstick, the ratepayers had invited the tribunal to take note of the assessments of certain modern houses but the valuation officer claimed that houses were in a different market from flats. The plain fact was that no means existed whereby the assessments of houses cited by the ratepayers could be used as a yardstick from which to derive the correct assessment of flats. Therefore, the tribunal found itself left with what were the assessments of flats provided by private developers and having regard to that evidence and its own inspection the tribunal determined lower figures, reducing the gross values by £35 in three cases and by £40 in the other six. Appellants allowed costs of £3 against the valuation officer in respect of each appellant. The valuation officer was commended for his impartial assistance and for sparing no pains to ensure that the ratepayers' case was as fully documented as his own.

(*Decision April 25, 1975*)

58

DETERIORATING LOCALITY NO JUSTIFICATION FOR REDUCED ASSESSMENTS BEARING IN MIND AVAILABLE RENTAL EVIDENCE.

The appeal *Ashberry* v. *Platt* (*Valuation Officer*) concerned a house in N.W. London where a valuation court had reduced the gross value from £790 to £780. The ratepayer had lived in the house for over 50 years and was over 90 years of age. He recalled the area when it formed part of what he called a nice residential district and the substance of his case was that this was no longer true. Houses were dilapidated, many in multiple occupation, gardens were neglected and the road was very noisy and often choked with traffic.

The valuation officer thought the court's decision to be fair and he presented details of six other rented properties in the locality. In addition he sought to rely on the fact that only one proposal had been made when the list came into force.

The tribunal (Mr. J. H. Emlyn Jones), having inspected the property and the rented properties referred to by the valuation officer, noted that the rents ran from dates between May 1967 and August 1972 and constituted evidence which, taken as a whole, supported the basic value attributable to the appeal property. There was nothing wrong with the court's decision. Appeal dismissed, ratepayer to pay £20 costs to the valuation officer.

(*Decision April 28, 1975*)

59

EVIDENCE OF REGISTERED RENTS DISPROVES CASE FOR REDUCTION ON GROUNDS OF TRAFFIC AND NEARBY DEVELOPMENT.

The appeal *Harris* v. *Coggins* (*Valuation Officer*) concerned a house at Luton, the end house of a block of four, where it was claimed that development in the form of construction of offices, warehouses and storage yards adversely affected the rental value. A valuation court had confirmed the gross value at £285 and the applicant's case was that under conditions existing before 1973 he would not be objecting to the assessment but since that time there had been a substantial increase in traffic and the property had been further depreciated by the development of a builders' merchants' premises at the rear of his dwelling.

In the view of the valuation officer these factors did not represent a disability so severe as to lead to a reduction in rental value and in support of this he submitted details of 13 rented properties in the same road, all very similar and in all cases rents payable were registered rents where registration had occurred between February 1972 and November 1973. The traffic was heavy but in the view of the tribunal (Mr. J. H. Emlyn Jones) it did not seem to be so excessive as to be distinguished from other main traffic arteries in and around industrial towns of this country. The rental evidence clearly supported the valuation officer's assertion that the rental value was not affected by the alleged disabilities. It was true that gross value for rating and fair rents had to be arrived at on different statutory formulae but the effect on value, however, of factors such as those described were properly to be reflected in both calculations. Appeal dismissed, costs £20 against the ratepayer.

(*Decision April 28, 1975*)

60

USE AND MISUSE OF FOOTPATH JUSTIFY ASSESSMENT REDUCTIONS. TRIBUNAL AFFIRMS VALUATION COURT DECISIONS IN DISMISSING VALUATION OFFICER'S APPEALS. RELEVANCE OF RENTAL EVIDENCE DENYING ANY EFFECT ON VALUES NOT UNDERSTOOD BY TRIBUNAL WHEN VALUATION OFFICER CONCEDES SOME ALLOWANCE.

The appeals *Levene* (*Valuation Officer*) v. *Sauer and Daniell* concerned houses in Wembley, houses which were typically inter-war end of terrace dwellings, between which ran a narrow pedestrian footpath, the use of which gave rise to the appeal proceedings. A valuation court had reduced by £20 gross value the assessments in each case confirming gross values of £380 and £345 respectively.

The valuation officer sought restoration of the original figures subject to half the allowance given by the court, so that gross values of £390 and £355 were substituted. According to the tribunal (Mr. J. H. Emlyn Jones) the matter ceased to raise any question of principle and became simply a question of degree. The valuation officer accepted that some allowance should be made but contended only that the gross reductions were excessive. That being so the tribunal did not understand the purpose of the valuation officer's evidence disclosing rents which purported to show no difference between houses adjoining the footpath and those which did not. All the houses concerned were on a comparable basis and all that could be deduced was that in those cases referred to, the existence of the footpath did not appear to have any effect on the annual value of the houses. In the tribunal's opinion the disability from the footpath in the present cases was worse than in any other cases to which attention had been drawn and the valuation court's reductions were not excessive. Valuation Officer's appeals dismissed and costs of £10 to each ratepayer awarded against the valuation officer.

(*Decision April 28, 1975*)

61

GENERAL MULTIPLIER INDICATING DIFFERENCES BETWEEN OLD AND NEW VALUATION LIST ENTRIES OF NO ASSISTANCE IN DETERMINING APPEAL. USEFULNESS OF EVIDENCE OF REGISTERED RENTS.

The appeal *Carman* v. *Henson* (*Valuation Officer*) concerned a bungalow in a village near Derby where a valuation court had reduced the gross value from £235 to £215. This reduction had been offered by the valuation officer to the ratepayer prior to the hearing by the court. The ratepayer contended that both the valuation list entry and the valuation court's determination were both in excess of the multiplier which the local rating authority had confirmed to be the average increase on revaluation. There were additional grounds of appeal based on criticisms of the valuation officer in failing to give details of properties and who had refused to answer vital questions. In addition he had presented a document which contained inaccuracies.

The valuation officer supported the court's decision and he relied on the assessments of comparables which, by acceptance, had by this time established the tone of the valuation list in the area. He referred to 14 bungalows and also produced a schedule of nine bungalows in respect of which the fair rents registered for June 1971 had not been available at the time of the preparation of the valuation list. The valuation officer claimed that having regard to the difference in the definitions of gross value and fair rent the registered rents supported the assessments of the appeal properties.

The tribunal (Mr. E. C. Strathon) was satisfied that the valuation officer's rental evidence established that the proper gross value was not less than the figure fixed by the valuation court and dismissed the appeal, awarding £10 costs against the ratepayer.

(*Decision April 30, 1975*)

62

LACK OF GARDEN AND SHARED ACCESS JUSTIFY TRIBUNAL INCREASING VALUATION OFFICER'S ALLOWANCE FOR SUCH DISABILITIES.

The appeal *Pennell* v. *Pellow* (*Valuation Officer*) concerned a cottage near Exeter where a court had reduced the gross value from £225 to £180. The valuation officer supported the reduced value in the appeal proceedings and both he and the ratepayer relied on comparisons with other cottages in the same village and in an adjoining village.

The tribunal (Mr. E. C. Strathon) was satisfied about the basic gross value being fair but when it came to the various adjustments, some of which were thought equally fair, there was a doubt about the valuation officer's allowance of £25 for the lack of a garden and for the fact that access to the appeal property was shared with others. Except for a small triangular patch which was not owned by the ratepayer anyway, the cottage was surrounded by paths, a road and a courtyard, all of which were used in common with others. This adjustment of £25 was insufficient in the view of the tribunal and he considered a figure of £40 to be appropriate, thus reducing the gross value to £165. Costs £10 awarded against the valuation officer.

(*Decision April 30, 1975*)

63

INTERNAL DIMENSIONS WRONGLY ASSUMED TO BE EXTERNAL. VALUATION COURT'S REDUCTIONS CANCELLED.

The appeal *Wrapson* (*Valuation Officer*) v. *Haines* and the ratepayer's cross appeal concerned a house and two garages in Wattisfield, Norfolk, assessed in the new list at £445 gross value. This was reduced by a valuation court to £400. However, the valuation officer had made a proposal to increase the gross value from £445 to £625 on the grounds that there had been an error in treating the internal area of the property as the exterior area, thus indicating that the property was smaller than it was. A valuation court fixed the gross value, following the valuation officer's proposal, at £520. Both parties appealed, the valuation officer against the earlier decision, the ratepayer against the later decision of the court. The house had a rather old-fashioned central heating system, the annual cost of oil for the minimum of heating being over £300, the cost of electricity being about the same. Extensive cellars were subject to flooding in heavy rain and there was dampness. The valuation officer considered that the hypothetical tenant would have readily paid a rent of £520, which was a fair and reasonable figure, well supported by comparables. There was evidence of nine comparables. The tribunal (Mr. J. Stuart Daniel) explained that when the true rents of comparable properties were scarce or non-existent it was normal to look at the assessments of such properties as providing the best evidence of the hypothetical rent under s. 19 of the General Rate Act 1967. The tribunal thought that the valuation officer's pattern of assessments was a coherent and sensible one into which the appeal property fitted well. The ratepayer's appeal was dismissed, leaving the gross value at £520. The valuation officer's appeal was allowed. No order as to costs as the ratepayer had, in reality, helped the valuation officer to correct the valuation list.

(*Decision May 1, 1975*)

64

VALUATION COURT'S REDUCTION ON ACCOUNT OF HEAVY TRAFFIC CONFIRMED.

The appeal *Molloy* v. *Haysom* (*Valuation Officer*) concerned a dwelling in Blackheath, assessed at £414 gross value but reduced following a ratepayer's proposal to £345. The ratepayer sought further relief on the grounds of noise, disturbance and dirt caused by heavy traffic along the road in question. The ratepayer was also concerned about the behaviour of local hooligans. The valuation officer presented, according to the tribunal (Mr. J. R. Laird), a well documented case based on statutory rent returns and assessments of comparable properties and the tribunal had not been persuaded by the ratepayer that a further reduction was warranted. Appeal dismissed. Costs £18 against the ratepayer.

(*Decision May 7, 1975*)

65

LOCAL AUTHORITY'S ALLEGED SHORTCOMINGS NOT A MATTER FOR THE TRIBUNAL.

The appeal *Beedie* v. *Leeds* (*Valuation Officer*) concerned two adjoining semi-detached houses in Lichfield, each being over 150 years old. One was assessed at £178 gross value, the other at £144. A valuation court had reduced the lower figure of assessment to £133 and confirmed the other. The ratepayer referred to the effect of smoke, fumes and dust from a nearby factory and an anticipated road widening scheme affecting property values. He was upset about alleged local government inefficiency, particularly in planning and public health. The tribunal (Mr. J. D. Russell-Davis) explained its jurisdiction, which did not include acting as an ombudsman in relation to local authorities. The valuation officer produced well-documented evidence indicating that the appeal assessments had been founded on rents passing for six similar hereditaments, rents fixed in 1967/69. Out of nearly 200 properties in the vicinity there had been only one appeal on the grounds of factory pollution. The tribunal came to the conclusion that the assessments of the two propetries were fair and reasonable. The ratepayer had failed to show that his appeal had any substance. Appeals dismissed. Ratepayer order to pay £10 towards the valuation officer's costs. (*Decision May 8, 1975*)

66

TRIBUNAL CONFIRMS VALUATION OFFICER'S ALLOWANCES ON ACCOUNT OF TRAFFIC, SHOP LAYOUT AND MIXED NATURE OF HEREDITAMENT, I.E. SHOP AND DWELLING.

The appeal *Kingston* v. *Houghton* (*Valuation Officer*) concerned a shop, houses and premises at Warminster. The gross value of £570 had been confirmed by a valuation court and the ratepayer appealed to the tribunal on the grounds of traffic noise, overlooking from offices, loss of an amenity in the shape of a nearby garden, revaluation increase out of proportion to trade turnover, the age of the property and its cost of upkeep and the effect on business of a new shopping precinct. No evidence was produced on the trading position nor did the ratepayer offer any comparables.

The valuation officer founded his assessment on rent returns for 11 comparables. He had made the same proportionate end deduction for the effect of traffic disturbance on the residential parts of premises and he quoted traffic statistics indicating a reduction in traffic overall between August 1970 and October 1974 although there had been an increase in heavy goods vehicles. The tribunal (Mr. J. D. Russell-Davis) confirmed from his own observations that the traffic past the appeal property was indeed heavy. However, examining each of the grounds for appeal the tribunal came to the conclusion that the ratepayer had not discharged the onus of showing the assessment to be excessive. Appeal dismissed. A nominal contribution of £10 against the ratepayer. (*Decision May 8, 1975*)

67

CONTRACTORS' ACTIVITIES IN LARGE NEARBY DEVELOPMENT, INVOLVING DIRT ON PAVEMENTS, GARDENS AND WINDOWS, JUSTIFIES VALUATION COURT'S ALLOWANCE BEING QUADRUPLED.

The appeal *Rahamin* v. *Pinder* (*Valuation Officer*) concerned a house in N.W. London where a valuation court had reduced the gross value from £450 to £425. The property was one of a row of ten similar houses and the road in which they stood had become one of the major traffic routes leading to the North Circular Road and the M1. Moreover, the appeal property backed on to land which was now being developed as a large shopping centre. The ratepayer sought a reduction beyond that conceded by the valuation court on account of the increase in traffic but, more importantly, because of the nuisance caused by the construction and site development of the shopping centre.

The valuation officer considered that the valuation court's allowance adequately met the ratepayer's complaint. However, the tribunal (Mr. E. C. Strathon), having made his inspection on a dry day, also noted that it had rained during the previous night. In the words of the tribunal, "the contractor's employee, with shovel and brush, waged a losing battle with dried mud, about 3 ins. thick, which he sought to move permanently from the pavement to the carriageway. Heavy traffic and a contrary wind ensured the return of the mixture in the form of clouds of dust to cover pavements, gardens, windows and the whole of the fronts of the affected houses". The appeal property clearly presented a most forlorn and dismal appearance and the valuation court's allowance was quite inadequate. The gross value should be reduced by £100 and determined at £350. Appeal allowed. £10 costs against the valuation officer.

(*Decision May 9, 1975*)

68

VALUATION OFFICER CONCEDES VALUATION COURT REDUCTION, ON ONE PROPERTY, TO OTHERS IN VICINITY. TRIBUNAL APPROVES REVISED ASSESSMENTS.

The appeal *Wall* v. *Gale* (*Valuation Officer*) concerned a bungalow and premises in Bournemouth where a court had reduced the gross value from £510 to £485. The ratepayer complained about the relative increase on revaluation compared with other properties including houses, that the area had lost its status, there was overlooking from nearby houses, an obtrusive extension to the adjoining bungalow and in support of these various complaints, the assessments of four bungalows, five semi-bungalows and five houses were cited.

The valuation officer said that in the preparation of the new valuation list it had been found that rental evidence in the residential sector had tended to come from inferior properties in inferior locations but basic evidence had been used in comparative form for the assessments of properties in other localities. He produced details of the assessments of eight bungalows. The tribunal (Mr. E. C. Strathon) said the comparison of new and old assessments was irrelevant and he was not satisfied that on the available rental evidence and on the evidence of the assessments produced by both parties, that the pattern supported the appellant's contention. The evidence of the valuation officer was found most convincing. On other matters the tribunal concluded that they would not affect rental values. Appeal dismissed. Costs £10 awarded against the ratepayer.

(*Decision May 9, 1975*)

69

AREA SCHEME FOR REDUCTIONS ON ACCOUNT OF TRAFFIC, BY SHADED ALLOWANCES, SLIGHTLY EXTENDED TO ENCOMPASS APPEAL PROPERTY.

The appeal *Pascoe v. Bartlett* (*Valuation Officer*) concerned a house and garage in Great Barr, Birmingham. A valuation court had confirmed a gross value of £425 notwithstanding the ratepayer's claim that an allowance should be made because of severe disturbance from heavy traffic. The court did not think the traffic volume sufficient to affect the rental value but the ratepayer quoted reductions of £10 and £15 determined by the same court in respect of nearby houses. He also referred to another decision of the court when over 700 cases had been heard following the opening of a section of the M6 motorway. In those instances the court had awarded percentage reductions related to disturbances from the motorway and even the last category obtained a 2½ *per cent.* reduction. The ratepayer thought the drawing of an arbitrary line led to injustice.

The valuation officer supported his basic assessment by reference to a schedule of these dwellings where rents were passing and, on the traffic point, he relied on the valuation court's decisions as these had been within a scheme whereby shaded relief was given according to the situation of various properties. He produced details of traffic counts and eventually concluded that the hypothetical tenant of the appeal property would not be affected by the traffic and he would not be as sensitive to traffic noise as the appellant.

The tribunal (Mr. J. H. Emlyn Jones) thought it could not be said that the basic level of values applied by the valuation officer was excessive. Undoubtedly the traffic in the affected road was heavy and it passed quite close to the appeal property. The tribunal had been left with the impression that the traffic in the particular road, taken by itself, must be very near the borderline to the point where a landlord might be compelled to admit some rent reduction and in the present appeal the scales were tipped because of the proximity of the M6 motorway. Taking into account traffic density and motorway disturbance there was justification for some reduction. An allowance of 2½ *per cent.* should be extended a little further to cover the appeal property. A gross value of £415 was determined. As the hearing had run to two days a considerable amount of time had been devoted to the valuation officer's basis of assessment and as on that part of the case the tribunal had found against the ratepayer there was no order as to costs.

(*Decision May 14, 1975*)

70

TRIBUNAL INCREASES VALUATION OFFICER'S ALLOWANCES FOR PROXIMITY OF NUCLEAR POWER STATION AND FOR SOAKAWAY DRAINAGE.

The appeal *Bamford* v. *Pryke* (*Valuation Officer*) concerned a house and garage at Leiston Common, Suffolk, where there were 3 acres of garden. The property was on an unmade track over 500 yards away from the Leiston to Sizewell road but was less than a mile inland from and in sight of the Sizewell nuclear power station which was on the coast. A valuation court had reduced the gross value from £750 to £700 because of the isolated situation, poor access and an over-large garden. The ratepayer appealed, considering that the new valuation list figure indicated an excessive increase.

The property was within the primary danger zone of the nuclear power station, its situation was isolated, it had a poor access involving heavy maintenance costs, the garden was extremely large and there was a lack of main drainage.

The valuation officer defended a gross value of £700 and he was in contention with a valuer called on behalf of the ratepayer who supported a figure of £540. The ratepayer submitted a letter from the planning authority from which the inference was drawn, and this was not challenged by the valuation officer, that in an emergency the area would have to be evacuated at minimum notice.

The tribunal (Mr. J. D. Russell-Davis) thought the lack of drainage for waste water to be a drawback and the soakways needed rodding and cleaning. The ratepayer had estimated that a gardener costing £12 a week was necessary and the cost of maintaining the approach road to the house was not less than £60 per annum. The valuation officer, on the other hand, maintained that the £40 reduction certainly covered the nuclear power station point and in support of his assessment he submitted a schedule of 16 comparable properties. Dealing with different items, the tribunal preferred the ratepayer's valuer's deduction in respect of the power station. The tribunal confirmed the valuation officer's allowance s for isolation, access and large garden but allowed a £15 gross value reduction because of the inadequate method for disposing of bath and sink waste to the soakaways. In all the additional relief totalled £25, leading to the determination of a gross value of £675. Appeal allowed to that extent. Valuation officer to pay £30 costs to the ratepayer.

(*Decision May 15, 1975*)

71

RESIDENTIAL CARAVANS AND PITCHES. RENTAL EVIDENCE JUSTIFIES RESTORATION OF VALUATION OFFICER'S ASSESSMENTS ON APPEAL.

The appeals *Baker (Valuation Officer)* v. *Horwell and Others and Halton Borough Council* concerned ten residential caravans and the pitches on which they stood at the Promenade Caravan Park, Halton, Cheshire. Five ratepayers had given notice of intention to appear but five other ratepayers did not respond. In all ten cases the rating authority supported the valuation officer. A valuation court had reduced the gross values by 25 *per cent.* and although the valuation officer now conceded small reductions in respect of two cases he sought restoration of his original assessments, whereas the ratepayers sought a reduction of 50 *per cent.* The grounds on which they sought relief were summarised under three main headings, i.e. lack of amenities in the neighbourhood, lack of jurisdiction over the camping ground by the local authority, the restrictive conditions imposed by the site owners and insecurity of tenure.

The caravans were of the type that because of their size could not be towed along the public highway by ordinary motorcar but could only be moved by loading on a lorry or transporter vehicle. Once installed on a pitch such mobile homes were seldom moved and owners were more likely to sell to the site proprietors or to someone else wishing to move in. The valuation officer explained that only in the new list had caravans been separately assessed and his approach to the revaluation was based on the case of *Field Place Caravan Park Ltd.* v. *Harding (V.O.)* (1965) where it was held that caravans permanently parked on a residential site were rateable, a decision subsequently confirmed by the Court of Appeal where it was held that a caravan was rateable, notwithstanding that it was a chattel on wheels, because it was placed on and enjoyed with land in such circumstances and with such a degree of permanence that the two could together be regarded as a unit of occupation. He had relied on certain rents actually paid as the best evidence of value, 14 in number, but some of these rents had been negotiated when some caravans had not been connected to the drainage system so that rents were subsequently increased. On the whole the gross values were well below the estimated rental values. In addition the valuation officer tendered a schedule of 13 sample assessments of hereditaments on a somewhat comparable residential site.

The tribunal (Mr. J. R. Laird) agreed with the valuation officer that this particular caravan site was attractively laid out and that some of the disadvantages prevailing were experienced at other caravan parks. This was one of the best the tribunal had seen. The tribunal also agreed that the best evidence in these appeals was afforded by the actual rents paid for pitches in 1970/72, rents reflecting local conditions and the advantages and disadvantages. The ratepayer had no rental evidence to refute that of the valuation officer and therein lay the weakness of the case for the ratepayers. The valuation officer thought that the valuation court had made the 25 *per cent.* reductions in all probability because the court had not been given the extensive rental evidence now presented to the tribunal and thus had not had the chance of studying such evidence. The tribunal was satisfied that the valuation officer had made out his case for restoration of the assessments and his appeals succeeded but there was no order as to costs.

(*Decision May 16, 1975*)

72

RATEPAYER FAILS TO CONVINCE TRIBUNAL THAT PROPORTIONALITY BETWEEN HOUSE AND SHOP IS WRONG.

The appeal *Green* v. *Wilkes* (*Valuation Officer*) concerned a shop and premises in Maldon, Essex, following confirmation by a valuation court of a gross value of £650. The premises were on the edge of a council housing estate and the ratepayer had put in a tender of £960 per annum for one of the properties which were built by the Maldon Corporation in 1968/69. This had been accepted so that the tenancy which covered both the shop, garage and flat commenced in April 1969. Two assessments had been raised because the shop and the flat were not interconnecting. The new valuation list included an entry of £650 gross value for the shop and £295 for the flat. These figures had been confirmed by a valuation court following a proposal by the ratepayer for figures of £500 and £280 respectively.

At the hearing by the tribunal the ratepayer accepted that the assessment of the shop was fair by comparison with the assessments of other shops and that the assessment of the flat (which was not surprisingly under appeal) was fair by comparison with other flats. In the ratepayer's view the assessment of the shop did not bear a fair relationship with the assessment of the flat. Briefly, the ratepayer considered that the relationship between the two in the 1963 valuation list should have been maintained in the 1973 valuation list resulting, in the tribunal's view, in gross values of £475 for the shop. The valuation officer had accepted the valuation court's decision and produced a detailed analysis of the rents of various comparables. The tribunal (Mr. R. C. Walmsley) came to the conclusion that the figure of rent apportioned to the shop was not out of line and that was sufficient to dispose of the appeal. However, the tribunal referred to an apparent misconception on the part of the ratepayer. Briefly, it was the ratepayer's belief that residential properties were assessed below their actual rental values, that shops were assessed up to their rental values and that the gross values of shops required to be reduced proportionately with any under-assessment of residential properties. In the tribunal's view this last submission was a non sequitur. Appeal dismissed. Gross value confirmed at £650, costs £25 against the ratepayer.

(*Decision May 19, 1975*)

73

RATEPAYER AGGRIEVED THAT ASSESSMENT REDUCTION TO OLD VALUATION LIST GROSS VALUE WAS NOT REFLECTED IN THE NEW VALUATION LIST.

The appeal *Hurford* v. *Sheil* (*Valuation Officer*) concerned a house and garage at Bishop's Stortford where a valuation court had reduced the gross value from £615 to £600. The ratepayer's main ground of complaint which the ratepayer had thought had not been dealt with by the valuation court was that the assessment of his house in the 1973 valuation list did not reflect a reduction granted by the local valuation court in 1967 of about 4½ *per cent*. The ratepayer explained that his appeal was on a point of principle. The circumstances between the two periods was in no way different and if the valuation officer was to be allowed to use a revaluation as a means of cancelling the benefit of an earlier reduction this really was circumventing the valuation court's decision.

The valuation officer explained his approach to the revaluation. There had been no rental evidence available for houses of the type in question and he had extrapolated the rental evidence which had been available for smaller houses. The tone of the list could now be regarded as established because only five other proposals had been lodged in respect of the 150-200 similar dwellings in the area and all had been disposd of without disturbing the level of assessment. In his opinion the appeal dwelling did not suffer any disadvantage by comparison with others in the same road and it was not overassessed.

The tribunal (Mr. R. C. Walmsley) having inspected the dwelling, agreed with the valuation officer. A prospective tenant would not be concerned with the fact that the appeal house had at some earlier date enjoyed an open outlook and a differential assessment. The valuation court's decision was neither incorrect nor excessive.

Dealing with the ratepayer's point about the old and new list, the tribunal found the valuation officer's evidence somewhat equivocal and noted from earlier valuation court minutes that the valuation officer in February 1975 had confirmed that a reduction in the 1963 list figure had been made in respect of the building of houses opposite the appeal property and for the inadequacy of the narrow and restrictive roadway. The tribunal noted these matters only out of courtesy since it was not necessary for the tribunal to make any finding as to what happened in 1967 and thereafter. The tribunal thought that the ratepayer had understood why his assessment had had to be confirmed. Although the appeal failed the ratepayer was entitled to come to the tribunal to have his unresolved point of principle investigated. A sum of only £5 costs was awarded against the ratepayer.

(*Decision May 19, 1975*)

74

RATEPAYER'S CASE, BASED PARTLY ON COMPARABLES AND ALSO ON THE EFFECTS OF PRICE RISES ON SPECIFIC COMMODITIES RELATING TO OCCUPATION COSTS, FAILS.

The appeal *Woods* v. *Turner* (*Valuation Officer*) concerned a house and garage at Itchingfield, Sussex, following confirmation of a gross value of £695 by a valuation court. The tribunal (Mr. J. Stuart Daniel) in summarising the ratepayer's grounds said that the ratepayer thought it reasonable to suppose that the location of the kind of house concerned involved the occupier having two family cars so as to travel some 5,000 miles a year to go to and get from Horsham and a further 1,170 miles for shopping in Billingshurst plus 1,070 miles for sundry other journeys. In attempting to show the need for this travel the ratepayer pointed out that there were no services or shops nearer than those two towns and no public transport available nearby. There was a primary school at Itchingfield but other schools were available only at the two towns mentioned or even further afield. Moreover, refuse was collected only fortnightly and doctors, dentists, the fire service and police and hospitals were all three to six miles away. There was no bread or newspaper delivery and garages made a collection charge for servicing. Finally, he had objection to aircraft noise from Gatwick airport. The ratepayer referred to various groups of comparable houses and also to a number of notable rating decisions in the courts.

The tribunal concentrated on one relatively recent Lands Tribunal case, *Delaney* v. *Bedbrook* (*V.O.*) (1974) where the tribunal had accepted that an 18 month period having elapsed since the 1973 valuation list came into force was a sufficiently long period for it to be said that the level of assessment could be regarded as settled and established. The ratepayer, however, suggested that this decision was of local and limited application and doubted whether the tone of the list in the Horsham area was by any means settled. The ratepayer sought a reduction of £40 in the gross value and produced a number of calculations based on the capital value of the property, comparable assessments and increases to various prices of commodities such as oil, electricity, petrol and so on.

The valuation officer, dealing with the *Delaney* case, said that the local valuation list had 38,600 hereditaments of which there were 31,800 dwellings and apart from the valuation officer's own proposals there had been only 1,451 ratepayers' proposals, of which 714 had now been settled, withdrawn or decided by the valuation court. Seven hundred and thirty-seven were outstanding and he considered that the valuation list was substantially correct. On details of the appeal property assessment he thought an addition of £50 was reasonable for the swimming bath and he found little wrong with the central heating system. He did not think aircraft noise was such as to affect the value and on the cost of motoring, he did not think the hypothetical rent would be altered on account of rising costs of commodities due to inflation and other costs. Everything else went up in price, including wages and salaries.

The tribunal found nothing in the comparables which made the appeal property assessment seem excessive and that view would conclude the matter unless the tribunal felt it should accede to the proposition that recent economic changes had so altered the equilibrium of the market that the hypothetical tenant, however much he loved the country, must be deemed by reason of financial stringency to have reduced his bid for a property of this kind which committed him to heavy expenditure on the more expensive fuel and energy. This was a proposition which had to be proved in the market and mere inference would not do. The tribunal was not satisfied that the valuation court's decision was wrong. Appeal dismissed. Nominal award of £10 costs against the ratepayer.

(*Decision May 19, 1975*)

75

CHILD MINDING IN UPSTAIRS FLAT AND FAULTY SOLID FUEL BOILER NOT REASONS FOR REDUCING ASSESSMENT.

The appeal *Harte* v. *Hillary* (*Valuation Officer*) concerned a purpose-built flat in a four-storey block of 16 flats in Haringey. A valuation court had reduced the gross value from £450 to £395 on the recommendation of the valuation officer, who had agreed with the ratepayer that the assessment was excessive on grounds of comparability. The ratepayer had claimed that there was no running hot water, no lighting on the landing and stairway and child minding in the upstairs flat created constant noise. In addition, car parking disturbed him.

The ratepayer referred to a local authority certificate of registration as a child minder referring to the number of children permitted under the Child Minder provisions. Indeed, the ratepayer considered that by granting such a certificate the local authority itself had broken the tenancy condition relevant to the flats, which had to be used only as private residences and that nuisances should be avoided.

The tribunal (Mr. J. R. Laird) agreed with the valuation officer that the landlord would not be expected to accept less rent from the hypothetical tenant because of the child minding activities, nor because of the car parking, which was a common experience all over London and elsewhere. On the lack of hot water, it appeared that a pipe on an Ideal boiler installation was loose and that there was some difficulty in obtaining supplies of solid fuel. However, in the rating context it had to be assumed that the landlord would make the necessary repairs to the hot water system and the difficulty of obtaining fuel was not a ground justifying a reduced assessment. The appeal was ill-founded and was dismissed with £25 costs being awarded against the ratepayer.

(*Decision May 20, 1975*)

76

RATEPAYER'S CASE BASED ON COMPARABLES AND ALLEGED STRUCTURAL FAULTS UNCONVINCING.

The appeal *Collins* v. *Cropper* (*Valuation Officer*) concerned an old list assessment of a self-contained flat in West London, one in a modern block of some 13 storeys in height. The original valuation list entry was for a gross value of £1,230 but subsequently the valuation officer had made various proposals, one of which was to reduce the assessment of the appeal flat to £990 gross value. Later the ratepayer sought a reduction of 50 *per cent.* on the grounds of poor construction features, an unfinished stairway which was poorly lit and other matters. However, a valuation court had considered that the possibilities referred to would not affect the rental bid of a hypothetical tenant. The ratepayer persisted before the Lands Tribunal on the question of comparability and also the structural problems.

The valuation officer cited the assessments of some 40 flats elsewhere similar in size and layout to the appeal property and all the assessments involved had been accepted by the ratepayers.

During the proceedings reference was made to registered fair rents but the tribunal (Mr. J. R. Laird) said that on the question of registered rents there were no firm conclusions that could be drawn from them for three reasons. Landlords had appealed on the score that the rent officer's determinations were too low so the rents cited were not final. There was no firm evidence as to the allowances for scarcity and as the present appeal concerned the tone of the valuation list in 1962/63, registered rents effective in late 1973 and mid 1974 were for periods more than ten years later. The tribunal examined in considerable detail the factors affecting the block of flats containing the appeal flat and other blocks but the tribunal considered that the ratepayer had failed to show that a reduction in rental value and, therefore, in the assessment, was justified. On those details of the statement of case dealing with structural and kindred matters, the tribunal found that all were common to all the other flats in the block and in some respects were the same as other cited blocks of flats. Taking everything into account the tribunal said that the appellant had failed to make out his case. Appeal dismissed, costs £25 awarded against the ratepayer.

(*Decision May 23, 1975*)

77

COMPARABILITY OF ESTATES OF DWELLINGS. VALUATION OFFICER'S OPINION CONFIRMED.

The appeal *Doyle and Others* v. *Bourne* (*Valuation Officer*) concerned three dwellings in Dawlish, Devon, following valuation court decisions reducing gross values of £415, £360 and £290 to £400, £345 and £285 respectively. Evidence was given about what was an extensive estate development but it was pointed out on behalf of the occupiers that one important requirement of the whole scheme was that of low-cost construction which, while providing an attractive external effect, had resulted in restricted internal lay-outs of poor design and of poor use of available floor area. The estate had not been completed and only 105 dwellings, less than one-quarter of the total planned, had been built since development started in 1970. Moreover, the planned development included the building of council houses on part of the estate.

The ratepayers' challenge was directed against the basic gross values and they cited other post-war estates in Dawlish which induced them to argue for a reduction of 10 *per cent.* in the gross values. On behalf of the ratepayers, reliance was placed on the assessments of 29 houses on other estates and it was certainly thought to be incorrect for the dwellings on the appeal estate to be assessed higher than others. The valuation court reductions had been given solely in respect of specific disabilities as recommended by the valuation officer. He had no rental evidence of post-war houses and he accepted that the details he had produced of the rents of six older houses were not adequate evidence on which to find a reliable basis. As with the appellants, he relied on comparisons but considered that properties in the appeal estate would command higher rents than those on four other cited estates.

The tribunal (Mr. E. C. Strathon) had been told that other outstanding appeals had been settled and that the valuation officer's proposals had been made to bring assessments into line with the revised basis decided by the valuation court. Moreover, a chartered surveyor resident on the appeal estate had agreed his assessment and had advised a number of other ratepayers on their assessments. In addition, the ratepayers' spokesman had agreed the assessment of his own house. The tribunal did not accept that as a result of the internal planning the rental values had materially suffered and the tribunal was not persuaded on the argument of comparables. In its opinion a more dependable yardstick was to be derived from a study of the generality of assessments on all the estates named and this led the tribunal to decide that the valuation court decisions were not incorrect or excessive. Appeals dismissed, costs £5 to the valuation officer from each of the appellants.

(*Decision June 3, 1975*)

78

ASSESSMENT OF FARMHOUSE. DISABILITIES FOR POOR APPROACH, REFLECTED IN VALUATION COURT'S DECISION, APPROVED.

The appeal *Kirkham* v. *Bailey* (*Valuation Officer*) concerned a farmhouse at Kirkham, Lancashire, assessed in the new list at £339 gross value, subsequently reduced by a valuation court to £315, a figure which still left the ratepayer dissatisfied. Reference was made to a disproportionate increase on revaluation by comparison to other farmhouses and it was also complained that the £24 allowance by the valuation court inadequately took account of the poor access, and an unmade narrow and unlighted public way. Moreover, there was frequent obstruction when church events took place nearby.

The valuation officer adduced a list of 12 post-war properties in respect of which rental evidence was available. These rents, suitably adjusted, constituted the foundation for the basis of assessment throughout the rating area and his assessment of the appeal property was supported by the assessments of eight other working farmhouses in the locality, figures agreed in all cases without proposals up to what was the third year of the revaluation.

The tribunal (Mr. J. D. Russell-Davis) thought the valuation court's allowance of about 7 *per cent.* was sufficient and it was concluded that the court's decision was fair and should be upheld. Appeal dismissed, costs £25 against the ratepayer.

(*Decision June 5, 1975*)

79

TIPPING AFFECTS NATURAL DRAINAGE BUT THIS OFFSET BY VIEWS OF OPEN COUNTRY.

The appeal *Griffiths* v. *Hughes* (*Valuation Officer*) concerned a house and garage at Wellington, Salop, assessed in the new list at £276 gross value. Subsequently the valuation officer made a proposal to increase that figure to £309 following the building of an extension of the kitchen and adjoining area at the rear of the house, a proposal confirmed by the valuation court. The only issue before the tribunal (Mr. J. H. Emlyn Jones) was the question of a disability suffered as a result of an apparent interference with the natural drainage of the land behind the property which had resulted in the rear garden becoming waterlogged when there was heavy rain. This adjoining land had been greatly built up by tipping and a stream which ran across this land had been culverted. One result was that the natural drainage was interfered with and water tended to collect at the rear of the appeal property. The valuation officer did not think that the rental value would be affected in any way by the occasional waterlogging and the tribunal was not persuaded of this either. Fear of future disabilities was not a factor which could affect the hypothetical rental value. On the whole it was thought that the benefit of the open view offset the disadvantages of occasional waterlogging. A reduction was not justified. Appeal dismissed, £25 costs against the ratepayer.

(*Decision June 9, 1975*)

80

RENTS AND COMPARABILITY OF SHOPS IN SAME AREA CONFIRMS FAIRNESS OF SHOP ASSESSMENT.

The appeal *Hayward Bros.* v. *Easterbrook* (*Valuation Officer*) concerned a shop at Benllech, Anglesey. A valuation court had dismissed a ratepayer's proposal to reduce the gross value of £590. The ratepayer presented figures indicating that the rates involved were more than the business could bear and that the basic gross value of local shops appeared to be nearly double those found in the neighbouring town of Beaumaris, whereas in his opinion the situation should be reversed. In addition, the ratepayer thought his own assessment to be excessive by comparison with other shops in the same locality. The valuation officer produced details of rents paid for 11 shops in the area, together with details of those shops and other shops which were either owner-occupied or for which no rental details were available.

In the light of all the evidence the tribunal (Mr. J. H. Emlyn Jones) felt quite unable to consider the assessment to be excessive. Appeal dismissed, £25 costs against the ratepayer.

(*Decision June 9, 1975*)

81

BUNGALOW. VALUATION OFFICER'S REDUCTION BASED ON COMPARABILITY HELD TO BE INSUFFICIENT.

The appeal *Parry v. Williams* (*Valuation Officer*) concerned a bungalow at Llangefni, Gwynedd, assessed in the new list at £156 gross value subsequently reduced by a valuation court to £134. The ratepayer was still dissatisfied but at the Lands Tribunal hearing the valuation officer supported an amended gross value of only £125. Even this was still thought to be excessive having regard to the assessments of three other rather similar bungalows in the same village. Moreover, there was concern about comparability of assessment between old and new valuation lists.

The valuation officer provided details of the three comparables cited by the ratepayer and justified the lower assessments of two of them on the grounds of inferiority, partly based on age. Regarding the third property, this had been recently modernised and he would be lodging a proposal to increase the assessment appreciably. In the valuation officer's opinion the rental evidence and the assessments derived from that evidence fully justified the revised gross value he was now supporting.

The tribunal (Mr. J. H. Emlyn Jones), having made his inspections, concluded that two of the three comparables were assessed on a basis which was less than half that which the valuation officer had put forward for the appeal property, a disparity which it thought too great and which enabled it to conclude that the reduction offered by the valuation officer was insufficient. In the tribunal's view the gross value should be reduced to £110. Appeal allowed, respondent valuation officer to pay £7 costs to the ratepayer.

(*Decision June 9, 1975*)

82

CAR RUN-IN AND GENERAL DETERIORATION OF LOCALITY HELD NOT TO JUSTIFY ASSESSMENT REDUCTION.

The appeal *Langworthy* v. *Rapps* (*Valuation Officer*) concerned a house in Bristol, the centre house of a terrace of three assessed at £320 gross value, this figure having been confirmed by a valuation court. The ratepayer referred to the adverse effect on her property value by the construction of a car run-in without a kerb crossing which was in front of and replacing part of the front garden of the immediately adjoining property. Additionally, it was the ratepayer's opinion that the amenities of the locality were deteriorating, otherwise she was not concerned about comparable assessments but on her second ground of deterioration she referred to hooliganism, kerbside parking, smell and fumes from a hospital chimney and the draughtiness of the nearest bus stop.

The valuation officer supported his evidence with full documentation and had been subject to extensive cross-examination, much of it irrelevant.

The tribunal (Mr. J. D. Russell-Davis) viewed the house under appeal and the general locality and could not find the garage run-in development either objectionable or un-neighbourly and if there had been some damage to a party wall, this was a matter for an alternative remedy. The tribunal was satisfied that the hypothetical tenant fresh upon the scene would not seek to reduce his rental offer because of the ratepayer's complaints. Neither would the hypothetical landlord concede a reduction. The valuation court's decision was upheld and the appeal was dismissed with £25 costs against the ratepayer.

(*Decision June 10, 1975*)

83

ADJOINING HOUSE USED BY SQUATTERS, BUT AFTER THE DATE OF THE RATEPAYER'S PROPOSAL.

The appeal *O'Riordan* v. *Cadogan* (*Valuation Officer*) concerned a house in Islington following a decision by a valuation court to reduce the gross value from £950 to £900. The ratepayer appealed on grounds of comparability and that an adjoining house had been occupied by squatters. Additionally, the road in which the appeal property stood was claimed to be used by goods vehicles and others as a short cut. Moreover, there were neighbouring unattractive uses such as a scrap metal warehouse, a public house, some cafes, a take-away food shop and a Turkish club. The ratepayer cited seven assessments of other properties in the same road which he claimed were on a lower basis.

The tribunal (Mr. J. D. Russell-Davis) was satisfied that at the date of the proposal the property claimed to be used by squatters was occupied by a single family and at that time there was nothing to influence the hypothetical tenant to reduce his rent offer on that account. The tribunal was concerned with conditions as they were at the date of the proposal and it would be up to the ratepayer, if he thought fit, to make a fresh proposal in respect of subsequent events. The ratepayer sought a reduction of a further £50 gross value.

The valuation officer said that the basis of assessment was founded on actual rents under leases granted between 1970 and 1973 for 18 three-storey non-basement houses about half the size of the appeal property but in the reasonably near neighbourhood. The houses concerned belonged to the GLC and were let but in an earlier appeal to the Lands Tribunal the rents were thought to be suspect as local authority rents and below open market value, because they ignored the element of scarcity. Nevertheless, as the lowest possible basis of value they were inadmissible for application to other houses in the area. He further supported his valuation by a table of 11 comparables.

The tribunal found that the appellant had not proved his case and the valuation court's determination was upheld. Appeal dismissed, ratepayer to pay £25 costs to the valuation officer.

(*Decision June 10, 1975*)

84

SCHOOL CAR PARK. DISADVANTAGE OFFSETS BENEFITS OF CONSERVATORY. COSTS AWARDED LESS THAN NORMAL AS RATEPAYER'S PROPOSAL LED TO CORRECTION OF VALUATION LIST.

The appeal *Griffith* v. *Abernethy* (*Valuation Officer*) concerned a ground floor flat of a property in Guildford following confirmation by a valuation court of a gross value of £280. In the spring of 1974 a car park was constructed on the school playing fields and not very far from the boundary wall of the garden of the appeal property. The car park was used by the staff of the sixth form scholars and also for evening class tutors. It was in use from 8.30 a.m. to 9.30 p.m. but rarely used at weekends or during school holidays. The ratepayer sought a reduction of £50 gross value because the car park had led to loss of privacy and amenity and had increased atmospheric pollution.

The valuation officer's evidence related to a number of rented flats in the same road as the appeal property and on analysis these showed that the tone of assessment for the 1973 valuation list had not been pitched above the level of actual rents. The valuation officer had, in effect, balanced the advantage of a conservatory, which had not been included in the assessment, against the disadvantage of the car park and to the tribunal that seemed very fair to the ratepayer. The ratepayer had failed to establish any error in the valuation court's decision and the appeal was dismissed with costs.

The valuation officer had sought a sum of £25 in costs but there was a complication in that due to an arithmetical error the conservatory value had not been added in. Inasmuch as the ratepayer's appeal had enabled the valuation officer to correct his valuation list the tribunal thought it appropriate to award only nominal costs in the sum of £10 against the ratepayer.

(*Decision June 12, 1975*)

85

VALUATION OFFICER'S FIGURES FOR ANCILLARY ACCOMMODATION AND END ALLOWANCE FOR DISABILITIES APPROVED BY TRIBUNAL.

The appeal *Star News Shops Limited* v. *Stamp* (*Valuation Officer*) concerned a shop and premises at Tettenhall, Wolverhampton, following the determination by a valuation court of a gross value of £3,075. The premises were an amalgam of two shops, both of two storeys but of a different age. The valuers, the one acting for the ratepayer and the valuation officer, had been able to reach agreement on all points except two. The first of these was the rental value attributable to certain ancillary accommodation and secondly the appropriate end allowance for certain disabilities.

The tribunal (Mr. R. C. Walmsley), dealing with the ancillary accommodation which was first floor, and outside store accommodation, preferred the valuation officer's method and adopted his gross value of £239 against the ratepayers' valuer's figure of £201. So far as disabilities were concerned, these were described under three headings. A broken frontage in that one shop front was set back appreciably, a divided sales area because of the poor connection between the two original premises and different floor levels. For the ratepayers a deduction of 15 *per cent.* had been made whereas the valuation officer considered that only 8 *per cent.* was justified. In neither case were figures supported by any external evidence. That being the case the only way the tribunal was able to "value the values" was to "value the valuers". The ratepayers' valuer was a young man with insubstantial grounds for offering his opinion as that of an expert whereas the valuation officer had been able to draw on 35 years professional experience. The tribunal considered the valuation officer's opinion to be more reliable. In adopting the 8 *per cent.* end allowance the tribunal added that it would have reached the same conclusion regardless of the weight of experience. The broken frontage seemed to present no serious disadvantage but the divided sales area was a factor which would have some significance so far as rental value was concerned. The different floor levels did not seem a great drawback and the layout of the combined shop had been designed by the ratepayers themselves. Appeal dismissed. £30 costs against the ratepayers.

(*Decision June 12, 1975*)

86

SHOP PREMISES. COMPARABLES. EVIDENCE OF AGREED SETTLEMENTS MORE RELIABLE THAN UNSUPPORTED OPINION EVIDENCE.

The appeal *Allied Carpet Stores Limited* v. *Culverwell* (*Valuation Officer*) concerned shop premises in Leicester entered in the old valuation list at £7,600 gross value. The originating proposal of March 16, 1973 referred to an assessment that was incorrect, unfair, grossly excessive, bad in law and calling for a substantial reduction. A figure of £5,000 gross value was sought. However, a valuation court reduced the gross value to only £6,800 but even then the ratepayers appealed. For the ratepayers a valuer spoke to a gross value of £4,000 but the valuation officer presented a valuation in a sum of £7,600. The valuer for the City Council spoke to a valuation of £6,845 gross value.

The tribunal (Mr. E. C. Strathon) said that the ratepayers' valuer had based his valuation on his general experience as a valuer, referring primarily to two comparables in the locality. The valuation officer relied on the assessments of nine comparable shops and he had taken the view that he derived no assistance from the ratepayers' valuer's two comparables. After examining in some detail the supporting data from the ratepayers' valuer the tribunal concluded that this left the valuer's opinion valuation unsupported by any comparable or by other recognisable valuation data, whereas the valuation officer had relied on a recognisable pattern of descending values to support the appealed assessment of £6,800 gross value. In the tribunal's judgment a valuation approach which embraced a review of the assessments of comparables, all of which had been agreed with, or accepted by, surveyors acting for the various ratepayers, and which went to make the tone of the valuation list, must be more reliable than an unsupported opinion valuation. The ratepayers had not persuaded the tribunal that the valuation court's decision was incorrect. Appeal dismissed. On the question of costs the decision was that the ratepayers should pay to the respondents only one set of costs, of which there should be apportioned to the valuation officer the sum of £25 and, to the second respondent, the remainder. If not agreed the costs were to be taxed on the High Court scale.

(*Decision June 19, 1975*)

87

VALUATION OFFICER'S ALLOWANCE FOR PROXIMITY OF GROCERY DISTRIBUTION DEPOT CONFIRMED.

The appeal *Clay* v. *Hardy* (*Valuation Officer*) concerned a house at Beverley in Yorkshire where the short point was the extent to which the assessment of the appeal property called for a reduction because of the presence of a transport depot on adjoining land. Following the erection of a garage and another structural extension the valuation officer had made a proposal increasing the new list gross value from £253 to £380 but he had agreed to reduce this latter figure to £374 because central heating had not been installed in the extension area. Eventually a valuation court determined the assessments at £240 and £362 respectively and it was against those figures on two proposals that the ratepayer appealed.

Had it not been for the existence of the depot the parties agreed that the assessments should be as the valuation officer had indicated, but in addition the house backed on to playing fields. The ratepayer said he suffered noise through the testing of diesel engines and the use of a compressor. Moreover, in the early hours of the morning there was a lot of movement and noise and he had been unsuccessful in seeking to eradicate this through action by the local planning authority. He sought a reduction of 25 *per cent.* and did not agree that his house enjoyed any advantage because of the outlook over a cricket ground.

The valuation officer said that the depot was used to distribute groceries and he had made six visits at various times, including one at 3.15 a.m. He had heard voices on the Tannoy system and engine and other noises as well as having seen lights on at night but he considered that his allowance of 5 *per cent.* was correct and this deduction had been accepted by other occupiers in the same road. Given that allowance, the gross values would be £240 and £356 respectively.

The tribunal (Mr. W. H. Rees) concluded on the evidence that the proper deduction was 5 *per cent.* and the appeal was allowed to that extent. In all the circumstances the tribunal thought that a proper costs award against the appellant was £10. The appellant had admitted that the valuation officer had offered, shortly after the valuation court's decision, to reduce the second assessment because of the lack of central heating in the extension.

(*Decision June 23, 1975*)

88

VALUATION OFFICER'S ADJUSTMENT OF VALUATION FOR SIZE OF DWELLING ACCEPTED BY TRIBUNAL.

The appeal *O'Mullane* v. *Ellerby* (*Valuation Officer*) concerned a house at Driffield, assessed at £310 gross value in the new valuation list, reduced by a valuation court to £305, a reduction suggested by the valuation officer after discovery of a minor arithmetical error in the area of the property. The ratepayer claimed that his property was one of the largest semi-detached houses in the area and that there was no direct comparable. He referred to the assessments of five dwellings in the locality. In the light of its inspection the tribunal (Mr. W. H. Rees) came to the conclusion that there was no reason to question the application by the valuation officer of his professional judgment. Appeal dismissed. Costs £25 against the rate-payer.

(Decision June 23, 1975)

89

EFFECT OF HOVERPORT. VALUATION COURT'S REDUCTION CONFIRMED.

The appeals in *Peacock and Another* v. *Paul* (*Valuation Officer*) *and the Thanet District Council* concerned two houses in Ramsgate where the ratepayers sought a reduction because of the effect of a nearby hoverport. They sought a 50 *per cent.* reduction. The valuation officer sought to uphold the valuation court's decision. In the new valuation list one of the two assessments involved was reduced from £447 gross value to £346 gross value, and the other from £423 to £343. The valuation officer conceded that a reduction should be made on account of vibration, noise, smell and pollution, but he had no rental evidence which could be regarded as reflecting these disabilities. In pre-revaluation proceedings the valuation court had reduced the assessments by 11.43 *per cent.* Because of the increased traffic he had considered a percentage of 15 to be appropriate. However, the later decisions by the valuation court, reducing the assessments by 17½ *per cent.* were within valuation tolerance and he had accepted the court's decisions. In the view of the tribunal (Mr. W. H. Rees) there was nothing in the evidence of the ratepayers to raise doubts about the correctness of the valuation officer's logical and objective approach and the use of his professional judgment. Appeals dismissed. Costs £20 against each of the two ratepayers.

(Decision June 23, 1975)

90

RATEPAYER FAILS TO JUSTIFY REDUCED ASSESSMENT ON THE GROUNDS OF PROFIT MARGINS, INTRODUCTION OF YELLOW LINES AND DESIGN OF PROPERTY.

The appeal *Playford* v. *Shadwell* (*Valuation Officer*) concerned a shop and house in Brighton, following confirmation by a valuation court of a gross value of £575. The ratepayer claimed that no consideration had been given to his profit margin, noise at traffic lights, the introduction of yellow lines and that there was no separate entrance to the dwelling part of the premises. A reduction to £517 gross value was sought. The valuation officer submitted details of five other shops in the locality, together with rental details covering the period 1962 to 1970. The valuation officer considered that the rent being paid, £400 per annum, was below what the landlord would have agreed with a new tenant in 1973. The tribunal (Mr. W. H. Rees) saw nothing on inspection indicating that the assessment was incorrect. The valuation officer had, by reference to other assessments supported by actual rents, proved the assessment of the appeal property. Appeal dismissed. Costs £20 against the ratepayer.

(*Decision June 23, 1975*)

91

RENTS AND UNCHALLENGED ASSESSMENTS HELD TO SUPPORT VALUATION OFFICER WHERE RATEPAYER SOUGHT REDUCTION ON GROUNDS OF COMPARABLES. LACK OF MAIN DRAINAGE AND UNADOPTED ROAD.

The appeal *Watt* v. *Sawyer* (*Valuation Officer*) concerned a house near Macclesfield, following confirmation by a valuation court of a gross value of £845. The ratepayer complained that insufficient consideration had been given to the lack of main drainage and that the highway had not been adopted. The valuation officer pointed out that following his inspection it had been discovered that no account had been taken of the value of a utility room and double garage; there was a proposal outstanding on a revised gross value of £900. In respect of the present appeal he submited details of 18 houses in the locality, but the tribunal (Mr. W. H. Rees) found none of this helpful. Additionally, the valuation officer gave details of the assessments of 23 houses in the area which included seven in the same road as the appeal property. These were of help to the tribunal. The valuation officer's evidence was preferred because it accorded with the unchallenged assessments of nearby properties, whereas the ratepayer's analysis and unsupported spot value was not convincing. Appeal dismissed. Costs £25 against the ratepayer.

(*Decision June 23, 1975*)

92

SMALL REDUCTION FOR DOUBLE GARAGE AFFORDING TIGHT FIT.

The appeal *Albiston* v. *Robinson* (*Valuation Officer*) concerned a house at Poulton-le-Fylde, Blackpool, following a valuation court reduction of gross value from £397 to £360. The ratepayer did not think the reduction sufficient and more specifically on account of the proximity of a new extension to a telephone exchange and the difficulty of using a room in the roof space because when the approach ladder was lowered it obstructed access to the kitchen-dining room and one bedroom. Moreover, the ratepayer complained that the revaluation increase was disproportionate. Then again there was a complaint about a free public car park and the assessment of what was thought to be a double garage as such, whereas it was difficult to accommodate two cars.

The valuation officer confirmed that the assessment was founded on limited rental evidence but was supported by the assessments of eight other dwellings in the same road, including two cited by the ratepayer. The reduction awarded by the court followed his suggestion to reflect the adverse effects of the telephone exchange and the room access. He did not think the car park could be regarded as detrimental and he was satisfied that the garage did afford accommodation for two cars.

The tribunal (Mr. J. D. Russell-Davis) stressed that comparisons between old and new assessments, although frequently raised before the tribunal, were irrelevant and inadmissible. The tribunal agreed with the valuation officer that the use of the car park presented an insignificant disadvantage and he also agreed that the garage would accommodate two family size cars even if the entrance was somewhat inconvenient. All the same, the car on the right hand side would have to be driven out before the one on the left hand side could be moved and the tribunal thought this justified a further deduction of £5, supporting a gross value of £355. Appeal allowed. No costs awarded.

(*Decision June 25, 1975*)

93

ERROR IN VALUATION LIST. VALUATION OFFICER'S APPEAL AGAINST VALUATION COURT'S DECISION ALLOWED BUT RATEPAYER AWARDED SMALL SUM IN COSTS.

The appeal *Gornall* (*Valuation Officer*) v. *Pierce* concerned a bungalow at Neston in Cheshire. A number of modern detached bungalows had been built in the locality and they comprised four types. These four types carried different gross values. Three had been entered in the list at £525 gross value, two at £485 gross value and the remaining two at £475 gross value. The ratepayer in the present appeal considered that his assessment should be brought into line with two identical bungalows at the lowest figure whereas his was assessed at the highest. In due course a valuation court came to the conclusion that the appeal property gross value should be £475 and in so agreeing they had adopted a deduction suggested by the valuation officer to reflect the disability of an approach over an unmade and unadopted road; this reduction was £10 gross value.

The valuation officer sought restoration of anything above his £10 deduction, seeking a gross value of £515. The issue was, therefore, whether a higher gross value of £515 was correct rather than a figure of £475. There was a discrepancy which the valuation officer agreed had arisen from a mistake in the valuation office but it was his duty to correct assessments and in this case he had found it necessary, to achieve correctness, to appeal against the valuation court's decision. Additionally he had made proposals to increase the assessments of the other bungalows which were equally under-assessed. He referred to the assessments of seven other detached bungalows in the immediate locality and it was on an examination of those other assessments that the decision of the tribunal (Mr. J. H. Emlyn Jones) had to rest and the tribunal came to the conclusion, although not without some reluctance, that the appeal must be allowed and the gross value determined at £515. The valuation officer had not asked for costs and the tribunal thought the ratepayer had been brought before the tribunal very largely because of the initial mistake in the valuation office and in those circumstances the tribunal directed that the valuation officer should pay £3 costs to the ratepayer.

(*Decision June 25, 1975*)

94

VALUATION COURT'S REDUCTION ON ACCOUNT OF NEARBY DEPOT, MOTORWAY TRAFFIC AND OTHER NUISANCES NOT CHANGED.

The appeal *Humphreys* v. *Rankin* (*Valuation Officer*) concerned a bungalow at Eastham, Wirral, assessed in the new valuation list at £380 gross value. The ratepayers sought a reduction to £261 but when the matter came before the local valuation court the valuation officer conceded the case for a reduction but only to a figure of £365 gross value. The valuation court thought that insufficient and determined a gross value of £355, leaving the ratepayers dissatisfied.

It appeared that industrial waste of various kinds, some of it highly offensive, was tipped nearby and dropped on to the road where mud formed and this was carried from the pavement into the house. In addition there was an open ditch which was full of rubbish and contained stagnant water. There was also a great deal of traffic on the ordinary highway as well as the nuisance from the noise and dust of traffic on the nearby motorway.

The valuation officer put in a schedule giving details of rents and assessments of comparable bungalows from which the tribunal (Mr. J. H. Emlyn Jones) was satisfied that the general basis of value was amply supported, a fact which the ratepayers did not seriously challenge. Their concern was the allowances for the various disabilities and although the valuation officer agreed about the mud and smells and also that the elevated motorway would be considered somewhat overbearing he did not consider that the traffic noise would be a problem and if litter tended to gather as the result of public use of a shop, it had also to be remembered that the shop was the only one in the district. It was open on Sunday mornings and would be found very convenient.

The tribunal said that the question of adjustment for various disabilities was necessarily a matter of impression. The valuation officer had suggested £15 but the valuation court thought £25 to be the right figure. The tribunal did not consider the presence of the shop to have any appreciable effect on rental value nor did the motorway fly-over cause excessive noise. It was true that there was annoyance from fumes and although the two depots were some distance away it was quite clear that the passing to and from the depots by lorries created disturbance and fouling of the carriageway. Taking everything into account the tribunal was not persuaded that the valuation court's reduction was inadequate. Appeal dismissed. £30 costs against the ratepayer.

(*Decision June 25, 1975*)

95

TRIBUNAL REJECTS VALUATION OFFICER'S APPEAL. VALUATION COURT'S REDUCTION MODIFIED. ALLOWANCE FOR DERELICT HOUSES AND NEARBY RAILWAY WORKSHOP.

The appeal *Rogers* (*Valuation Officer*) v. *Lederer* concerned a house in west London, assessed at £1,025 gross value, reduced by a valuation court to £925 because of the disadvantageous position of the house in relation to the railway, and Paddington Station. The valuation officer sought a gross value of £1,100. Noise of trains and motor traffic, together with day and night working at a nearby railway workshop. There were signs of settlement in the structure of the house. The valuation officer supported his case by reference to analyses of assessments of three houses in the same road and two others quite near, all five of which were assessed on the same basis as the appeal property and with deductions of 11 *per cent.* and 12½ *per cent.* for the effect of the motorway and railway in the case of the three houses. With a gross value of £925, as determined by the valuation court, the equivalent deduction was over 19 *per cent.* In his opinion neither the derelict houses—also a complaint by the ratepayer—nor the railway workshop affected the rental value of the appeal property. The tribunal (Mr. W. H. Rees) accepted the valuation officer's 12½ *per cent.* deduction and considered the building defects to be covered by the rating hypothesis *Wexler* v. *Playle* (*Valuation Officer*), (1960), but thought that the derelict houses and railway workshop would affect the rental value and allowed £25 on that account. Gross value £975 determined. Appeal allowed to that extent. No costs award.

(*Decision June 30, 1975*)

96

TRAFFIC AND ESTATE DEVELOPMENT NUISANCES HELD NOT TO JUSTIFY REDUCED ASSESSMENTS.

Two appeals in *Baker and Another* v. *Havard* (*Valuation Officer*) concerned houses at Ellesmere Port, Cheshire, following confirmation of the gross values of £356 by a valuation court. The question raised in the appeals was the amount of an allowance in respect of certain disabilities. One concerned the use of the road in which the properties stood by much heavy traffic using it as a short cut to two major roads, substantial housing development and the consequential inconvenience from building operations which among other things had led to the blocking up of a drainage ditch. The valuation officer considered the traffic not to be such as to influence the hypothetical tenant in his rental bid and most of the building operations had ceased before the proposals were served by the ratepayers. Certainly there had been temporary flooding of the rear gardens but they had dried up very quickly and the damage was purely temporary in any case.

The tribunal (Mr. V. G. Wellings) following his visit to the locality saw no evidence of serious nuisance or annoyance from either traffic or building operations and there was certainly no evidence of damage from flooding. The valuation officer's evidence and arguments were accepted and the appeals dismissed with an award of £15 costs against each of the two ratepayers.

(*Decision July 2, 1975*)

97

GENERAL CLAIM BASED ON LOCAL REVALUATION INCREASES COMPARED WITH NATIONAL PERCENTAGE REJECTED. OIL-FIRED BOILER NOT A NUISANCE JUSTIFYING A NEIGHBOUR'S ASSESSMENT REDUCTION.

The appeal *Marshall* v. *Webber* (*Valuation Officer*) concerned a house and garage at Wickham Bishops, Essex, assessed in the 1973 valuation list at £485 gross value. The ratepayer sought a considerable reduction based on two proposals. The first was a comparison of the average national increase in rateable values compared with a much higher local increase. The second point concerned the presence of an oil-fired boiler with an external chimney at a neighbouring house where it was claimed that sulphur dioxide fumes regularly and frequently swept over the appellant ratepayer's garden. A valuation court had reduced the gross value to £475 but gave no written reasons for so doing. The ratepayer thought the assessment should be reduced by 20 *per cent*.

The valuation officer said it had been impossible to find rental evidence and he had, therefore, relied on the assessments of similar houses and more particularly ten other houses in the same road. He considered that the valuation list had by now settled down and did not think it appropriate to take into account a national average difference between valuation lists. He much doubted whether the hyothetical tenant would have obtained a lower rental on account of the alleged nuisance from the oil-fired boiler and although he had been surprised by the valuation court's decision he had not thought it appropriate to challenge such a small reduction.

The tribunal (Mr. J. Stuart Daniel) said he could not possibly be satisfied that an allowance of more than £10 should be made. Appeal dismissed. Costs £25 against the ratepayer.

(Decision July 3, 1975)

98

TRIBUNAL ALLOWS AN APPROXIMATE REDUCTION OF 5 *PER CENT.* ON GROSS VALUES OF DWELLINGS AFFECTED BY DUST AND FUMES FROM A PHURNACITE PLANT.

The appeal *Pritchard and Others* v. *Williams (Valuation Officer)* concerned 13 appeals against the assessments of properties in the same road at Mountain Ash, Glamorgan. A valuation court had reduced the gross values by a nominal £2 on account of a narrow and badly surfaced access to the road. The ratepayers appealed on the grounds that the valuation court had failed to recognise the evidence of pollution due to fumes and dust fall-out arising from the Aberaman Phurnacite Plant between Mountain Ash and Aberdare. The phurnacite plant was about a half mile distance from the properties and all the ratepayers spoke from first hand experience of the pollution, presenting one exhibit of a box containing dust collected the same morning from a porch roof of one of the houses. The valuation officer admitted the extent of the pollution and that the appeal properties were modern dwellings in a good situation. Except for the pollution complaint there was no dispute about the assessments. He put in a list of six comparable properties and contended that the pollution was widespread throughout the area and it had not been conclusively proved that the appeal properties suffered to a greater extent than properties anywhere else. The tone of the list had become established through acquiescence in valuation list assessments by ratepayers generally and the hypothetical tenant would accept the physical conditions in the locality as he found them.

The tribunal (Mr. J. D. Russell-Davis) accepted evidence that dust conditions were fairly bad and he was not altogether persuaded that a would-be tenant of these properties would not be fairly discriminating and he believed that such a tenant would seek to obtain a rent reduction, which the landlord might well concede. The tribunal concluded that the gross values should be reduced in each case by a flat rate sum of £12 each, in broad terms, or equivalent to approximately 5 *per cent.* of those originally in the new valuation list. Appeals allowed. Valuation officer to contribute £2 costs to each of the ratepayers. The valuation officer was congratulated on his fairness and helpfulness.

(Decision July 7, 1975)

99

NO REDUCTION ON ACCOUNT OF AIRCRAFT NOISE, NEARBY COLLEGE AND ABSENCE OF LOCAL POLICEMAN.

The appeal *Ricardo* v. *Meek* (*Valuation Officer*) concerned a house and two garages at Cookham, Berkshire, where a valuation court had confirmed a gross value of £540. Separated from the garden of the appeal property by a public footpath was a college known as Moor Hall.

The ratepayer contended for a reduction of a considerable amount by reference to the noise of aircraft, the presence of Moor Hall and the absence of a local policeman who had been replaced with a Panda car service. On the question of aircraft it was claimed that aircraft passed over every three or five minutes from 5 a.m.-11.30 p.m. The college of Moor Hall was occupied by the Institute of Marketing and the owners had a club licence and were apt to hold dances on the college premises or to allow local bodies to hold dances.

The valuation officer had no rental evidence but did stress that for purposes of the new list consideration had been given to the whole of the available rental evidence for all types of dwellings and a tone of value had been decided, a tone which had now become accepted and established. He gave the appropriate statistical facts in support of this claim. So far as aircraft noise was concerned the valuation officer said that the presence of London Airport was a factor which tended to maintain, rather than to reduce, the rental value of houses in the Thames Valley because 50,000 jobs existed at Heathrow. So far as records of house sales were concerned these showed that the price trend in Cookham was no different from the trend in the area as a whole. The atmosphere of Moor Hall was academic and tranquil and the police factor was general to all houses in the Thames Valley police area.

The tribunal (Mr. R. C. Walmsley) spent over two hours in the locality and found that the noise of aircraft was not obtrusive and was apt to be subordinated by the noise of passing vehicles. The valuation officer had not made any reduction for the aircraft noise factor. A number of earlier decisions by the tribunal were examined and the tribunal was satisfied that on the evidence the tone of the valuation list for Cookham was well established and the basic gross value of the appeal property was not above that tone. There were circumstances which could be regarded as normal to the locality and in this instance included the absence of a local policeman and the presence of aircraft noise. This left only the question of the neighbouring Moor Hall and the tribunal agreed with the valuation officer that there could well be prospective tenants who would regard Moor Hall as not being a disadvantage at all. The ratepayer had failed to establish an error in the valuation court's decision. Appeal dismissed. Costs £25 awarded against the ratepayer. The tribunal noted that the valuation court had been unaware of the existence of central heating and it seemed that a proposal had now been lodged to increase the assessment.

(*Decision July 7, 1975*)

100

LESS ATTRACTIVE SITUATION OF DWELLING COMPARED WITH NEIGHBOURING DWELLINGS AND DIFFERENCE IN PURCHASE PRICE WARRANT SMALL ASSESSMENT REDUCTION.

The appeal *Barnard* v. *Walker* (*Valuation Officer*) concerned a house and garage at Woburn Sands, Bedfordshire, where there was a gross value of £540, a figure which the ratepayer considered to be out of line with the assessments of neighbouring houses. However, a valuation court confirmed the assessment and before the Lands Tribunal (Mr. J. H. Emlyn Jones) the valuation officer supported the court's decision by a schedule of assessments of other houses in the vicinity and in an adjoining cul-de-sac. These, he claimed, showed a consistent pattern of values which had become generally accepted, thus establishing the revaluation level of assessments.

The ratepayers contended that their garden plot was smaller, that their house was overlooked and that they suffered considerable disturbance from heavy traffic. Their claim was supported by the fact that in 1968 the valuation officer had then agreed to a small reduction on these grounds, a differential also supported by the fact that the purchase price for their house was £450 less than the amount paid for other houses on the estate.

The valuation officer submitted that a purchase price was not a reliable guide in considering annual value, since personal considerations might have intervened.

The tribunal did not think the valuation officer was right to dismiss the 1968 adjustment as being irrelevant. When it came to a consideration of differentials in the old valuation list it seemed to the tribunal that there must be a presumption that those differentials were correct. In the present case the valuation officer had failed to persuade the tribunal that there had been any material change in the circumstances justifying the application of a different differential in the new list, for if it was correct to make an adjustment in 1968 then it was still correct to do so for the new list. So far as capital values were concerned the tribunal said it was quite true that the considerations affecting purchase price were not necessarily those relevant to annual value but the personal considerations referred to by the valuation officer which he detected in capital transactions could also apply to some extent to rents. That factor in itself did not inhibit the use of rental evidence as a means of arriving at rental value. Where the houses were all newly built and broadly similar, indeed some were identical, a differential in purchase price certainly provided some indication that a difference might also be expected in annual value. The evidence all pointed in the same direction, something confirmed when the tribunal viewed the property. The appeal property did not enjoy the same pleasant setting shared by the other houses and its situation was appreciably less attractive. Appeal allowed. Gross value reduced to £520, £10 costs against the valuation officer.

(*Decision July 10, 1975*)

101

RESTRICTED DEMAND FOR FIRST FLOOR SPACE OVER SHOP JUSTIFIES ASSESSMENT REDUCTION.

The appeal *Hardy & Co.* (*Furnishers*) *Limited* v. *Lenton* (*Valuation Officer*) concerned a shop in Farnborough, a valuation court having reduced the gross value from £6,600 to £6,500. The element of value which was in issue was the gross value of the first floor space. The ratepayers' valuer supported a figure of £1,292 for this space but the valuation officer supported £1,641.

For the ratepayers it was argued that there was a lack of demand for first floor showroom space in Farnborough and apart from the appeal property there was no first floor showroom or retail sale space in either Queensmead or in other shopping areas of Farnborough. The valuation officer had taken the view that competition could be expected from two other firms of furniture dealers, each of whom occupied two ground floor shops in Queensmead, also from two firms of furniture dealers who occupied shops elsewhere in Farnborough. Additionally, the appellants themselves would also be in the market. His selection of a value of one-sixth of zone A for the upstairs space was not a matter of rule of thumb but emerged from an analysis of rents paid in the valuation area of which Farnborough was part.

The tribunal (Mr. E. C. Strathon) pointed out that in the Queensmead precinct, where the appeal property was situated and in the rest of Farnborough no other shop was occupied with a first floor used for a showroom for retail sales and the tribunal accepted the ratepayers' contention that this pointed strongly to a lack of demand for those uses. In the tribunal's judgment it should not be assumed, as the valuation officer had assumed, that demand would come from other furniture dealers who now occupied ground floor shops but not first floor showrooms in Queensmead and elsewhere in Farnborough. The tribunal adopted intermediate values for the disputed area and finally determined a gross value of £6,270. The valuation officer was ordered to pay the ratepayers' costs on County Court scale 4 if not agreed.

(*Decision July 14, 1975*)

102

VALUATION OFFICER'S PROFFERED REDUCTION ON ACCOUNT OF CENTRAL HEATING ADDITION CONFIRMED.

The appeal *Strong* v. *Phillips* (*Valuation Officer*) concerned the assessment of a first floor flat in a three-storey building in Beckenham built in 1971 following confirmation by a valuation court of a gross value of £316. The ratepayer complained about traffic noise from parking and the arrival and departure of vehicles which was a particular nuisance considering that the windows of a living room and bedroom overlooked the roadway, where the parking, etc. occurred, and were set back less than 3 ft. from the pavement.

The valuation officer, after the valuation court hearing, had found that the amount included for central heating was excessive and he had informed the ratepayer that he would be defending a gross value of only £304 before the Lands Tribunal.

The tribunal (Mr. E. C. Strathon) observed that the valuation officer had relied for support on the assessments of 12 comparable flats in the locality and was satisfied that an assessment of £304 gross value would fall properly into the pattern of assessments of all these flats and the appeal flat would command a rent of not less than the gross value of £304. There was no order as to costs, a decision based on the suggestion of the valuation officer.

(Decision July 14, 1975)

103

RATEPAYER FAILS IN CLAIM FOR RELIEF BECAUSE OF NEARBY RECREATION GROUND.

The appeal *Swan* v. *Hunt* (*Valuation Officer*) concerned a house near Rochester following confirmation by a valuation court of a gross value of £237. The ratepayer complained about a recreation field at the bottom of his garden which was used by children and was apparently so used with out any control by council staff or through byelaws. The ratepayer thought that the nuisance warranted a rate reduction but the valuation officer's documents showed the same basic values throughout the estate and the ratepayer did not challenge this apart from the recreation ground's use.

In the view of the tribunal (Mr. E. C. Strathon) there would be potential tenants for the appeal property who would not regard the recreation field as the nuisance the appellant considered it to be, and in making their rent bids they would not seek a reduction from the general level of values prevailing on the estate as a whole. Appeal dismissed. £25 costs against the ratepayer.

(Decision July 14, 1975)

104

RESIDUAL METHOD OF VALUATION FOR PART OF HOUSE COMPRISING FLATLETS REJECTED. GROSS RENTS, LESS OUTGOINGS. DIRECT APPROACH PREFERRED. RATEPAYER FAILS TO SHOW VALUATION OFFICER'S PROFERRED REDUCTION LEAVES ASSESSMENT STILL EXCESSIVE.

The appeal *Cliffe* v. *White* (*Valuation Officer*) concerned a house mainly comprising flatlets in South East London where the owner resided in the basement which was self-contained, and where the ground and two upper floors comprised separately let out flatlets.

Following some reconstruction the valuation officer made a proposal for a gross value of £1,200 but a valuation court reduced this to £874. The ratepayer was dissatisfied and sought a reduction on the grounds of mistaken description, excessive rental value estimate for ground floor, inadequate regard to the cost of the landlord's outgoings and to certain comparisons in the vicinity. Since the ratepayer had appealed to the Lands Tribunal the valuation officer had offered a further reduction to £700 gross value. In addition, the valuation officer had offered to make an inclusive composite assessment for the whole house but this had not been accepted. Indeed, the ratepayer had declined even to agree a statement of facts but it was not in dispute that the property had been well adapted for its purpose and was in a sound condition. The nub of the appeal was in the description of the ground floor where the architect's plans showed the accommodation as two bedsitters.

A surveyor had advised the ratepayer that as a furnished flat it would be a better letting proposition. However, no evidence was called from his surveyor on this point and the valuation officer explained that each room had separate electric and gas meters and he accepted that they could be let together depending on the tenant found for them.

It seemed to the tribunal (Mr. J. D. Russell-Davis) that the ground floor had been adapted as single flatlets even if by a particular arrangement of the door it could be used, as at present, as a flat. It was clear that the landlord retained a large measure of control so that the valuation officer would be justified in exercising his discretion under s. 24 of the General Rate Act 1967 in treating the whole of the appeal hereditament as a single hereditament. So far as the rental value was concerned the estimated rent for the floor as bedsitters or flatlets semed to be in correct relationship with the rents received from the other seven letting rooms.

The tribunal could find no fault with the valuation officer's estimated gross income, although it did go on to make certain adjustments to the outgoings. Little assistance was derived from any of the valuation officer's comparables and equally, the appellant's comparables were of little assistance. It had often been said that the Lands Tribunal treated residual values with a great deal of reserve, especially when arriving at capital value and the same could be said, except in a few special cases, in reaching an annual value for rating purposes. The tribunal considered that a residual valuation could be adjusted to produce whatever result was desired and it was particularly unreliable when it was applied only after a short period of trading as in the present case. The question was whether the appeal property, vacant and to let, on a year to year basis, was worth to a tenant in the business of letting bedsitters or flatlets a rent of £14 per week, the tenant paying rates and the landlord insuring and carrying out repairs. The ratepayer had declined to answer that question but the tribunal thought that at the date of the new valuation list the answer must clearly be in the affirmative.

The tribunal upheld the gross value of £700 offered by the valuation officer and allowed the appeal to that extent. No costs were asked for so no order was made.

(*Decision July 21, 1975*)

105

LACK OF PRIVACY. NEARBY WAREHOUSE. TEMPORARY LOSS OF AMENITIES AND SALE OF PRIVATE HOUSES TO THE LOCAL COUNCIL INSUFFICIENT GROUNDS FOR REDUCING HOUSE ASSESSMENT.

The appeal *Price* v. *Sellick* (*Valuation Officer*) *and the Borough of Thamesdown* concerned a house and garage in Swindon following confirmation by a valuation court of a gross value of £412. The valuation officer supported his assessment by comparison with two other houses in the area and eight other similar properties in two groups nearby. The ratepayer complained about the building of a balcony in an adjoining house which overlooked the back garden and nearby rooms but the tribunal (Mr. J. D. Russell-Davis) did not think that would affect the hypothetical tenant's bid. Nor, in the tribunal's view did a large single-storey building used as a Post Office warehouse justify a reduction. Additionally, failure on behalf of a public authority to provide an infants' school was not a valid ground of appeal and there seemed to be a fairly universal acceptance by other ratepayers that this omission would be remedied when better times came. On the question of the lack of a pavement, this, too, was a matter which would be rectified and did not constitute a ground of objection. Finally on the complaint that the council's purchase of 17 out of 22 town houses in the area had affected the residential standards, the rating authority representative explained that with the encouragement of the Department of the Environment the Council had purchased about 200 houses in the Swindon area which had been completed but which were not selling very well. The appeal property was an attractive and well designed one and standing in pleasant surroundings. The drawbacks had been over-emphasised and some were only temporary; none were substantial. The valuation officer had satisfied the tribunal that the assessment was fair and reasonable. Appeal dismissed. The valuation officer had asked for costs of only £10 and this sum was awarded. No costs were due to the Thamesdown Borough Council.

(*Decision July 21, 1975*)

106

NO CHANGE IN CIRCUMSTANCES SINCE TRIBUNAL DECLINED TO REDUCE HOUSE ASSESSMENT ON ACCOUNT OF NEARBY COAL DEPOT. NO CHANGE IN ASSESSMENT.

The appeal *Kendall* v. *Shadlock* (*Valuation Officer*) concerned a house at Bexleyheath. In 1972 a co-operative society had erected some coal hoppers at a nearby coal depot so that coal could be placed mechanically by way of a scoop and funnelled into waiting lorries. A valuation court had confirmed the gross value at £310.

The ratepayer was concerned that the Bexley Council had served an enforcement notice seeking removal of the coal yard and his contention was that the council were not going to pursue the matter while both the council and the co-operative society were deriving income from the existing development.

The valuation officer produced plans and schedules and explained that in the last three valuation lists a small allowance had been made on account of the coal yard for certain occupiers but the appeal property was considered to be far enough away not to justify an allowance. All the neighbouring houses had the same gross value as the appeal property.

The tribunal (Mr. J. Stuart Daniel) thought that the appeal was misconceived. The valuation court's decision was not wrong. Appeal dismissed. £25 costs against the ratepayer.

(*Decision July 22, 1975*)

107

RECENTLY FIXED LEASE RENT AND OBLIGATIONS. NO ALLOWANCE FOR DISABILITIES ALREADY REFLECTED IN RENT. AMORTISATION OF TENANTS' EXPENDITURE, IN ADDITION TO RENT, LIMITED TO TERM OF LEASE, THUS DISREGARDING POSSIBLE RENEWAL UNDER LANDLORD AND TENANT ACT 1954.

The appeal *Edma* (*Jewellers*) *Limited* v. *Moore* (*Valuation Officer*) concerned a shop in a new covered pedestrian shop precinct in Luton. The first phase of extensive development comprising 34 shops, together with a market hall, public house, office block and multi-storey car park. The shop was entered in the valuation list at £8,000 gross value but following an objection by the ratepayers the valuation officer submitted to the local valuation court a revised gross value of £7,650 whereas the ratepayers contended for a gross value of £6,750. The court determined the gross value at £7,500.

The ratepayers occupied the premises under an agreement made in February 1972 whereby they undertook an underlease for a term of 21 years from March 1972 at a rent of £4,500 for 1½ years, £5,250 for the next 5½ years and then £6,250 for the next seven years. There was provision for an upward revision after 14 years to the then prevailing market rent but disregarding the effect on rent of any improvements carried out by the tenants at their own expense otherwise than in pursuance of any obligation under the agreement. The tenants were required to install a suitable shop front and floor, wall and ceiling surfaces and all usual tenants' shop fixtures, fittings and decorations, electric lighting and power fittings and such other fixtures and fittings as might be necessary for the proper occupation and trading in the shop. The tenants were to pay rates and to repair and maintain the interior of the premises and also to pay a service charge which included the apportioned costs of the landlord's repairing and maintenance expenses so far as the shopping centre was concerned. In effect, the ratepayers held the premises on a full repairing and insuring lease. They had expended approximately £18,000 including £16,000 for a shop front and internal finishings, £1,200 on a sprinkler system and £800 on electrical installations.

The ratepayers' valuer supported a gross value of £6,600 and the valuation officer supported a gross value of £7,500. In their valuations there were three points of disagreement. Firstly, whether there should be any allowance for alleged disabilities; secondly, whether the tenants' expenditure was to be taken to include the sum of £1,200 spent on the sprinkler installation and, thirdly, the period over which the tenants' expenditure was to be amortised. The alleged disabilities related to the shape, size and position of the appeal hereditament within the centre, it being claimed that a jeweller (this was the ratepayers' trade) was the only likely tenant. The valuation officer merely conceded that a jeweller would be the most likely tenant but not the only one.

The tribunal (Mr. J. H. Emlyn Jones) observed that the rent represented the negotiated figure by the jeweller with all the physical factors already determined, so that any effect those factors might have on the value of the premises must clearly be reflected in the negotiated rent. The tribunal could see no justification, therefore, for an end allowance for disabilities which the ratepayers' valuer had included. So far as the sprinkler system was concerned the ratepayers' valuer submitted that this system had no value to the tenants since it protected the landlord's property, and its presence led to a reduction in the insurance premium, which under the rating hypothesis, was a landlord's responsibility. However, the tribunal stated that it had not been convinced that it was proper to exclude that item of expenditure and it did not accept the valuer's opinion that the sprinkler system had no value for the tenants since among other things, it provided some protection to their stock. The remaining point was the length of time to be allowed for the amortisation of the expenditure by the tenants so as to arrive at an annual equivalent to be added to the rent reserved. The valuation officer thought the correct term was the term of the lease, i.e. 21 years, but the ratepayers' valuer argued for 35 years because of the protection afforded to the tenants under the Landlord and Tenant Act 1954, whereby a further 14 year term could be anticipated. Attention had been drawn to an earlier decision of the Lands Tribunal, i.e. *Shell-Mex and B.P. Ltd.* v. *Harding (Valuation Officer)* (1958) where a similar argument had been rejected in respect of capital expenditure by a tenant in installing partitions. Counsel for the ratepayer conceded that the decision was against him but submitted that the question had been wrongly decided. The valuation officer relied on the case.

Looking at the realities of the situation, the tribunal thought it quite appropriate to consider some of the expenditure as being something which enhanced the value of the hereditament on a semi-permanent basis, and of which the tenant could expect to enjoy the benefit for a period longer than the 21 year term of the lease. For example, the installation of a mezzanine floor. However, the tribunal did not think that the *Shell-Mex* case could be taken as authority for the proposition that in rating cases, as opposed to revenue cases, no expenditure could in any circumstances be amortised over a period longer than the term of the lease. Conversely, there might be some expenditure for which the full term of the lease was too long a period to take. For example, in the present case much of the expenditure, including the installation of the shop front and surfaces for the floors, walls and ceiling was carried out by the tenants in pursuance of lease obligations. The lease itself provided that in calculating the rent for the purposes of possible review at the 14th year any increase in value due to tenants' improvements, apart from lease obligations, should be disregarded. The clear inference was that where the improvement was being undertaken in pursuance of a lease obligation it was to be reflected in the calculation of rent during the last seven years of the lease.

Looking, therefore, at all the circumstances in the present case the tribunal was satisfied that the ratepayers' valuer was wrong in adopting 35 years for amortisation purposes. The tribunal was of the opinion that the annual equivalent put forward by the valuation officer on the basis of 21 years' amortisation was, if anything, favourable to the ratepayers and no further reduction could be justified. The appeal was dismissed and the valuation court's decision determining a gross value of £7,500 was upheld. The ratepayers were ordered to pay the valuation officer's costs on the High Court scale failing agreement.

(*Decision July 25, 1975*)

108

CLAIM FOR REDUCED ASSESSMENT BASED ON PARTICULAR TYPE OF CENTRAL HEATING FAILS. ALSO NO REDUCTION ON ACCOUNT OF TRAFFIC AND ELECTRICITY DEPOT.

The appeal *Debell* v. *Turner* (*Valuation Officer*) concerned a house and garage at Pinner, Middlesex, following confirmation by a valuation court of a gross value of £640. The ratepayer contended that an addition for central heating was excessive, the basic gross value was excessive bearing in mind the heavy traffic, and the proximity of an electricity board depot detracted from the rental value.

The tribunal (Mr. R. C. Walmsley) did not regard the depot as a significant rental factor and on the traffic point he stressed that traffic had to be of a most unusual character before a reduction in assessment was justified. Moreover, he had been impressed by a schedule produced by the valuation officer giving particulars of eight rented houses in the locality. Four of these were on traffic routes and the other four were in quiet side roads, yet the rents of the houses fronting traffic were seen to be no lower than the rents for similar houses in quieter surroundings. The tribunal did not think that the property was affected detrimentally by traffic. The tribunal was quite satisfied that the tone of value adopted for the 1973 valuation list was sufficiently supported by the evidence of rents passing in 1971/72 and specifically, it considered that the basic gross value of the appeal property fitted comfortably within the tone of assessment for the locality.

On the central heating point, the valuation officer explained that he drew no distinction between a system which provided "topgear" heating and a system, as with the appeal property, which provided only "background" heating. The tribunal thought this to be a realistic approach. The ratepayer had failed to discharge the onus of establishing any error in the valuation court's decision. A gross value of £640 was confirmed and the appeal dismissed with £25 costs against the ratepayer.

(*Decision July 31, 1975*)

109

SEASONAL TRADING UNSUCCESSFULLY CITED. DEFINITION OF GROSS VALUE WOULD EMBRACE SUCH A FACTOR IN PARTICULAR CIRCUMSTANCES. RENTAL EVIDENCE CONCLUSIVE.

The appeal *Hapston* v. *Thompson* (*Valuation Officer*) concerned a shop and house at Cromer which, it was claimed, was used mainly for the holiday trade. The property had been assessed in the 1973 valuation list at £415 gross value but at the valuation court hearing the valuation officer had offered a reduction to £370. This was not acceptable to the ratepayer but was nevertheless approved by the valuation court. The ratepayer considered the assessment to exceed the rent at which the premises could be let, situated as they were in a secondary thoroughfare and enjoying only seasonal trade. The ratepayer was not in dispute about the part of the assessment applicable to the dwelling but he did dispute a value of £276 applicable to the shop.

The valuation officer presented evidence of rents of six other premises in secondary thoroughfares and supported his valuation by comparison with assessments of six other properties. The ratepayer was not prepared to accept that the definition of gross value was realistic when applied to a shop with only seasonal trade but the tribunal (Mr. J. D. Russell-Davis) explained that the definition in s. 19(6) of the General Rate Act 1967 required the gross value to be based on the rent payable by a hypothetical tenant from year to year and such a tenant would clearly take into account the limited trade potential when making his offer, and certainly the landlord would bear it in mind. The actual trade carried on was immaterial and the question to be asked and answered was quite simple: "Was the shop worth a rent of £5·30 per week on the basis of the statutory definition"? The tribunal concluded that the answer must be yes. The assessment was founded on adequate rental evidence and there was a fair measure of consistency in the rating assessments in the street in which the property stood and where there seemed to have been a degree of acquiescence by other ratepayers. Appeal dismissed. Costs £25 awarded against the ratepayer.

(*Decision July 31, 1975*)

110

UNDER-ASSESSMENT OF OTHER PROPERTIES NOT A MATTER OF JURISDICTION FOR THE LANDS TRIBUNAL.

The appeal *Hopkirk* v. *Dodd* (*Valuation Officer*) followed confirmation by a valuation court of a gross value of £600 on a house in Hammersmith. The ratepayer thought the assessment excessive by comparison with comparable properties. The house is on the Peterborough Estate, which, together with Moore Park Estate and the Hurlingham Estate, is regarded as an extension of the high-class residential district of Chelsea. Actual rents of seven houses in this same area formed the foundation of the area valuations in the 1973 valuation list. The ratepayer did not admit that the appeal property was worth an annual rent indicated by the gross value. The tribunal (Mr. J. D. Russell-Davis) accepted that rental evidence was scarce but considered that there was a consistency of valuation throughout the estate and a large measure of acquiescence by ratepayers in their assessments. The property would, in the tribunal's view, let readily at £600 per annum. The ratepayer's comparables were not helpful. Moreover, the tribunal was primarily concerned not with consistency of assessments generally but whether upon the evidence the appeal property assessment was correct. The ratepayer had not convinced the tribunal otherwise. Appeal dismissed. Costs £25 against the ratepayer.

(*Decision July 31, 1975*)

111

INSUFFICIENT ALLOWANCE FOR TRAFFIC NOISE AND HAZARDS.

The appeal *O'Dowd* v. *Stokes* (*Valuation Officer*) concerned an attractive well-maintained cottage in 2 acres near Kidderminster, assessed at £640 gross value. The property was built about 1740. It is on the A449 which carries much traffic and near the cottage was a bend in the road which resulted in a poor and potentially dangerous sight-line at the cottage. From the evidence and its own inspection the tribunal (Mr. Douglas Frank, President) concluded that the valuation officer had made insufficient allowance for the extent of the traffic noise and hazards compared with the comparable properties and for the generally lower quality of the environment at the cottage site. Gross value of £528 determined. Appeal allowed. Costs against the valuation officer on County Court scale 3 if not agreed.

(*Decision July 31, 1975*)

112

NO REDUCTION ON ACCOUNT OF NOISE OF AIRCRAFT FROM NEARBY AIRFIELD.

The appeal *Collier* v. *Chandler* (*Valuation Officer*) concerned a semi-detached house in High Wycombe assessed at £437 gross value, subsequently reduced on the valuation officer's recommendation to £425 by a valuation court. The ratepayer thought his assessment excessive by comparison with cited properties and he also suffered nuisance and disturbance by the noise of aircraft using a nearby airfield, principally at weekends. Amongst other things the flight path had been diverted three years ago which had tended to bring more aircraft directly over his dwelling.

The valuation officer stated that there was no rental evidence but he produced a schedule of rents and assessments of houses up and down the town. He confirmed that there had been no proposals or appeals in respect of the 1973 assessments of houses, save the appeal house, in the vicinity of the airfield.

The tribunal (Mr. E. C. Strathon) said that the merits of the comparables on which the valuation officer had relied for support of his valuation were virtually unchallenged and he accepted that the general level of assessments prevailing in the locality took account not only of various disabilities suffered, including the airfield factor, but also the advantages such as the existence of the recreation field adjacent to the appeal house. The appeal house could not be identified as a special case. Appeal dismissed, ratepayer to pay £25 costs to the valuation officer.

(*Decision August 22, 1975*)

113

CAR ACCESS BLOCKED BY POST AND CHAIN FENCE. ALTERNATIVE ACCESS THROUGH GENEROSITY OF NEIGHBOUR. VALUATION COURT REDUCTION REINSTATED.

The appeal *Gunter* (*Valuation Officer*) v. *Dodwell* followed a valuation court decision reducing the gross value of a bungalow near Ryde, Isle of Wight, from £300 to £225. The ratepayer claimed that the bungalow was unsaleable and unlettable because of posts and chains being erected across the driveway which he had thought to be his land at the time of purchase. This was not the case.

The valuation officer contended that, in the rating hypothesis, the circumstances described would not affect bidding for the house at the date of making his bid since it would be seen that there was adequate access even if made by way of other arrangements between the landlord and third parties. With some reluctance the tribunal (Mr. E. C. Strathon) found that the decision of the valuation court could not be sustained and he directed reinstatement of the gross value of £300 but no order was made as to costs.

(*Decision August 22, 1975*)

114

RISK OF FLOODING AND LACK OF SECLUSION WARRANT SMALL REDUCTION IN HOUSE ASSESSMENT.

The appeal *Blum* v. *Clegg* (*Valuation Officer*) concerned a house and garage near Stamford, Lincolnshire, following confirmation by a valuation court of a gross value of £485. The ratepayer referred to certain comparables, houses built by the same builders to the same design but in another valuation area. He also claimed that there had been changes in education structure to the detriment of his neighbourhood and there was no adequate bus service, street lighting or road maintenance. The ratepayer submitted ten schedules, five graphs and plans as well as 13 batches of other material but unfortunately in the view of the tribunal (Mr. J. R. Laird) this had been, to a large extent, wasted effort primarily because valuation was more of an art than a science and valuations could not be read off graphs, useful though they might be in special circumstances.

On the evidence the tribunal was satisfied that the valuation officer had made out his case for the tone of the list ascribed to the particular part of his valuation area and although the tribunal could well understand the ratepayer's annoyance when he saw smaller properties only four miles away valued on a different basis and assessed at £70 gross value less. This would be especially so as the particular estate enjoyed superior advantages to dwellings on the estate in which the appeal property stood and in particular so far as drainage, roads, footpaths and street lighting were concerned. The tribunal thought that each of the estates had advantages and disadvantages but had come to the conclusion that a hypothetical tenant attracted to a property in the vicinity of the appeal property would not be so interested in a similar house at Barnack.

There were two other matters referred to by the ratepayer, one being a degree of overlooking from other houses and the other being a risk of flooding. So far as the latter was concerned, he produced a comparatively recent letter from the River Authority in which it was stated that the county planning officer had not consulted the River Authority on the proposed development which included the appeal property and had he done so the Authority would have advised that development should not be permitted as the site was liable to flooding following exceptional rainfall. The tribunal thought that this letter would have alerted the hypothetical tenant to the possible risk. The tribunal was also satisfied that the ratepayer had a case on overlooking. Some allowance should be made for both the risk of flooding and the lack of seclusion and the tribunal thought that a fair gross value would be £470. Appeal allowed, £25 costs against the valuation officer.

(*Decision August 26, 1975*)

115

REJECTED GROUNDS: CENTRAL HEATING VALUE RELATED TO REVALUATION MULTIPLIER AND OVERLOOKING, NEARBY SUBSTATION, SHARED ACCESS AND ABSENCE OF MAIN DRAINAGE.

The appeal *Apperly* v. *Clee* (*Valuation Officer*) followed a valuation court reduction in the gross value of a house near Stroud, Gloucester, from £477 gross value to £453. The ratepayer was concerned about the addition in respect of central heating and that the valuation officer had not made allowances for certain disabilities.

So far as these various grounds were concerned the tribunal (Mr. R. C. Walmsley) came to the following conclusions. He was satisfied that an addition of about 4 *per cent.* for partial central heating was recognisably part of the established tone of the 1973 list for houses in the particular locality and the ratepayer's arithmetical challenge was rejected. So far as overlooking was concerned the evidence of the valuation officer was accepted, that assessments of houses in the locality had not been pitched any higher because of an open view so nothing having been included for a view nothing fell to be deducted when that view was partly lost.

The tribunal did not regard the presence of a small substation to have any significant rental disadvantage and equally the tribunal saw no rental significance in the fact that there was a shared angled entrance to garages. On the question of the lack of main drainage the tribunal noted the words of a local valuation court decision, that in all the cases where the evidence showed septic tanks to be functioning efficiently, the valuation court had approved the valuation officer's practice of not making any allowance so far as the lack of main drainage was concerned. As the valuation officer had conceded a reduction to £445 gross value the appeal was allowed to that extent and £25 costs were awarded against the ratepayer.

(*Decision August 27, 1975*)

116

DEVELOPMENT TAKES AWAY A VIEW. NO ADDITION MADE ON ACCOUNT OF THE VIEW, SO NO DEDUCTION WHEN IT IS LOST.

The appeal *Re Corser* (*Valuation Officer*) concerned a bungalow at Winchcombe, Gloucester, following a valuation court decision to reduce a gross value of £425 to £410. The issue concerned the effect of development and the loss of a view but the valuation officer confirmed that nothing had been included in the assessment of the appeal property by reason of its former fine view so nothing fell to be deducted when that view no longer existed. The tribunal (Mr. R. C. Walmsley) allowed the appeal and ordered restoration of a gross value of £425.

(*Decision August 27, 1975*)

117

UNATTRACTIVE SURROUNDINGS AND POOR AMENITIES JUSTIFY REDUCTION IN ASSESSMENT OF NEW HOUSE.

The appeal *Miller* v. *Corser* (*Valuation Officer*) concerned the assessment of a house near Cheltenham, the assessment of which was £575 gross value as proposed by the valuation officer and following consideration by the valuation court. The valuation officer stated that there was no direct rental evidence so the question fell to be resolved, stated the tribunal (Mr. R. C. Walmsley), by reference to the settled assessments of other houses in the locality. There was a problem in respect of one of the ratepayer's comparables because the assessment was still under consideration by way of appeal so it was not possible to use that as any kind of yardstick. The tribunal noted that the assessments of a group of 12 modern detached houses which both the ratepayer and the valuation officer regarded as comparable presented useful evidence. The tribunal thought that the surroundings of the appeal property to be comparatively unattractive and that the property lacked amenities. It was approached by way of a long and narrow country lane, the nearest bus route was nearly three miles away, the nearest school more than a mile away and there was no gas, no pavements or street lighting. Having regard to all the evidence the tribunal settled a gross value of £550 and allowed the appeal with £10 costs against the valuation officer.

(*Decision August 27, 1975*)

118

VALUATION COURT'S LARGE REDUCTIONS ON ACCOUNT OF GROSS NUISANCES ON LAND USED BY GIPSIES REDUCED ON APPEAL.

Five appeals in *McLean* (*Valuation Officer*) v. *Hubble and Others* concerned houses in York where appreciable reductions had been made by a valuation court ranging from £87 gross value to £62 gross value on original gross values ranging from £193 to £274. The valuation officer subsequently sought restoration of his original figures but in three cases he now supported small reductions of £10 gross value in two cases and £7 in another.

It was not disputed that the locality was a pleasant one but nearby there was an area of open land owned by the local authority across which there was a footpath leading to a river. On the western edge of this particular land there were two areas, one owned by the local authority and the other owned by a private individual. Both of these were used as caravan sites by gipsies and other travelling folk. For a long period up to 1965 the privately owned land housed three caravans but thereafter a planning permission was sought for 15 caravans and following the lodging of an appeal against the planning authority's refusal, the planning authority accepted that there had been existing use rights so the appeal did not proceed. At the beginning of 1975 an attempt had been made to close the land owned by the local authority. This had been abortive in spite of the erection of bollards and the dumping on the site of a large amount of rubble. Therefore, part of the site seemed to have been rendered unusable and at the date of the hearing ten caravans remained on the local authority owned land and 20 on the privately owned land. It was not seriously disputed that at various times, particularly in the winter, the sites had been grossly overcrowded by up to as many as 80 caravans. The main complaints concerned nuisances by animals, noise, pollution, uncontrolled tipping, vandalism, thieving, threats, victimisation and intimidation. All the respondents claimed that conditions were intolerable and tended to become worse in the winter months. The valuation court said that the environment presented a situation which no hypothetical tenant would be prepared to tolerate.

In his evidence the valuation officer presented three examples of other environmental disabilities where the courts had given much smaller reductions. These included a brewery and loading yard, a working men's club and a plant hire depot.

The tribunal (Mr. J. D. Russell-Davis) said that both sites presented an appearance of extreme squalor and devastation. It needed little imagination to accept that there was a gross environmental nuisance. So far as a prospective tenant was concerned, he would no doubt learn that the planning authority had failed to secure discontinuance. The use of an alternative gipsy site was still in the balance. A further extension of use of the local authority's land might have to be conceded and there had been a complete failure to close the local authority's land as intended. The tribunal awarded gross value reductions of £40 in four cases and £45 in the remaining one. The appeal of the valuation officer was allowed to that extent but no order was made as to costs.

(*Decision September 30, 1975*)

119

PROXIMITY OF OPENCAST COAL SITE ADEQUATELY ALLOWED FOR BY VALUATION COURT. NO REDUCTION IN RESPECT OF TRAFFIC OR SETTLEMENT CRACKS.

The appeal *New* v. *Binney* (*Valuation Officer*) concerned a bungalow in Wakefield, following the determination by a valuation court of a gross value of £430. The ratepayer considered that to be excessive by comparison with other properties in the vicinity. There was heavy traffic, dirt and noise from an opencast coal site, the partial loss of a view because of a spoil heap and the house suffered from settlement. The valuation officer did not think the traffic to be exceptional but he had allowed adequately for the disability of the coal site. In the absence of rental evidence he had had regard to the assessments of four post-war detached bungalows in the locality. He also considered that the tone of the list had become established since only about 1,000 ratepayers had made proposals out of a total of about 53,000 domestic properties, and only 100 of those were still outstanding. The tribunal (Mr. J. D. Russell-Davis) was not concerned with the settlement cracks since that would be the hypothetical landlord's responsibility, the traffic was not exceptional, in the tribunal's view an adequate allowance had been made for the opencast site. The ratepayer had not persuaded the tribunal that the gross value of £430 was other than fair. Appeal dismissed. Ratepayer to pay £25 costs.

(*Decision September 30, 1975*)

120

TRIBUNAL INCREASES ALLOWANCES FOR OLD-FASHIONED SHOP PREMISES.

The appeal *Newman* v. *Baker* (*Valuation Officer*) concerned a shop and premises in Godalming, assessed at £1,300 gross value, a figure confirmed by the local valuation court. The ratepayer thought the figure to be too high, excessive by comparison with other properties but only so far as the trading part of the premises was concerned. An offer to reduce the gross value to £1,200 from the valuation officer was declined by the ratepayer. The valuation officer supported that figure before the tribunal (Mr. J. D. Russell Davis). The valuation officer's basis of assessment rested on the rents of five nearby properties and others which were less comparable. These justified a zone A figure of £20. The tribunal had heard nothing to show that this was excessive. There had been a fair measure of acquiescence by ratepayers in the shopping area basis of assessment. So far as the appeal property was concerned there were two differing display fronts, a narrow opening and different floor levels. The valuation officer's allowance of 10 *per cent.* was insufficient. The tribunal increased it to 17½ *per cent.* and determined a gross value of £1,130. Appeal allowed to that extent. Costs of £68·50 awarded against the valuation officer to cover the ratepayer's expenses on plans, photographs, travelling and the statutory fees.

(*Decision September 30, 1975*)

121

CONSIDERABLE REDUCTION IN ASSESSMENT TO REFLECT OCCUPIER'S RESPONSIBILITY FOR OPERATING SLUICE GATES AT FREQUENT INTERVALS TO GUARD AGAINST FLOODING.

The appeal *Eccles* v. *Hanford* (*Valuation Officer*) concerned a house at Padworth, Berkshire, assessed in the 1973 valuation list at £761 gross value. The valuation officer had offered a reduction to £700 but this was not accepted. Before the valuation court hearing the valuation officer offered a reduction to £640 gross value. Subsequently the court reduced the gross value to £615. The property was on the northern bank of the River Kennet and within the curtilage of the property there were seven sluice gates. Every time the flow of water changed these seven gates had to be re-set to avoid the risk of flooding. Sometimes there had to be three changes a day. Additionally there were three sluice gates on an adjoining property, presently unoccupied, so that the appellant ratepayer had to ensure supervision of these gates too. Each gate weighed about half a ton. To turn the handle to open each gate properly involved 190 turns. The tribunal (Mr. V. G. Wellings) said it was unrealistic to expect the hypothetical landlord or any person other than the occupier of the subject property to operate the gates. It was a most onerous burden. A valuer for the ratepayer spoke to a gross value of £336. The valuation officer questioned if the sluice gate responsibility rested on the hypothetical occupier, but even if it did the valuation court's allowance was adequate. The tribunal preferred the evidence of the ratepayer's valuer. The valuation officer's comparables were not helpful. The tribunal could not regard the operation of the sluice gates as the hypothetical landlord's obligation. The gates might well be plant and machinery and as such not part of the rateable hereditament but that point had no relevance to the disability arising from the gates. Appeal allowed. Gross value of £425 determined. Valuation officer to pay the appellant ratepayer £54 costs.

(*Decision October 1, 1975*)

122

BUNGALOW APPEAL FAILS ON GROUNDS OF COMPARISONS AND DISABILITIES DUE TO STRUCTURE AND LOCATION.

The appeal *Stewart* v. *Page* (*Valuation Officer*) concerned a bungalow near Wendover assessed at £550 in the 1973 valuation list but reduced by a valuation court to £510. The ratepayer thought that even then the assessment was excessive by comparison with other properties in the locality.

The property was approached by an unmade track about 200 metres in length from a parish road. The disabilities cited referred to the absence of public transport or nearby shops, limited milk deliveries and refuse collections, noise from a farming contractors, corrosion due to a nearby salt tip, inaccessible cesspool and poor insulation of the main room in the bungalow. The ratepayers sought a gross value of £380. The valuation officer testified that his valuation list for bungalows in the area could be traced back to rent returns for two bungalows, but in the ratepayers' view these were not comparable. The tribunal (Mr. V. G. Wellings) said that the ratepayers had failed to show that the court decision was wrong. Appeal dismissed. Ratepayers to pay £25 costs.

(*Decision October 1, 1975*)

123

SHOP OPERATED FROM FRONT ROOM OF BUNGALOW. TRIBUNAL CONCEDES REDUCTION IN ASSESSMENT ON ACCOUNT OF ISOLATED POSITION, SETTING BACK OF PREMISES AND SMALL WINDOW.

The appeal *Harvey* v. *Alexander* (*Valuation Officer*) concerned premises in Rayleigh, described in the new valuation list as "shop, bungalow and garage", assessed at £750 gross value. A valuation court reduced this figure to £590. The front room of the premises was used as a retail shop. The ratepayer complained that his forecourt was used for unauthorised parking, the accommodation was poor and the room floors were on different levels. The parties had agreed the total value for the office and garage and the tribunal (Mr. W. H. Rees) was satisfied with the valuation officer's figure for the living accommodation. So far as the shop space was concerned the tribunal took account of the isolation, setting back and small window space. It was thought that the unauthorised parking was balanced by the convenience to the appellant of the parking space. Appeal allowed. Gross value reduced to £535. Costs in a sum of £9·50 awarded against the valuation officer.

(*Decision October 13, 1975*)

124

NO ALLOWANCE BASED ON COMPARABLES, INADEQUATE CENTRAL HEATING, EFFECTS OF TREE ROOTS AND PHYSICAL DEFECTS. SMALL ALLOWANCE FOR STEEP DRIVE.

The appeal *Knight* v. *Canavon* (*Valuation Officer*) together with a cross appeal concerned a house in Wolverhampton. A valuation court had reduced the gross value from £427 to £398. The ratepayer complained that he had not agreed the accommodation area with the valuation officer and that a diminished vehicle access was a source of potential damage to both the garage and vehicle. The valuation officer sought reinstatement of the original gross value. The ratepayer sought a gross value of £222. He referred to tree root growth, a curved drive and building defects. The valuation officer gave details of the rents of four houses in the same locality. The ratepayer submitted a list of eight houses in the locality and pointed out examples of uneven treatment to properties in the new valuation list, but the tribunal did not agree that differences in assessment in the old valuation list should necessarily be repeated in the new list. The tribunal (Mr. W. H. Rees) did not think that the ratepayer's view about an allowance for the steepness of the drive was correct, but saw no reason for upsetting the valuation court's allowance of a small increase because of a front porch. There was nothing wrong with the valuation officer's figure for central heating and the tree roots did not warrant any deduction from the value. There were cracks in the walls, springing of pipe joints and ill-fitting doors, the result of some settlement. There was no evidence of structural danger. There was an inherent defect but not sufficient to warrant a deduction from the gross value. Valuation officer's appeal allowed to the extent of substituting a gross value of £424. Ratepayer's appeal dismissed. Costs £30 awarded against the ratepayer. The ratepayer had taken up much time in submitting documents relating to measurements and assessments which might have been avoided if he had troubled to agree the facts with the valuation officer.

(*Decision October 13, 1975*)

125

VALUATION COURT'S DEDUCTION INCREASED ON ACCOUNT OF OVERLOOKING FROM NEIGHBOURING HOUSES ON HIGHER LEVEL.

The appeal *Wilson* v. *Whyment* (*Valuation Officer*) concerned the assessment of a house in Liphook, the gross value of which had been reduced from £345 to £325 by a valuation court. Two houses had been built on a higher level at the rear of the appeal property and this resulted in some overlooking. The valuation officer had offered a gross value reduction of £15 both before and at the court hearing, but now accepted the court's allowance of £20 gross value. The dispute before the tribunal (Mr. E. C. Strathon) was the quantum of allowance on account of the building of the two houses. The tribunal did not think the court had allowed enough for this disadvantage. A reduction of £35 was more realistic. Gross value reduced to £310. Costs £5 awarded against the valuation officer.

(*Decision October 16, 1975*)

126

FURTHER REDUCTION, BEYOND VALUATION OFFICER'S PROPOSITION, MADE BY TRIBUNAL ON ACCOUNT OF NEARBY ACCESS ROAD FOR SUBSTANTIAL DEVELOPMENT SCHEME.

The appeal *Ashcroft* v. *Braxton* (*Valuation Officer*) concerned the assessment of a bungalow at High Wycombe, assessed in the new valuation list at £496 gross value. The ratepayer and valuation officer agreed that the gross value should be reduced to £405 and this basis of agreement was subsequently accepted by the valuation court. However, the ratepayer had an unsettled second proposal and sought a further reduction on fresh grounds. Primarily these related to the making of a new road directly opposite the appeal dwelling. This was presently used by lorries carrying materials for the development of a large housing estate, and would eventually be serving that estate. A valuation court confirmed the gross value of £405. There was claimed to be noise, dust and dirt and these inconveniences would be likely to continue into 1977. The valuation officer explained that in the built-up area of High Wycombe hereditaments suffered from disabilities such as hills, sloping sites, heavily trafficked roads, noise and smell from factories and the intermingling of residential, commercial and industrial properties. The tribunal (Mr. J. R. Laird) said that such disadvantages as he had found to exist could not be regarded as transient or temporary even in the rating hypothesis of a tenancy from year to year. A reduction to £390 gross value was warranted while the effective part of the new estate was under construction. Costs £10 awarded against the valuation officer.

(*Decision October 17, 1975*)

127

BUILDING DEVELOPMENT NEARBY JUSTIFIES A TEN *PER CENT*. ASSESSMENT REDUCTION.

The appeal *Steward* v. *Ardern* (*Valuation Officer*) concerned a house near Great Yarmouth, assessed at £146 gross value in the 1973 valuation list, a figure confirmed by a valuation court. The ratepayer had sought a reduction to £102. He complained about the loss of amenity and privacy as a result of the building of a new estate. He also thought that reductions in rating assessments had been made for lesser reasons. It was also out of date that the valuation officer should argue that old and new assessments and percentage increases had no relevance. The tribunal (Mr. J. Stuart Daniel) thought the inferences on temporary disabilities in other villages were too intangible and uncertain. The tribunal could not heed arguments about old and new list contrasts. However, on the question of the new nearby estate the tribunal noted that until recently the land in question was meadow land. The valuation officer had been short of rental evidence but he had had regard to the assessments of comparable properties and the valuation list had by now become established. However, the tribunal, commenting on the building development near the appeal property, said that the hypothetical tenant was not stone deaf and came to the conclusion that such a tenant would seek and obtain a rent reduction on account of this development. Ten *per cent*. reduction made. Gross value fixed at £130. Appeal allowed. Costs £10 awarded against the valuation officer.

(*Decision October 17, 1975*)

128

NO REDUCTION FOR TWO GRASS STRIPS USED AS AIRFIELD. VALUATION OFFICER'S OFFER BEFORE VALUATION COURT HEARING AN ERROR OF JUDGMENT.

The appeal *Sheffield* v. *Millwood* (*Valuation Officer*) concerned a house near Ashford, Kent, assessed at £320 gross value, a figure confirmed by a valuation court. About a mile away were two grass landing strips constituting an airfield, known locally as Headcorn or Shenley. The airfield was owned by a local farmer and was a licensed aerodrome. Operating there were a flying club and a parachute club. Aircraft were serviced and the aerodrome also provided a base for a firm of crop sprayers. The valuation officer confirmed that there had been no similar appeals. Only light aircraft used the airfield, there were no facilities for night flying and the take-off direction was away from the appeal property. He did not consider that the rental value of the appeal property would be affected by the airfield. The ratepayer accepted that his assessment was reasonable as at April 1973, but conditions so far as the use of the airport had greatly changed since then, something which the valuation officer had not appreciated. However, this operated against the ratepayer because his proposal had been made in 1973. In that sense the tribunal (Mr. R. C. Walmsley) noted, the ratepayer's own evidence was fatal to his appeal. Gross value confirmed at £320. Costs £25 awarded against the ratepayer. One interesting fact emerged during the proceedings. It seemed that a representative of the valuation officer had offered a reduction of £20 in the gross value when he had called prior to the valuation court hearing. That offer was now, on reflection, an error of judgment. Disappointing to the ratepayer but not a matter for criticism of the valuation officer in the context of the present appeal.

(*Decision October 22, 1975*)

129

ASSESSMENT REDUCTION ON ACCOUNT OF ADJOINING UNTIDY NURSERY.

The appeal *Clark* v. *Beasley* (*Valuation Officer*) concerned a house near Wolverhampton, the occupier of which complained about the depreciating effect of a nursery which adjoined the house. The erection of unsightly greenhouses, the use of low grade fuel excessive in sulphur, litter and the building of an unsightly bungalow. A valuation court had reduced the gross value from £740 to £700. The valuation officer accepted the court's decision and thought that a hypothetical tenant coming fresh on the scene in April 1973 would know that the action which the appellant had taken in complaining to the authorities, would be available to him too. The tribunal (Mr. W. H. Rees) thought that the effect of the nursery was substantial but not as devastating as the ratepayer's case indicated. Appeal allowed. Gross value of £680 determined. Costs £12 against the valuation officer.

(*Decision October 28, 1975*)

130

UNSUCCESSFUL APPEAL BASED ON DISTURBANCE AND NUISANCE.

The appeal *Davies* v. *Bailey* (*Valuation Officer*) concerned a house at Stoke-on-Trent, assessed for the first time at £232 gross value, reduced by a valuation court to £216. The ratepayer complained about disturbance from a public house almost opposite, disturbance from building operations, the erection of local authority bungalows opposite as well as almost adjoining, vacant sites used for unauthorised tipping, childrens' playground, car parking and bonfires. In addition there was the odour and litter associated with a fried fish shop nearby and the roadway and pavements were in poor shape as a result of the building operations. The valuation officer pointed out how general were some of the disadvantages in an industrial community. He advanced evidence of seven rented properties and the assessments on seven others. Appeal dismissed. Costs £30 against the ratepayer. Tribunal (Mr. W. H. Rees).

(*Decision October 28, 1975*)

131

SHARP REDUCTION ON FLAT ASSESSMENT IN AN EXTREME STATE OF DILAPIDATION.

The appeal *Black* v. *Oliver* (*Valuation Officer*) concerned the assessment of a first-floor flat in a two-storey house in North Kensington. A gross value of £260 appeared in the 1973 valuation list but a valuation court reduced this to £100. The flat was considered by the court to have been in a deplorable state of repair. The ratepayer considered the flat to be unfit for human habitation, she had been subjected to considerable harassment from a family living in overcrowded conditions on the ground floor and, in fairness, the assessment ought to be reduced to nil. So far as harassment went the tribunal (Mr. J. D. Russell-Davis) pointed out that the remedy lay elsewhere. The flat was indeed in an extreme state of dilapidation. Defective windows, dampness, rot to architraves, floorboards and joists, a large hole in the floor, defective wall and ceiling plaster, no hot water, collapsed sink, broken w.c. cistern and no electricity supply due to unsafe wiring. The valuation officer conceded that the state of disrepair went further than that which the hypothetical landlord would expect to carry out before granting a tenancy, but the present occupier stood to pay an inclusive statutory rent equivalent to £113 gross value. The tribunal was in no doubt that the flat was unfit and dangerous for occupation. The rent was suspect. The tenant was anxious to retain protection under the Rent Acts and if occupation was continued there was a chance of re-housing when a closing order was eventually made. The tribunal also thought that a prospective tenant would have regard to the likelihood of a closing order being made within a short time. Gross value of £70 determined. Appeal allowed. No costs asked for or awarded.

(*Decision October 29, 1975*)

132

MODERNISATION OF DWELLING AND EXISTENCE OF GARAGE OVERLOOKED IN OLD VALUATION LIST. REDUCTION MADE BY TRIBUNAL BY REGARDING THE VALUE OF THE GARAGE AS INCLUDED IN THE APPEALED ASSESSMENT.

The appeal *Rank* v. *Baker* (*Valuation Officer*) concerned a house at Cranleigh, the gross value of which had been reduced by a valuation court from £510 to £425. This was on the recommendation of the valuation officer. Nevertheless, even this figure was five times the old list figure, yet no improvements or alterations had been done. The valuation officer explained that up to the 1950's the occupiers of country cottages were from the lower income groups. But later these cottages became much sought after for occupation by higher income groups. So far as the appeal cottage was concerned modernisation would have been carried out shortly after 1962 but the valuation officer was not informed. Had he been aware of the renovation of the appeal property then the 1963 list assessment would have been increased, so that the 1973 list figure would not have come as such a surprise. The tribunal (Mr. R. C. Walmsley) thought that although sparse the rental evidence supported the tone of valuation adopted for the type of hereditament which comprised the appeal property. The valuation officer's figure of £450 gross value had been pitched a little high and that a more appropriate figure would be £425. The valuation court's determination was not excessive. But the valuation list description required correction from "house" to "house and garage". Appeal dismissed. No costs award in view of the circumstances.

(*Decision November 4, 1975*)

133

QUESTION OF ASSUMED ERECTION OF FENCE. ABSENCE OF FENCE A TEMPORARY FACTOR LIKELY TO BE REMEDIED BY THE TENANT.

The appeal *Roberts* v. *Turner* (*Valuation Officer*) concerned a house at Harrow, assessed at £465 gross value, but reduced by a valuation court to £440. The ratepayer sought a reduction on the grounds of traffic and the use of a sports ground at the rear of his property. The Tribunal (Mr.

R. C. Walmsley) found no substance in that ground relating to the traffic. The sports ground was well used, with a busy car park. The valuation court's reduction of £25 seemed to the ratepayer to be inadequate. The valuation officer assumed that the landlord would put up a fence along the back boundary of the ratepayer's garden in order to maintain the rental value. The tribunal (Mr. R. C. Walmsley) recalled an earlier tribunal decision in point and explained that with an adverse factor of a temporary nature a year to year tenant could reasonably be expected to set about remedying matters. In either event the present appellant was not assisted. The court's decision seemed to the tribunal to have been reasonable. Appeal dismissed. Costs £25 against the ratepayer.

(*Decision November 4, 1975*)

134

STREET PARKING AN UNMITIGATED NUISANCE. ASSESSMENT ADDITION FOR GARAGE AND ACCESS REDUCED ON ACCOUNT OF OBSTRUCTION.

The appeal *Smith v. Thornton* (*Valuation Officer*) concerned a house at Barkingside, Essex, following confirmation by a valuation court of a gross value of £365. The dispute centred on the question of a reduction because a shared driveway was subject to obstruction by parked cars in the roadway. There was considerable parking on account of the nearby bingo hall. The ratepayer had difficulty in getting into his own garage, or out of it. The valuation officer thought the parking hazard something which might befall any householder and any disadvantage was offset by convenience in situation in relation to transport and shopping. The tribunal (Mr. R. C. Walmsley) found there was substance in the appeal. The width of the roadway, the use of street parking, the absence of restrictions on street parking and the use every day of the week of the hall for bingo meant that the obstruction was an unmitigated nuisance. Reduction to £350 gross value. Appeal allowed. Costs £10 against the valuation officer.

(*Decision November 4, 1975*)

135

ASSESSMENT REDUCTION FOR OLD, COLD AND DRAUGHTY VILLAGE HALL.

The appeal *Downe Village Residents Association* v. *Valentine* (*Valuation Officer*) concerned the assessment of the village hall at Downe, near Orpington, Kent. In the 1973 valuation list this stood at £285 gross value, ten times greater than the old list figure. A valuation court reduced this to £180. The ratepayers had declined an offer by the valuation officer to reduce the gross value to £150. Emphasis was laid on the hall being old, cold and draughty and the facilities generally inadequate. Inefficient heating, dark kitchen, a single lavatory, no car park, and no stage. There was no rental evidence so the question was one of comparability of assessments of similar properties. Seven other halls were taken into account by the valuation officer. The tribunal (Mr. J. Stuart Daniel) thought that all the disadvantages of the appeal property distinguished it from others. The gross value should be further reduced to £120. Appeal allowed to that extent. Costs £10 awarded against the valuation officer.

(*Decision November 6, 1975*)

136

RATEPAYER'S ADMISSION OF RENTAL VALUES RESULTS IN DISMISSAL OF APPEAL, NOTWITHSTANDING TRIBUNAL'S CRITICISM OF BOTH THE VALUATION OFFICER AND THE VALUATION COURT.

The appeal *Eyre & Others* v. *Benson* (*Valuation Officer*) concerned the assessments of five caravans at Falmouth, with gross values ranging from £100 to £180. The valuation officer said she was content to rely on s. 20 of the General Rate Act 1967 (valuation according to the tone of the valuation list) indicating the extent to which assessments of residential caravans had been accepted, agreed or settled. The tribunal (Mr. Douglas Frank, President) pointed out that that section had nothing to do with evidence, there was direct evidence and the tribunal had been deprived of the benefit of such evidence. The valuation court also came under criticism for having set up the correct statutory basis of assessment, they did not apply it, or did not say so in giving reasons for their decisions. The tribunal had been concerned to the point of considering adjourning the hearing so that the valuation officer could produce the factual evidence. Unfortunately for the appellants the spokesman, acting as both advocate and witness for all the appellants, conceded that the gross values as determined by the valuation court would not exceed the amount of rent paid. The tribunal, offered this admission, had no alternative but to dismiss the appeal. There was, however, no costs award.

(*Decision November 6, 1975*)

137

RATEPAYER'S FIGURE FOR DISABILITIES ALLOWANCE, SLIGHTLY IN EXCESS OF ALLOWANCE BY VALUATION COURT, ADOPTED BY TRIBUNAL.

There were two appeals in *Bentall* v. *Dewar* (*Valuation Officer*) concerning a house at Tonbridge. The 1973 valuation list included a gross value of £445 for the property. Following structural alterations the valuation officer later proposed a gross value of £501. Later he made a further proposal to increase the figure to £521 on the grounds that the lower figure of assessment was incorrect and insufficient. In due course the valuation court determined gross values of £486 on the first proposal and £506 on the second. The ratepayer appealed on grounds related to comparability with adjacent properties, absence of full central heating, and inconsistency in the valuation court's decision, and thought that the allowance by the valuation court for these disabilities to be too small. The valuation officer submitted details of three rented houses and details of 33 houses' assessments. He sought a gross value of £506 on each appeal. The tribunal (Mr. W. H. Rees) thought the house suffered from a poor position, but did not find that such inconsistencies as there might be in the 33 assessments invalidated comparisons. The tribunal also saw no reason why the valuation officer should not amend figures he put forward at the valuation court. The tribunal concurred with the valuation officer that attempts to value houses by reference to capital value should be rejected in this instance. Gross value of £500 determined in respect of each proposal since the parties agreed that there was no material difference in the property between the dates of the two proposals. However, the valuation officer had not appealed against the valuation court's figure of £486 in one instance, so that figure must stand. But in any case the decision on the later proposal would overtake the first proposal, so effectively a figure of £500 would apply throughout. Costs £20 against the valuation officer.

(*Decision November 10, 1975*)

138

NO REDUCTION OF DWELLINGHOUSE ASSESSMENT ON GROUNDS OF MERGED BEDROOMS, ABSENCE OF LEAN-TO STRUCTURES AND OVERLOOKING WINDOW.

The appeal *Husbands* v. *Owens* (*Valuation Officer*) concerned a house in Addiscombe, Croydon, assessed at £280 gross value, a figure confirmed by a valuation court. The ratepayer complained that the house had been assessed as having five rooms, but two had been converted into one. Other comparable houses had additions and lean-to structures, but his had none. There was also overlooking from a neighbour's window. The valuation officer cited seven comparables in the same road, four of which would involve reconsideration as they had had bathrooms formed. The tribunal (Mr. W. H. Rees) considered that the number of rooms had no significance, as the floor area was unchanged. Nothing had been added to the assessments of adjoining houses on account of lean-to structures. The window disadvantage was too small to affect the annual value. Appeal dismissed. Costs £25 against the ratepayer.

(*Decision November 10, 1975*)

139

VALUATION COURT'S ALLOWANCES FOR NOISE FROM SHUNTING YARD, OVERHEAD ELECTRIC CABLES AND STATE OF ROAD ENDORSED.

The appeal *Rushton* v. *Townend* (*Valuation Officer*) concerned a bungalow and garage in Horbury, Wakefield, assessed at £520 gross value, reduced by a valuation court to £490. The court thought this reduction justified in view of the disabilities from a shunting yard and high tension electricity cables. The ratepayer sought a further reduction, referring to comparable properties and a poor access road. The valuation officer submitted an analysis of the rents and assessments of four bungalows within reasonable reach of the appeal property, the assessments of six bungalows in the same locality and a house and three bungalows in a different valuation area. He agreed that the valuation list had been built up from the rents for smaller properties. The valuation list had been generally accepted and less than one *per cent.* of properties in Horbury were still the subject of outstanding proposals. The tribunal (Mr. W. H. Rees) was not convinced that the valuation court's allowance was inadequate and dismissed the appeal. No order as to costs as there were special circumstances.

(*Decision November 10, 1975*)

140

EVIDENCE OF SHOP RENTS AND ACCEPTED ASSESSMENTS PREFERRED TO ALTERNATIVE CALCULATIONS.

The appeal *Clinkard Ltd.* v. *Hodgson* (*Valuation Officer*) concerned shop premises in the main shopping centre of Northallerton, assessed at £2,650 gross value, reduced to £2,500 by a valuation court. The ratepayer, on appeal, contended for a zone A price of £20 per square metre, the valuation officer contending for £25. For the ratepayer it was argued that the shop position was a secondary one, but this could not be supported by reference to relevant rental evidence or to an analysis of assessments. For the ratepayer certain calculations were offered in evidence, one being based on the aggregate lease rent payable over ten years, suitably adjusted for the repairing obligation by the lessee, the intention being to claim that the amount to be invested each year to produce that aggregate in ten years represented the gross value, subject to an addition to reflect the lessee's obligation to fit out the premises. Another calculation was based on the concept of a profit rental, which in turn depressed the amount of the annual value. The valuation officer supported his assessment by reference to six shop assessments and the rents of five shops, all on the same side of the street as the appeal property. He conceded that the appeal property was not in the best position, but he had allowed for that. The tribunal

(Mr. W. H. Rees) preferred the valuation officer's figures, based as they were on rents and assessments, and rejected the calculations presented on behalf of the ratepayer. Appeal dismissed. Costs £30 against the ratepayer.

(*Decision November 11, 1975*)

141

UNSUCCESSFUL CLAIM THAT BLOCK OF FLATS ADVERSELY AFFECTED MIND OF HYPOTHETICAL TENANTS OF PRIVATE HOUSES.

The appeal *Hill and Another* v. *Griffiths* (*Valuation Officer*) concerned two houses in Thornbury, Avon, following confirmation by a valuation court of gross values of £294 and £286 respectively. Both ratepayers sought reductions on account of the erection, in 1974, of a three-storey block of 15 flats nearby. This involved some element of overloking, car noises and car lights. There was also the loss of a view following construction of the flats. The local environment had been changed. The valuation officer did not consider that the presence of the flats would have the disadvantageous effect mentioned. The tribunal (Mr. E. C. Strathon) did not think a tenant, coming fresh to an established residential area, would be deterred by finding there is a three-story block of flats such as the one in question. The court had not come to a wrong conclusion. Appeals dismissed. Costs £25 against each ratepayer.

(*Decision November 14, 1975*)

142

FACTORS INCLUDING ASBESTOS WALL, CESSPOOL DRAINAGE, RELATIVE REVALUATION INCREASE AND PARKING OF COACHES IN RESPECT OF WAREHOUSE ASSESSMENT APPEAL, UNACCEPTABLE OR UNCONVINCING.

The appeal *Trevor Toys Ltd.* v. *Aplin* (*Valuation Officer*) concerned a warehouse in Worthing, built on a trading estate in 1970, and assessed at £2,400 gross value. It was used for the bulk storage of toys. The ratepayers sought a reduction to £1,714 gross value on the grounds that the revaluation increase was excessive in relation to other properties, the premises had access only to a cesspit, one of the warehouse walls was asbestos and there was a dangerous entry to the premises. The tribunal (Mr. J. R. Laird) did not consider a reduction warranted in respect of the asbestos wall, thought a £20 allowance sufficient so far as drainage disabilities were concerned, pointed out that comparative revaluation increases were irrelevant where adequate rental evidence was available as in the present appeal and was satisfied that occasional parking of a motor coach on the public highway in front of the subject property would not affect the rental value in the rating context. Appeal dismissed. Costs £30 against the ratepayers.

(*Decision November 14, 1975*)

143

APPEAL ON FLAT ASSESSMENT MULTIPLIER ON REVALUATION HELD TO BE MISCONCEIVED.

The appeal *Hartley* v. *Phillips* (*Valuation Officer*) concerned a flat in Shortlands, Bromley, assessed at £335 gross value, reduced by a valuation court to £325. The ratepayer's sole ground of appeal was that the assessment had been increased by about 200 *per cent.* on revaluation, whereas the flat below had suffered an increase of only about 150 *per cent.* Both flats formed part of a three-storey detached house, several of such houses in the locality having been converted into three self-contained flats. The valuation officer provided details of five comparable flats. The tribunal (Mr. R. C. Walmsley) thought the ratepayer's grounds to be misconceived. If the effect of a revaluation was to produce uniform increases of assessment as between any two hereditaments, the whole exercise would be unnecessary and pointless. Appeal dismissed. Costs £25 against the ratepayer.

(*Decision November 18, 1975*)

144

LONDON FLAT. UNSUCCESSFUL APPEAL ON GROUNDS OF TRAFFIC NOISE, STREET VENDORS AND COMPARABILITY.

The appeal *Woolf* v. *Mooney* (*Valuation Officer*) concerned a second floor flat in north west London, one of a seven-storey block built between 1969 and 1971, assessed at £1,825 gross value in the new valuation list, confirmed by a valuation court. The ratepayer considered the assessment to be excessive by comparison with more expensive flats in the same block, increased traffic followed the opening-up of Westway and the proximity of Madame Tussaud's encouraged the presence of street vendors. The purchase prices of cited flats were offered in evidence, the ratepayer contending that there could be no better guide to relative values than the asking prices for the flats. Additionally, the revaluation increase was excessive. The valuation officer said that there was no rental evidence in the valuation area of flats in blocks the size of the subject block. Reliance had been placed on rents passing in other named blocks. On the traffic point the tribunal (Mr. E. C. Strathon) said there was abundant evidence that neither noise nor danger to children affected rental values in populous areas unless they were quite out of the ordinary. The tribunal could not find any evidence to support the contention about the proximity of Madame Tussaud's exhibition. The tribunal was satisfied from the valuation officer's analysis, presented in great detail, that the assessments of the comparable flats supported the assessment of the appeal flat. There was nothing in the ratepayer's point about the percentage increase on revaluation. The valuation court had come to a correct conclusion. Appeal dismissed. Costs £25 against the ratepayer.

(*Decision November 24, 1975*)

145

NO REDUCTION ON FLAT ASSESSMENT ON ACCOUNT OF NOISE AND NUISANCE FROM PUBLIC HOUSE, LOCAL DERELICTION AND TRAFFIC VOLUME.

The appeal *Fenner-Fownes* v. *Walker* (*Valuation Officer*) concerned a flat at Ealing Common, assessed at £490 gross value, a figure confirmed by a valuation court. For the ratepayer it was stated that customers at a nearby public house were noisy and committed nuisances in the front garden of the flat. Music from the pub could be heard in the subject flat. The road was subject to heavy traffic and the parking of vehicles. There was a derelict house opposite, entered by trespassers, and another house opposite was in multi-occupation and was also used as a car workshop. He sought a reduction of £20 in the gross value, but the valuation officer thought the existing figure to be supported by unchallenged assessments and there was no evidence of any fall in rental values on account of the matters mentioned by the ratepayer. The tribunal (Mr. W. H. Rees) agreed. Appeal dismissed. Costs £25 against the ratepayer.

(*Decision November 25, 1975*)

146

UNSUCCESSFUL APPEAL ON HOUSE ASSESSMENT BASED ON PLOT SIZE, SMALLER NEIGHBOURING DWELLINGS, INFREQUENT BUS SERVICE, NARROW ROAD AND OVER-LOOKING.

The appeal *Marguerie* v. *Salvoni* (*Valuation Officer*) concerned a house at Heswall, Wirral, following confirmation by a valuation court of a gross value of £675. However, the valuation officer subsequently conceded a reduction to £658 gross value following recalculation of the external floor area. The ratepayer was concerned about the size of the house plot and the smaller size of neighbouring houses. The bus service was infrequent and the bus stop was some distance away. Walkers used a nearby undeveloped plot to the detriment of the ratepayer's privacy. The tribunal (Mr. R. C. Walmsley) found the gross value to be in tone with the assessments of other modern detached houses in the same locality and allowed the appeal to the extent conceded by the valuation officer. The ratepayer had been aware of this concession about a month before the hearing. Costs £25 against the ratepayer.

(*Decision November 25, 1975*)

147

UNSUCCESSFUL FLAT APPEAL. ALLEGATIONS OF ARBITRARY PERCENTAGE INCREASES ON REVALUATION UNSUPPORTED. COMPARABLES CHALLENGED BY RATEPAYER. CONTROLLED RENT SUBMITTED BY RATEPAYER AS JUSTIFICATION FOR REDUCTION.

The appeal *Rubin* v. *Dutnall* (*Valuation Officer*) concerned a Hampstead flat on the top floor of a converted house. A gross value of £400 was confirmed by a valuation court. The ratepayer had not accepted an offer by the valuation officer to agree facts before the tribunal hearing and time was lost in disputation about floor area which was as stated by the valuation officer. The ratepayer argued that the valuation officer had to assess each hereditament individually. As there were, in the ratepayer's view, 31,000 flats in Hampstead, it was impossible for the valuation officer personally to carry out a task of such magnitude. He criticised the valuation officer's comparables. There was no thermal insulation to the roof so the flat was cold in winter and expensive to heat. Because of this disadvantage the ratepayer claimed that the landlord was not able to obtain a qualification certificate which would enable him to increase the present rent. The rent, therefore, was an open market rent of £123 per annum. In supporting a gross value of £400 the valuation officer cited nine other third floor flats in nearby houses. The gross value of one of them was supported by a rent fixed in the open market in 1964 of £455 per annum. In another case a registered rent supported the gross value. Additionally, he submitted a list of 30 assessments on residential properties in the immediate locality. The tribunal (Mr. W. H. Rees) said the ratepayer had been confused between services and the cost of repairs and other expenses. The ratepayer had failed to show that the valuation court's decision was incorrect. Appeal dismissed. Costs £20 against the ratepayer.

(*Decision November 25, 1975*)

148

ASSESSMENT REDUCED FURTHER THAN VALUATION COURT'S FIGURE. SETTLED ASSESSMENTS NOTED IN THE ABSENCE OF DIRECT RENTAL EVIDENCE. RATEPAYER'S FOUR PROPOSALS.

The appeal *Wilimowski* v. *Bonner* (*Valuation Officer*) constituted four separate appeals by the ratepayer which had been consolidated. A valuation court had reduced the gross value of a house in Ealing from £705 to £670. The first of the proposals by the ratepayer, in August 1973, claimed a reduction on account of proposed developments on the adjoining site, which would effectively convert the appeal property from a semi-detached to a terrace house, there would be interference with natural light, overlooking and the blocking of light to windows. In October 1973 a proposal was supported on the grounds that the present assessment was incorrect and excessive. In August 1974 it was claimed that the assessment was out of line with the general tone of the new valuation list. Another proposal dated the same day in August 1974 referred to disruption due to the nearby development. The tribunal agreed that the vicinity gave the impression of being run down. Values ascribed to a porch and bin store were considered by the tribunal (Mr. R. C. Walmsley) to be excessive. An allowance in respect of the temporary disability arising out of the adjoining development was confirmed. Clearly there was a dearth of rents. The ratepayer thought modern terrace houses to be excessively assessed in the area concerned. The tribunal said that in the absence of rental evidence the next best guide was in settled assessments of comparable properties and referred to several groups of these dealt with in evidence. Based on what were considered by the tribunal to be the best guides in such evidence a gross value of £560 was thought to be right for the appeal property. Appeal allowed. Costs against the valuation officer £25. For the record the tribunal treated as irrelevant the first proposal related to prospective disabilities. The time to contest an assessment on such grounds was when development actually took place.

(*Decision November 25, 1975*)

149

RATE INCREASES NOT A GROUND FOR APPEAL. AIRCRAFT NUISANCE COMMON TO MANY PROPERTIES NO REASON FOR TREATING ONE PROPERTY IN A DIFFERENT WAY.

The appeal *Clarke* v. *Rutherford* (*Valuation Officer*) concerned a house at Redmarley, near Ledbury, assessed at £219 gross value. The ratepayer sought a considerable reduction on the grounds that there was no garage, despite the valuation list description to the contrary, and the property was not on main drainage. A valuation court directed an amendment of the list to exclude the garage and to enter a lower gross value of £206. The difference lay in the value attributed to an asbestos and timber garage. The ratepayer also referred to the lack of amenities such as footpaths and street lighting. A comparable property was also cited in support of a reduction. Finally, the noise of aircraft was mentioned as a further justification for a reduced assessment. At the hearing it seemed that the ratepayer's main complaint was in regard to the actual rate increase he faced. The tribunal (Mr. J. R. Laird) could not accede to a reduction on that account. It agreed with the valuation officer regarding valuation in accordance with the tone of the list and was satisfied that that requirement had been met. The ratepayer had not adduced any evidence, so far as aircraft noise was concerned, why he should be singled out for special treatment. Appeal dismissed. Nominal costs £5 against the ratepayer.

(*Decision December 2, 1975*)

150

NEARBY DEVELOPMENT. VALUATION COURT'S REDUCTION APPROVED.

The appeal *Davis* v. *Bellamy* (*Valuation Officer*) concerned a house at Shurdington, near Cheltenham, assessed in the new valuation list at £203 gross value. After completion of structural alterations and additions this was increased to £410. A valuation court reduced this by 5 *per cent.* to £390 on the valuation officer's recommendation. This was to recognise the loss of annual value due to nearby development which had deprived the ratepayer of an open view. A new house had been built near the appeal property. The county council had refused planning permission but had been overruled by the Secretary of State who had given permission for the erection of an agricultural worker's dwelling. A bungalow had been intended but in fact a house was erected and of a size and nature to justify a gross value of £595. However, the valuation officer testified that the house was not assessed or entered in the valuation list as an agricultural dwelling. Enforcement notices had been served by the local planning authority in respect of unauthorised windows and unauthorised use of part of the dwelling. Two of the offending windows had subsequently been blocked up. The ratepayer also complained about heavy main road traffic, but the tribunal (Mr. J. R. Laird) agreed with the valuation court that this was a common factor to all properties fronting on to the Shurdington Road. And the traffic volume was not so out of the ordinary as to warrant an assessment reduction. The tribunal thought the 5 *per cent.* reduction by the valuation court was adequate and dismissed the appeal with £25 costs against the ratepayer.

(*Decision December 4, 1975*)

151

TRIBUNAL GIVES FURTHER REDUCTION IN ASSESSMENT ON ACCOUNT OF TRAFFIC NOISE AND ALLOTMENTS EYESORE.

The appeal *Dix* v. *Kent* (*Valuation Officer*) concerned a house in Ipswich entered in the 1973 valuation list at £650 gross value, subsequently reduced by a valuation court to £600. The various disabilities alleged by the ratepayer to justify a further reduction included traffic noise from the nearby A12, allotments involving the erection of ugly sheds, bonfires and manure heaps, a children's playground abused by older children and a car park used in connection with a church. A reduction to £522 gross value was sought. In the absence of rental evidence the valuation officer relied on the assessments of comparable properties. He had allowed in his assessment for traffic noise, had no evidence that the allotments were a nuisance and considered them, together with the playground, incidents of urban life. The tribunal (Mr. J. Stuart Daniel) thought the noise from the by-pass to be appalling, rejected the contention on the playground but thought the allotments to constitute a multi-coloured eyesore. A further 10 *per cent.* reduction was warranted. Gross value £540 determined. Costs £12 against the valuation officer.

(*Decision December 5, 1975*)

152

COUNCIL LEASED SHOPS IN THE DOLDRUMS. RENTS REDUCED AND THESE ACCEPTED AS GOOD EVIDENCE. VALUATION COURT'S REDUCTION APPROVED.

The appeal *Heap* (*Valuation Officer*) v. *Barrass* concerned a shop in Great Cornard, Suffolk. Following residential development, mainly by the local authority, a parade of lock-up shops had been built and leased on tender by the authority. Although some shops prospered there were others, including the appeal property, in the doldrums. One bankruptcy and a succession of assignments were proof of the economic problems. The local authority had acted reasonably and between 1973 and 1975 various rent reductions had been granted on the basis of disclosure of books and records. The idea was to insist on reversion to the original rent if the trading situation justified this. All the shops had been assessed at £1,000 gross value in the new valuation list. Following an assignment to him the ratepayer in the present appeal contracted to pay £750 per annum rent, but this was later reduced by the local authority to £500. A valuation court reduced the gross value to that figure. The valuation officer appealed, seeking restoration of a gross value of £750. He tendered a schedule of eight shops virtually identical with the appeal property. The revised rents reflected a council policy and were not rents fixed in the open market; they were not the best evidence for rating purposes. The tribunal (Mr. J. Stuart Daniel) found it a puzzling case. The valuation officer had tried to stabilise the situation with gross values of £750. That might be convenient but the tribunal was not sure that it was right. The tribunal was unable to satisfy itself that the valuation court's decision was wrong. Appeal dismissed. Costs £10 against the valuation officer.

(*Decision December 5, 1975*)

153

RATEPAYER'S CASE FOR ASSESSING ON QUALITY OF STRUCTURES WHEN DEALING WITH DOMESTIC PROPERTIES NOT ACCEPTED.

The appeal *Leverton* v. *Cooley* (*Valuation Officer*) concerned a bungalow at Belper, following confirmation by a valuation court of a gross value of £346. The valuation officer said that the only rental evidence available in the area comprised three 1969 rents in an inferior locality. After the new lists had been put on deposit two further rents emerged. This evidence, it was claimed, confirmed the assessment of the appeal property. Additionally, the valuation officer relied on the assessments of 22 nearby bungalows. The ratepayer contended that true comparison was by reference to the quality of building. He referred to the assessments of eight houses. He complained that it was impossible to ascertain how the assessment of any one property had been fixed except by comparison with assessments already fixed by the valuation officer on an unrevealed basis. This was nonsense and left him with no other course but to compare building quality as a basis. The tribunal (Mr. E. C. Strathon) was in no doubt in the present appeal that the valuation officer's comparables were to be preferred and there was evidence of the general acceptance by local ratepayers of the general level of assessment. The ratepayer had failed to show that the valuation court had come to a wrong conclusion. Appeal dismissed. Costs £25 against the ratepayer.

(*Decision December 5, 1975*)

154

LACK OF SERVICES. A GENERALLY SHARED DISADVANTAGE. NOT A REASON FOR REDUCING THE ASSESSMENT OF A COUNTRY HOUSE.

The appeal *Minchinton* v. *Wrapson* (*Valuation Officer*) concerned a cottage in Preston St Mary, Suffolk, a comparatively ancient building in grounds of about one and a half acres, assessed in the new list at £375 gross value. A valuation court, on the valuation officer's recommendation, reduced this to £350 on the grounds of a disfiguring corrugated roof to part of the structure. The ratepayer had complained about a long delay in bringing the matter before the valuation court. He also wished to insist on the personal presence of the valuation officer at the court hearing. Failing to secure this he elected to leave matters to the Lands Tribunal. The authorised officer of the Inland Revenue was heard in his absence. Traffic in the lane, no verges, no pavements, no lighting, poor transport, no school and other facilities far removed led the ratepayer to suggest a gross value of £200 as reasonable. The valuation officer explained his unsuccessful attempts to discuss matters with the ratepayer and supported his assessment by reference to five comparable properties. Most of the disadvantages cited were common to country folk and in any case the hypothetical tenant was not necessarily an old age pensioner without a car. The tribunal (Mr. J. Stuart Daniel) saw nothing wrong with the assessment. Appeal dismissed. Costs £25 against the ratepayer.

(*Decision December 5, 1975*)

155

THREE BEDROOM SEMI-DETACHED HOUSES NO MORE VALUABLE THAN FOUR BEDROOM HOUSES LINKED TOGETHER.

The appeals *Evans (Valuation Officer)* v. *Start and Others* covered four houses in Selsdon, South Croydon, which had been assessed for the first time at gross values ranging from £465-£480. A valuation court had reduced all these gross values to a common figure of £450 and the valuation officer sought to restore the original assessments except in the case of one at £480 which he was content to be settled at £475, due to the discovery of a small error in measurements.

During the course of the hearing it was clear that the valuation officer was contending for the same figures as those determined by the valuation court. Normally that would have resulted in the instant dismissal of the appeals but it appeared that the valuation officer had obtained further information regarding building operations subsequent to the hearing by the local valuation court. The valuation officer supported his assessments by reference to the rents and assessments of six houses at Crystal Palace. There was no evidence of rents of modern semi-detached houses. Additionally, reference was made to the assessments of 11 houses on an adjoining estate. The valuation court decision indicated a certainty that the three bedroom houses could not be let at a higher rent than the four bedroom linked houses and with that the tribunal (Mr. W. H. Rees) was in entire agreement, bearing in mind that the linked houses were 67 sq. ft. larger than the largest of the appeal properties.

The appeal in respect of all the properties was dismissed and gross values of £450 were confirmed in each case. The ratepayer in one case had not sought costs so there was no costs order. In another, the valuation officer was ordered to pay £21·60 costs to the ratepayer. No costs were ordered in the other two cases, in one instance because the valuation officer had offered a settlement at the gross value ultimately agreed well before the hearing and in the other the ratepayer had not responded to the valuation officer's appeal.

(*Decision December 9, 1975*)

156

DISPUTE ON COMPARABLES AND DIMENSIONS DECIDED IN VALUATION OFFICER'S FAVOUR.

The appeal *Parker* v. *Morton (Valuation Officer)* concerned a house at Preston. A valuation court had reduced the gross value from £340 to £330, the valuation officer having offered to reduce the assessment in that way before the court hearing. The appeal property was an an estate of about 328 dwellings of various types and the appellant contended that as the bungalow was at the far end of the estate it was in the least valuable position on a low lying site subject to mist and damp. Moreover, it was close to a brook which gave off an unpleasant smell. The ratepayer claimed that there was no rental evidence and he referred to the assessments of four houses and bungalows on the same estate and to 12 sited elsewhere.

The valuation officer had measured the first floor of the appeal property internally and had added the hypothetical thicknesses of walls so that comparisons could properly be made between bungalows and bungalows with dormer windows in the roof space. His valuation was supported by reference to an analysis of the assessments of 14 dormer windowed bungalows, ten of which were on the subject estate. He had also included four comparables in a neighbouring area and explained the reduction offered before the court hearing by reference to an area in the roof space which had been included at full charge whereas it should have been omitted. The brook, in his opinion, was irrelevant. It was 160 ft. away with a row of houses in between and from those houses only one proposal had been made.

The tribunal (Mr. W. H. Rees) said that the ratepayer's basis of comparison was false since the areas of supposedly comparable properties had been computed differently. The tribunal agreed with the valuation officer that comparables on the subject estate were to be preferred and, in any case, the tribunal preferred the valuation officer's approach both for measuring the first floor space and his adoption of two-thirds of the area to give a proper basis of comparison. The tribunal saw nothing wrong with the central heating addition and the value of the garage had been agreed. Appeal dismissed. Ratepayer to pay £30 costs.

(*Decision December 9, 1975*)

157

NO REDUCTION ON ACCOUNT OF DEVELOPMENT OF NURSERY SITE FOR HOUSING.

The appeal *Shorrock* v. *Bain* (*Valuation Officer*) concerned a house near Southport and followed confirmation by a valuation court of a gross value of £465. The issue was whether or not housing development at the rear of the appeal property warranted any reduction in a gross value agreed by the parties to be correct apart from this matter of development. The ratepayer sought a reduction of £20. A year or two ago there was a nursery at the rear of the house. Later, 14 houses were built on the site, three backing on to the appeal property. The nearest point between the new and the appeal properties was 140 to 150 ft. with a row of poplars in the ratepayer's garden forming something of a screen. The valuation officer said he had had no other proposals on the same point. He submitted details of assessments of nine houses in the same road, none of which were under attack. The value to be considered was that to a newcomer to the scene without the appellant's hindsight. The tribunal (Mr. W. H. Rees) said that the valuation officer's approach was the correct one. Appeal dismissed. No costs awarded in view of the possibility that an incorrect plan had misled the ratepayer because it was inaccurate.

(*Decision December 9, 1975*)

158

BIG REDUCTION BY VALUATION COURT GREATLY MODIFIED. SMALL PRIVATE ESTATE BASIS OF ASSESSMENT SAME AS ADJOINING COUNCIL ESTATE, BUT ALLOWING FOR DETACHMENT. TRIBUNAL FINDS OFFSETTING DISADVANTAGES COUNTER-BALANCING THE VALUE OF DETACHMENT.

In *Mundy* (*Valuation Officer*) v. *Page and Others* eight appeals arose, affecting seven houses at Cowley, Oxford. A valuation court had reduced the gross value of each by £100. The private houses formed part of an enclave of residential development. There was a nearby local authority housing estate of 2,500 houses and flats. A small self-build housing group had purchased the land for the private estate of 24 houses which the tribunal (Mr. J. R. Laird) found pleasing in appearance, a credit to those concerned. One factor in the assessing of the appeal properties was that the valuation officer regarded them as more detached than semi-detached because each house of a pair was linked only by their single storey utility rooms. The valuation officer did not seek full reinstatement of the original gross values. His proposition was for gross values £40 less than the original figures. It was noted that on the north of the enclave there was a timber merchant's sawmill and premises, on the south and west council houses and on the east an electricity grid transformer station. The valuation officer contended that it would be wrong if the appealed assessments were lower than those of adjacent council houses. The tribunal agreed. It was clear that the revised figures supported by the valuation officer were no greater than those for the council houses. The tribunal thought that some disadvantages in the locality generally were more pronounced at the enclave. These included traffic, noise, unsightliness and hooliganism. These, in the tribunal's view counter-balanced the greater degree of detachment the privately owned houses enjoyed. The tribunal lowered the valuation officer's revised figures by a further £10 gross value in each case. Appeals allowed to that extent. The valuation officer had not asked for costs but as the tribunal had derived assistance from the evidence and attendance of six ratepayers it was thought appropriate to award each £2 costs against the valuation officer. In respect of two other appeals one award of £2 costs was made in favour of the ratepayer.

(*Decision December 12, 1975*)

159

HEARSAY EVIDENCE ABOUT SELLING PRICE OF HOUSES REJECTED. VALUATION OFFICER'S GROSS VALUES THOUGHT TO BE ABOVE THE TONE OF THE LIST. SMALL REDUCTIONS.

The appeals *Finance & Security and Another* v. *White* (*Valuation Officer*) related to two houses in Fulham. They were identical and were built in a terrace about 1973. In the valuation list both were entered with a gross value of £1,190. A valuation court reduced this to £1,075. Following discovery of an error in dimensions the valuation officer defended gross values of £1,050. In support of further reductions reference was made to excessive heavy traffic in Fulham Road, the proximity of the Chelsea football ground generating crowds, noise, nuisance and vandalism and to selling prices. The valuation officer could not produce rental evidence except for two rented houses in an adjoining borough. He drew attention to the assessments of a number of modern houses in Hammersmith quite near to the appeal property which he considered establishing the tone of the valuation list. So far as the cited disabilities were concerned he had allowed a total deduction of 18·6 per cent. from the gross value in arriving at the revised gross values of £1,050. The tribunal (Mr. J. H. Emlyn Jones) thought that allowance sufficient on the assumption that the starting figures were correct. On the basis of comparisons the gross values of the appeal properties were too high. So far as hearsay evidence on selling prices was concerned the tribunal could not derive any assistance therefrom. Appeals allowed. Gross values of £1,000 determined. Costs £15 to each of the two appellants against the valuation officer.

(*Decision December 19, 1975*)

159

HEARSAY EVIDENCE ABOUT SELLING PRICE OF HOUSES REJECTED. VALUATION OFFICER'S GROSS VALUES THOUGHT TO BE ABOVE THE TONE OF THE LIST. SMALL REDUCTIONS.

The appeals *Finance & Security and Another* v. *White* (*Valuation Officer*) related to two houses in Fulham. They were identical and were built in a terrace about 1973. In the valuation list both were entered with a gross value of £1,190. A valuation court reduced this to £1,075. Following discovery of an error in dimensions the valuation officer defended gross values of £1,050. In support of further reductions reference was made to excessive heavy traffic in Fulham Road, the proximity of the Chelsea football ground generating crowds, noise, nuisance and vandalism and to selling prices. The valuation officer could not produce rental evidence except for two rented houses in an adjoining borough. He drew attention to the assessments of a number of modern houses in Hammersmith quite near to the appeal property which he considered establishing the tone of the valuation list. So far as the cited disabilities were concerned he had allowed a total deduction of 18·6 per cent. from the gross value in arriving at the revised gross values of £1,050. The tribunal (Mr. J. H. Emlyn Jones) thought that allowance sufficient on the assumption that the starting figures were correct. On the basis of comparisons the gross values of the appeal properties were too high. So far as hearsay evidence on selling prices was concerned the tribunal could not derive any assistance therefrom. Appeals allowed. Gross values of £1,000 determined. Costs £15 to each of the two appellants against the valuation officer.

(*Decision December 19, 1975*)

